Inn
Peace

CW00500504

Lim Kean Siew

Inner Peace

A Source of Chinese Philosophic Meditative Practice

Pelanduk
Publications

Published by
Pelanduk Publications (M) Sdn. Bhd.,
(113307-W)
24 Jalan 20/16A, 46300 Petaling Jaya,
Selangor Darul Ehsan, Malaysia.

Address all correspondence to:
Pelanduk Publications (M) Sdn. Bhd.,
P.O. Box 8265, 46785 Kelana Jaya,
Selangor Darul Ehsan, Malaysia.

All rights reserved.
Copyright © 1994 Lim Kean Siew.
Cover design © 1994 Pelanduk Publications.
No part of this book may be reproduced in any form or by
any means without prior permission from the Publisher.

1st printing 1994
2nd printing 1997

Perpustakaan Negara Malaysia   Cataloguing-in-Publication Data

Lim, Kean Siew, 1922—
Inner peace/Lim Kean Siew.
Bibliography: p. 253-254
Includes Index.
ISBN 967-978-474-6
1. Meditation—Buddhism. 2. Buddhist meditations.
3. Peace of mind—Religious aspects—Buddhism.
I. Title.
294.3443

Printed by
Eagle Trading Sdn. Bhd.

CONTENTS

PART II – PEAKS OF POWER

THE AUTHOR

Born in 1922, the author comes from one of the most distinguished families of Malaysia. Educated in Raffles College, Singapore, before the Second World War, he went to Cambridge where he obtained a double honours Tripos in English and Law. He went on to follow the footsteps of his father, who was a well-known advocate and who served on the legislative council in Colonial times, to become a barrister-at-law of Gray's Inn.

Returning to Malaysia after a short practice in London, he was admitted as an advocate in the Malaysian Bar, went into politics and became a leader of the Labour Party, the Socialist Front, the Socialist Conference, holding many positions including that of Secretary-General in all the three organisations. With the demise of those Parties, he joined the Malaysian Chinese Association as the Presidential Adviser and member of the Presidential Council and Central Committee.

His interest in law and literature stems from his lifelong interest in philosophy and poetry. An accomplished photographer, writer and poet, he studied philosophy whilst at Cambridge but never took a degree in the subject.

Malaysia, in line with other colonies of the British empire, was then moving towards independence. He joined the Labour Party and became a member of Parliament and leader of the Opposition, and years later, a Senator. Perhaps, reflective of his Buddhist beliefs, the author turned down a ministerial post in 1960 and that of a judge of the Appellate Court in 1965.

1965 was a year of political turmoil during which Singapore was expelled from Malaysia. Although he was at that time the Secretary General of the Socialist Front, he was offered the post of the leader of the Malaysian branch of the Peoples Action Party, a post which he declined. That was before Singapore was cut off from the Malaysian Federation.

In l975, he was approached to join the Malaysian Chinese Association when the Socialist Front and the Labour Party were defunct. On a promise that his views on equality for all races would be accepted, he joined the MCA as a Presidential adviser and became a member of the Presidential Council and Central committee member. Unfortunately his blueprint for basic equality was never fulfilled for Dato Lee San Choon suddenly, though not surprisingly, resigned from the Presidency in 1983. He resigned from the party and all political positions in 1983. He is now a legal advisor of the Malaysian Buddist Association Meditation Centre (MBMC) at Penang.

He took up politics at a time when there was the universal struggle for equality and independence for all, irrespective of race. He believed that only a truly democratic society could guarantee human rights and equality of opportunity.

This work is written from the point of view of one who has seen how the human mind works in a political environment. The author had lived through the Japanese Occupation and was investigated by the Japanese military police. Two members of his family were imprisoned by the Japanese authorities. Because of his Socialist beliefs and later conversion to Buddhism, the author has steadfastly refused political honours and high office.

He comes from an interesting family. All of them are professionals who have served their offices with distinction. His brother and sister, also from Cambridge, are lawyers. His sister became an Ambassador to the United Nations, Yugoslavia, Austria, Belgium and the EEC. She is now the Director of the Regional Centre of Arbitration, Malaysia. His eldest brother retired as a Consultant of the North London chest hospital. Another brother served in the RAAF during the War and saw service in London as a bomber pilot.

The author's background should make this work interesting reading.

PREFACE

If there is something that is universally accepted without argument, it is the everpresent conflict between opposites in a perpetual struggle for unity. This, translated into moral philosophy, is accepted as the perpetual struggle between good and evil forces.

This central theme can be found in the Indian concept of Brahma, which is unity itself, from which evolved the individuals, or altman, which struggle to return to the unity. Thus, the Chinese refers to the conflict between the yang and ying forces and the way of Tao, which is the path to bring about harmony in the universe to end disturbances due to the division of unity into its opposites of ying and yang.

It is also the theory of the opposites, the positive and the negative, the male and the female, which strive to rejoin together. This theory of the opposites, their mutual attraction and repulsion and relativity, has brought together modern thinking of the physicists and the older philosophies of the East.

In human society, this conflict is found in our attempts to understand right from wrong, spiritualism and materialism, the concept of the common good and attempts to explain the meaning of life, the reason for our existence and how life on earth is ended.

Buddha, in an extension to the vedic philosophy, sought to apply this argument of opposites to explain this and used meditation as the instrument to find awareness of this reality, using awareness of voidness and "soullessness" (anatta) to bring about the end of this perpetual struggle of the opposites so that we may reach cessation and thus reach nibbana which is causeless and therefore without end.

Thus, to him, everything has a cause and all human behaviour arise from the three roots of greed, illwill and delusion and the achievements of their opposites of generosity, universal love and kindness and the removal of the atta will bring about eternal peace and the end of the cycle of births and deaths of the formations, of which we are a part.

Of all such philosophies seeking to provide answers to our questions and doubt of the meaning of life, our unhappiness and dissatisfaction, Buddhism is perhaps the greatest attempt. For it attempts to show that all this is due to our vanity of ego, greed and illwill which has been developed due to our ignorance of the truth of the illusion of all thought formations; indeed all formations arising out of such causes.

Some two thousand five hundred years ago Buddha propounded that all aggregates come from causes in which there are also resultant effects of disintegration. His law of dependant origination is similar, though wider than Pavlov's theory of conditioning of our minds and its reflexes.

To him, attachment to our desires of greed, illwill and delusion of the truth of the permanent ego, gives rise to all our suffering. To find inner peace, we must therefore understand that all formations we experience and subjective to the nature of our minds so that we can remove them as impermanent and empty meaningless formations which we have taken to be the truth.

The method to discover their innermost truth is insight meditation. This method and the meaning of insight, on which this writing is based, is to be found in the Tipitaka, consisting of three baskets of books written in Pali by a monk who sought refuge in the ancient Kingdom of Sri Lanka, apparently in the sixth century or thereabouts.

Together with the Visuddhi Magga (Path to Purity) and the Vimmuthi Magga (Path to Freedom), they form the Pali Canon, the only authenticated books on this subject.

Pali was the language used by Buddha but we do not know if that was the language of his people or that of the monks.

Unfortunately, the original Pali version of the Vimmuthi Magga was lost and the version we now have is the Chinese translation and it would be interesting if this monk who spent thirteen years in India in the seventh century translating the text, may be the original inspiration of the Chinese legend of the bodhisatva who came from India to spread Buddhism in China.

Meditation, indeed, existed before Buddha. The hermits, as they do today, also sought inner peace to escape from the unsatisfactory condition of their lives. But their meditation for peace was and still is by the temporary suppression of the defilements of the desires through concentration on a subject such as "Nothingness" and "Perception and non-Perception".

Though their concentration exercises in the material state, as we shall see, could develop supranormal powers, it gave no insight to the truth, which was the discovery of the Buddha.

It is the purpose and intention of the book to provide a bird's eyeview of Buddhist meditation according to the Pali Canon, providing, at the same time, a picture of samatha and vipassana and a clear picture as to the meaning of meditation and inner peace. This is the Theravada and belongs to the Hinayana tradition to be found in Ceylon, Burma and Thailand.

It is also hoped that through this book, we may remove some of the misunderstandings that have grown like cobwebs throughout the centuries to cloud the true nature of meditation through indifferent explanations and some of the many superstitions and mysteries surrounding the subject due to the use of animal symbols and animism to explain abstract and philosophic thought to primitive people, for how do we describe lack of faith and understanding to the superstitious people of those days other than referring to such as the monkey in us or the machinations of the fire god? Thus, in a sense, this book is a restatement of the teachings of Buddha.

No political change can result unless there is a change of outlook and the value system of the individuals in the society. The failure of the Communist systems has shown this as the people resurrect racialism and materialism after some seventy years of its rule. Soviet Russia which speaks out loudly that there was this failure.

But whether Buddhist philosophy is a solution, I cannot say. But it is an attempted explanation. Its hypothesis is that each has to find his own answer to his greed and illwill and the delusion of a permanent "self" and their derivatives such as jealousy, possessiveness, vanity and conceit, envy and spite through the development of their opposites.

This simple argument carries a great deal of sense, but can the human being, possessed with natural instinct of survival and its supportive characteristics of desire for security and so on, reduce this galloping consumption which will eventually succumb us?

What makes Buddha's teaching different from the other religions is that he puts the entire blame on our suffering and unhappiness upon ourselves and not upon a superior being, basing his argument on the concept that everything that arise, arise through its own causation.

Though he never denied the existence of god, he starts his teaching with the cycle of life, concerned only that the perpetual struggle will end only when we have ceased this cycle of cause and effect by reaching the nibbana which because it is causeless, is without end.

Expounded some two thousand five hundred years ago, we find the Abhidhamma, its view of physics to be surprisingly Aristotelian and his theory of cause and effect surprisingly modern.

Though his teaching has a moral purpose, by not depending upon a god it does not suffer any loss as a consequence of growing disbelief in the sanctity of religions due to the advancement of science; and the baby is thrown out with the wash, so to speak .

To understand Buddha's teaching, there is the need to understand the laws of dependent origination and its laws, called the dhamma, and how the consciousness, the centre of his belief of the important entity in us which is constantly fluxing and flexing due to its laws.

Like the river and the flame, which remain the same and yet are different because of the change of the water and fuel, so also is the consciousness that remains the same and yet is constantly changing as the formations rise and fall within it.

We also have to understand the meaning of kamma in Buddhism. In this context means the resultant of our intention when thinking and carrying out our own past acts. It is not what we do but why we do it and how it affects the subject of our acts that give rise to kamma. Inoperative acts have no kammic resultant (kriya) such as those without intention or is the resultant of past kamma or that of the arahant. Sometimes the kamma may be mixed where there is mixed intentions behind the act.

Acts influence contiguous, associated, proximate, supportive, related and connected acts and they all add up to make up the total kamma.

Where the kamma is so strong that one cannot avoid its resultant, it has been likened to "fate". But since there are other forms of kamma that can be affectecd by our present behaviour and since our present behaviour can change our future kamma, it is not fate.

Since the question as to whether there is a god in the teaching of the Buddha I have to refer to the Pattika Sutta, apparently told shortly before Buddha's death.

To a question put to him by Bhaggava, the Wanderer, on the truth as to why a disciple, Sunakkhata, had left him, Buddha recounted the conversation with Sunakkhata as follows:

> "But, Sir, the Exalted one does not reveal to me the beginning of things?"
> "Why now, Sunakkhata, have I ever said to you: Come, Sunakkhata, be my disciple and I will reveal to you the beginning of things."
> "Sir, you have not."
> "Or have you ever said to me: I will become the Exalted one's pupil, for he will reveal to me the beginning of all things?"
> "Sir, I have not."
> "But if I have not said the one and you have not said the other, what are you and what am I, foolish man, that you talk of giving up on that account? What think you, Sunakkhata? Whether the beginning of things be revealed or whether it be not revealed is the object for which I

> teach the Dhamma this: that it leads to the thorough destruction of ill for the doer thereof?"
> "Whether, Sir, they are revealed or not, that is indeed the object of the Dhamma taught by the Exalted One."
> "If then, Sunakkhata, it matters not to the object whether the beginning of things be revealed, or whether it be not, of what use is it to you to have the beginning of things revealed? See, foolish one, in how far the fault here is your own."

Thus, Buddha dismissed this impossible to understand question as not being in fact relevant to his teaching. Again, Buddha dismissed the account how the world began as being as irrelevant in the Patikka Suttanta in the following manner:

> "The ultimate beginning of things, I know Bhaggava, and I know not only that but more than that. And while I know it I do not pervert it."

Perversion here probably means that he would not explain it as it would not be understood without perversion. As for Brahma being the creator of all things, he answered the recluses and Brahmans appearing in the same sutta as follows:

> "Is it true that when the reverend teachers when asked, declared that it is their traditional doctrine that the beginning of things is the work of Brahma, the overlord?"

to which question, Buddha said:

> "There comes a time, friends, when sooner or later, after a long epoch, the world is dissolved and evolved. When this takes place, one of the beings in the World of Radiance (this refers to the superior beings of the highest plane) is reborn, the time for rebirth having come, is reborn in the world. Because of his loneliness he wishes for companions and, as the others are reborn in this world after him, he believes wrongly that the other beings were created by him."

The entire teaching of Buddha starts and ends with the mind. This writing reflects this and it is difficult to repeat oneself during explanation. It is called Inner Peace and is written in two parts:

Part I – Monuments of Peace
Part II – Peaks of Power

About one hundred years after Buddha's death, the Buddhists were divided into two schools – the Mahayana and the Hinayana. The Mahayanese school spread to China and thence to Korea and Japan giving rise to various schools of meditation there.

But the Pali Texts are the inspiration of this writing and it belongs to the Hinayana practice and, before I end, I would like to add that this book is more a guide for the benefit of those interested in inner peace and meditation and less a pretence to scholarship.

INTRODUCTION

In Buddhism, virtuous behaviour, or sila, is fundamental for achievement in meditation. Knowledge of sila is fundamental as also its effect. Awareness of jhanas and nanas (the stages in development of practice) are confirmation of progress. Meditation requires not only the practice of sila but also the development of not just any concentration but that of certain qualities suitable for the purpose of obtaining the jhanas and the nanas which require different levels of concentration with their various attributes from which the levels of concentration is discovered.

Not only that but these levels of concentration also bring about various states of consciousness and levels of mental attainment which levels and states of mind also have their different attributes and factors. However, concentration requires the use of certain subjects of meditation, even if it is the abstract nothingness, to produce the results wanted.

Since not all subjects can equally provide the same results, it is therefore necessary to know the subjects and what levels of concentration they can give.

Furthermore, wisdom in insight meditation not only requires certain subjects used in a certain way but also knowledge of the attributes of the mental attributes found in the various nanas and states of purity of mind, for which we need to know the mental factors and the attributes of the consciousness in each of those states.

Without knowledge of the subjects, not only may the meditators not progress as they should but also, understanding of meditation and discussion will be shallow.

For example, right from the beginning, the meditator is made to understand that the ultimate heaven is not a final resting place of a permanent soul but a state of mind when the consciousness, through realisation of the truth of all suffering and the awareness of the three characteristic marks of all formations which are that of anicca, dukkha and anatta, has come to a permanent rest in a never ending state called nibbana.

Again, in emphasis to the consciousness being the center of everything to do with our lives, in the Digha Nikaya II 305, Buddha asked: "Monks, what is the noble truth about suffering? Grief, lamentation, discomfort, unhappiness and despair is suffering; to wish for something and not obtain it is suffering; briefly, the five factors of attachment are suffering."

And, in answer to himself, answered, "Ananda, that is the reason for all our ills. Through this delusion, which is the cause of ignorance, arise birth and all its suffering. From, the realization of the truth, the darkness is dispelled, and the light of enlightenment and the end our suffering is achieved".

His emphasis on delusion and enlightenment and wisdom of the liberation of the rise and fall of formations, require this acceptance. Panna is discerned through the mind expressed as the nanas can therefore be described as insight from which the mind can discern the wisdom of the truth.

For nana we need to know more than the attributes of concentration. We need to perceive the various states of the consciousness itself, the psychological factors developed through meditation and the mental attributes involved in the process and in the various nanas.

Vipassana meditation and the meaning of its purities are also that of the purity of concentration and the consciousness which are complicated and more psychological than superstitious; more dependant and defined by psychology and mental logic than by religious rites and ceremonies.

Hinduism believes that Brahma created the world. Buddha, whose ideas were developed from Hinduism and from whom he borrowed many of his terms and definitions, held that assumption was incorrect and that impression had been given only because he was the first to finish his lifespan in the Brahma world and to be reborn in this world era after the world before had been destroyed by the flood.

Religion normally requires the concept of sin and salvation through a god. In his teaching, there is no concept of "sin" as an offence against ethics provided by a god but merely transgressions which develop the three roots of greed, illwill and delusion which are the causes of all our suffering.

Sin is a religious concept. Sila is not. It is sometimes argued that without the concept of a god and sin, there is no incentive to do good, much less to meditate.

That is not true, Buddha argued. A human, to be born a human, needs two mental roots of metta and karuna which distinguishes him from other beings. His volitions to do sila or not depends upon his volition and the strengths of these roots.

Emphasis on this and the third root of the acceptance of the sasana and understanding of the dhamma to know the effects of such sila acts upon his consciousness for emancipation, all revolve around the mind and the attributes which are affected by meditation.

That is to say, there are the mental attributes and faculties to do good in all humans and those of faith and the knowledge of the laws of the dhamma for meditation whilst past practice or paramis and his kamma will ultimately decide how far he can progress.

Namarupa, paticcasammupada and kamma are all attributes of the mental processes where kamma means the registered reaction of all acts except the acts of the arahant.

Panna, a state of mind, also takes place when the mental factors of enlightenment are found. It requires the factor and faculty of mindfulness providing detachment and bare attention.

This can result in purity of purity of mind by the shutting down of all his sense doors, leaving only his mind door open so as to see the formations to achieve nibbana through panna.

Panna is a resultant state of mind through the development of mental attributes of purity of mind which removes the veils of darkness referred to in the opening stanza of the Visuddhi Magga. It comes as a series of realizations which strikes the mind with sudden awareness and lifts the veil of ignorance.

In the description of how the mind is cleansed, we also find the description of resulting changes that take place in the factors and mental attributes in the various resultant states.

To see how this also relates to the mind instead of a "soul" we learn that the consciousness is in a mind incapable of awakening until it is impinged upon in its state of bhavanga, or life's continuum. When that happens, it goes first into the manodvara state, which is the threshold between somnolence and awakening.

Provoked into activity, conditioned by preconditioning due to paticcasammupada and kamma, it is directed to the point of its awakening and the object is identified and at once subjected to analysis according to its preconditioning.

Reaction then takes place, according to this preconditioning and the subject can either be rejected or acted upon. The reaction depends upon how the mind has been preconditioned since a resultant effect is the cause of the next resultant. Through the practice, it is possible to break this chain through non-attachment to the formations as they arise and so bring about the proximate cause for the next arising.

In this way, the mind is influenced and the kamma created. How does this reconcile with genes?

Both provide a theory. Whilst natural selectivity and environment which the Darwinians relate inherent characteristics to natural selectivity, kamma is also the resultant effect of past actions. Whilst genes and natural selectivity can explain certain results, it cannot explain the differences in the results from similarity of situations and persons.

Nor does it adequately explain the different characteristics of the different animals of the same species or different species with different characteristics with the same rate and possibility of survival.

However, there is no need to go into such controversies. The argument here is that the doctrines of kamma and paticcasammupada, explained by Buddha deals with the mind and its consciousness, relating its argument only to that of the mind and to its preconditioning due to voluntary behaviour.

The Buddhist doctrine of kamma, the concept of rebirth-linking and the cycle of life is not related to any spiritual being but to the inherent characteristics consciousness in constant flux up to the moment of death which interrupts the completion of the seven thought impulsions at the third or fourth impulsion, leaving it to be completed in the next new life.

Death coming before the end of a complete thought moment allows the consciousness to leap, at the moment of death, like a flame so to speak, to complete its seven impulsions in another existence, be it in the material or immaterial plane of existence.

Just as the flame is not a new flame crossing over to continue in its new base is but the same flame, so also is the new consciousness nothing more than the continuance of the old.

Where the death is smooth and there are no shocks, more of its memories remain. Where there are disturbances, what is carried over are affected resulting in changes or even loss so that little is carried over to the next life, including the skills gained.

This explains why not all persons have the same mental characteristics though they may have stemmed from the same parents and why people are born differently and according to their kamma.

All living beings are those which have consciousness and therefore are subject to kamma. Those with no consciousness but have genes and are the result of heat, water, air and the earth elements for their creation, such as trees and such like, are not considered to have kamma.

Kamma results only when the acts are voluntary. This shows the importance of knowing the attributes of the mind when it goes into action. An unconscious or accidental act cannot have an effect. A Kriya acts of the arahants, also have no effect.

It is important that effects on the mind and the resultants of kamma must arise from kammic resultants. Postures, for example, are not important kammically.

Thus, when asked why Buddha said that an arahant who was supposed to be mindful, was in the habit of jumping over streams, Buddha explained that the elder had been a monkey in his previous life and that his act of jumping was not the result of unwholesomeness as it was only a posture.

So also, on a complaint that Sariputta, an arahant, had rudely brushed his cloak against another monk when rising from his seat, without apology. Buddha explained that there was no kamma involved in that incident and that he was sure that Sariputtra had no intention of doing so and had behaved in that way because he had been born a person of nobility of some five hundred times in the past and that it was only a kind of posture.

Indeed, when confronted later on his return by the affronted monk, Sariputta at once apologized and stated that he had not intended to be rude but had thought that it was the wind that brushed against his cloak as he was throwing it around his shoulders.

The importance of knowing what acts have what attributes is also demonstrated in the explanation of mixed kamma results when the act is both done with wrongful and right intentions.

To kill is wrong, but if it is done for humane reasons or for the cause of medicine, a mixed kamma arises and the kammic effect is dependant upon the weight of both and which is the predominant intention.

Kamma can also be of immediate, intermediate or future effect; it can be supportive, proximate, actual or immediate cause of a resultant effect. It can be heavy, medium or light, mixed, of immediate, delayed till the next or later life, or it is such as can be affected and altered by counteracting behaviour.

The kammic resultants cannot be avoided in meditation except those of the slightest kinds. But mindfulness enables the meditator to develop the mental attributes to see the rise-and-fall of the formations and their three characteristic marks of anicca, dukkha, and anatta and discard them as being fearful attractions for salvation.

This path to salvation are marked by seven purities. which again reflect the attributes of the mind and the states of consciousness.

PART I

MONUMENTS OF PEACE

Powers of mind over matter through subjects of meditation

1
NEED TO MEDITATE

Meditation means so many things to so many people and is used for so many purposes and there are so many different levels of achievement that it is important first to define what it is before we can know exactly the kind of meditation we want.

To some, it is only concentration for calmness and peace of mind that is required. With others it may be spiritual powers or emancipation from pain and suffering and peace of mind. Whilst the Zen Buddhists speak of the achievement of "nothingness" through meditation as a means of Buddhist enlightenment, the rest are interested in meditation for insight that leads to emancipation through the removal of unwholesomeness through vipassana as found in the Pali Canons of the Tipitaka, the authenticated Buddhist texts.

Apart from a general desire of the need to meditate for mental improvement, the reasons for meditation are normally vague. The reason for this is the lack of a definitive writing on the subject in its entirety so that there is confusion as to a clear picture of what it is.

There is a desire to look for the meaning to our lives and how we can gain inner peace and escape from doubts and fears and distractions which cause us so much pain and suffering. Hence a reason for this book through which it is hoped that clearer understanding of the immense and interesting practice will emerge.

The development of mental concentration is the simplest result of meditation. But once concentration is developed, it can easily develop clarity of mind that will allow the meditator to perceive things beyond those normally perceived more clearly. Further development through exercises in the "skills" in the kasinas brought on "supranormal", or "divine" powers.

But above all, it can bring about a more calm and a brighter mind with a sense of inner peace. This is samatha. Buddha, introducing the element of mindfulness and focusing this mindfulness on formations which rise and fall during meditation as thoughts go through our mind, brought about inner peace and knowledge of the truth of the emptiness, impermanence and voidness of the aggregates leading to emancipation from all suffering.

There is a moral purpose, however, in this effort. For the discovery of this understanding of life requires the understanding of the reasons for virtuous behaviour as well. This is the highest form of Buddhist meditation.

As for Zen Buddhist meditation on "nothingness", we will see that it is samatha and has limitations. Both the meditation techniques have a great deal in common, in the search for inner peace and the method of concentration technique as well as purpose, at least in the concentration required up to the fourth jhana of absolute detachment and mental calm.

But, Zen Buddhist meditation appears to be samatha. Nothingness is its seventh jhana. The sense of absolute nothingness is brought about through absolute one-pointed concentration which suppresses and removes all mental formations and distractions through this absolute and exclusive concentration upon the subject of meditation. Buddha found it unsatisfactory because the lack of distractions came, not from the absence of desires but through their suppression. Thus the defilements which have to be removed for emancipation from our suffering remain.

Thus he introduced vipassana meditation with its mindfulness for this purpose. Through it and knowledge of the dhamma, defilements and desires can be removed and emancipation achieved. The difference between these two types will be discussed later as it cannot be understood without knowing more of the nature of vipassana meditation.

It is the inborn desire to look into the truth of our sufferings and the wish to escape from them that brings the meditator to meditation. In other words, he is interested in it if it is in his kamma (or mental makeup) and he is interested to search for the truth. Without such inherent desire for the truth, he would not be interested.

The first common requirement in all meditation, no matter how limited, is the development of a concentration. This is achieved when we can hold the subject of our concentration to the exclusion of all else in absolutely calm and detachment absolutely without any distraction whatsoever. It is a concentration which is oblivious of anything outside his subject of concentration. This brings about the anti-stress character of meditation recognized by the medical world. This is good therapy.

This is the basic step in meditation. Without it there can be no further achievement which meditation is capable of. The mind has to be absolutely still, pellucid, malleable and liable for it is required, in insight meditation to maintain a mindfulness and look into itself to see the formations rise and fall as thoughts pass through his mind.

When the concentration is established, there is a unique calmness that has lightness and peace of mind. This first feeling is that of complete relaxation and release of all tension. This is what the doctors look for.

But, to the meditators, this is only the starting point of his practice.

In samatha, which is the highest form of practice before Buddha, the meditator is required to be entirely concentrated on his subject through the suppression of all else and then, either practice for the skills of abhinna which will give him supranormal mental powers or enter into the immaterial states leading to nothingness or perception and non-perception.

Samatha and is excellent for the training for concentration and can provide mental powers superior to those of ordinary persons.

But suppression of the distractions of mental formations is not the same as the removal of the causes of their presence. To those looking for a permanent way out, this is not the answer. The permanent way out is what appeals to those looking for an answer to the unsatisfactoriness and the meaning of life.

When there is interest in moral virtue, generosity, charity, lovingkindness, feeling of virtue and a feeling for knowledge of inner peace and emancipation from our suffering, vipassana meditation is indicated. This is the meditation taught by Buddha and set out in the Tipitaka.

Vipassana means Insight. It is meditation is expounded in various suttas in the Tipitaka and the Visuddhi Magga and the Vimuthi Magga. It is the practice of the Theravada tradition followed by the monks of that Order to be found in Burma, Sri Lanka and Thailand.

To understand vipassana, understanding of samatha meditation helps, since there are common elements between both though the ends are not the same. For samatha provides great supranormal mental powers whilst vipassana targets itself at moral purity of the mind. But both require great powers of concentration but samatha concentration is one-pointed (ekaggata) whilst that of vipassana has the added factor of mindfulness (satipathana).

Samatha therefore lacks an important element of insight since there is no mindfulness and therefore there can be no penetration into the truth of the formations which arise during meditation. Because it depends upon suppression, its purification is not permanent but temporary, lasting only for the duration of the meditative practice. Unwholesome desires and temptations are therefore not removed. This could explain why samatha meditators can become conceited and showy and boastful and require constant sila practice to maintain their wholesomeness.

Buddhism, on its moral stand is a direct challenge to the age of materialism that is now sweeping through the world. It has developed the concept of a sage owning no more than his necessities living remotely and at peace with himself, found from the foothills of the Himalayas to the furthest corners of Japan.

Unlike materialism, which attempts to satisfy desires with indulgence which can lead to ever growing demands, Buddhism attempts to extinguish desires and thus satisfy demands by extinguishing them.

"Do not address me as friend or Gautama", he said, when he was greeted by his first five disciples, who had thought to ridicule him, when he went to meet them after his Enlightenment. "For I am now a Buddha. I have seen the truth and I will tell you what it is."

These words, uttered in the deer park at Benares some 2,500 years ago, started a practising moral philosophy which the world is still trying to understand today but which have given birth to the philosophies of ancient China and Japan and the recluses of India.

What is so interesting in this teaching that we should try to practise meditation?

Firstly, is it a religion? If the definition of religion depends upon a God as the fountainhead of all morality, it cannot be a religion by that definition. Furthermore, it attacks all forms of religious rites and ceremonies as being empty and meaningless as a means to salvation. In that sense it is not a religion.

Yet, it has a monkhood, a systematic order, and it deals with morality and the achievement of nibbana, defined as the final resting place of a consciousness that has ceased to function. These, with its morality (though not dependent on a god) and provision for a life after death prevents us from saying that it is not religious.

Secondly is it a philosophy? It is a moral philosophy but with all the trappings of religion. So we cannot say with full conviction that it is only a philosophy unless we can say that it is a religious philosophy.

Thirdly, and this is most important, it needs practice, not prayers as in other main religions, for salvation from all suffering. One does not reach heaven by prayers alone, is a phrase that can well apply to his teaching.

Though God does not feature in his teaching but the immutable scientific laws of cause and effect, and he does not deny God's existence. But it is not to God that we must look for salvation but to ourselves and through the practice of virtue and the understanding of the dhamma.

Thus, we can conclude that Buddhism is a religion by its own right and definition and that its salvation needs the practice of virtue based upon laws as immutable as the laws of the universe, to be discovered only through the perception of meditation.

The central theme of meditation is that everything is the result due to a past cause which is its conditioning. Because of this, every thought is the result of a past action.

This logic, extended to rebirths, means that since every rebirth is due to attachment to desires, as long as these desires are not extinguished, rebirths will continue. Since everything born is subject to decay and eventual death, there is constant suffering.

Only when the desires, which many think are natural, are extinguished will nibbana is attained. Since nibbana has no cause and therefore no beginning and end, it is achieved when all the formations of the consciousness are forever stilled.

All things must begin through a cause and will eventually have an end. Inanimate things happen without germination, such as rocks and so on. Animate things happen when there is germination, such as trees and so on. All living things are those with the additional factor of consciousness.

Of all living things, the human is the only one with volition. The others have to live out their kamma, including the highest living spiritual beings such as the Brahmas. The consciousness is the beginning of our living existence. We start to live at the moment when there is consciousness and die when the consciousness leaves us.

It is with this consciousness that meditation is concerned. For it is this that is affected by all our conscious acts which are both the results of our past kamma and which shape it for our future.

We are what we have done in the past and what we do at the present affect our future. Thus, we ourselves are to be blamed for what happens to us and no one else. This theory of cause and effect finds echoes in the modern theory of dialectics and dialectic materialism and conditioned replies.

That is the truth and this will be perceived only through insight meditation. Everything born is subject to suffering and decay, the eventual end of suffering is to escape this cycle of rebirths.

Through insight we will have insight to the meaning of suffering; know its causes; know that there can be an end; and discover for ourselves the Way to end it.

"There is but one way to the Path, and that is by way of vipassana meditation."

We reap what we sow, kammically. The human being is the only living being that is capable of choosing what he desires to be in the future. Through virtuous practice and meditation, he can build his paramis or virtues. Or he can continue to live out his kamma and do nothing to improve his kamma. But, as a human being with volition, he has this chance to condition his future. It is up to him.

Thus, crime and punishment come not from a Higher Authority but through oneself.

To understand how meditation affects his mind, we have, first of all, to understand how consciousness works.

Modern science refers to the different aspects as the conscious, unconscious and subconscious and accept that thoughts cannot arise without signals through one of the six sense organs. How does this square up with the psychology of the Abhidhamma?

In the Abhidhamma, Buddha refers to the mind as a consciousness in a state of somnolence (bhavanga) till awakened by one or more of these sense organs without which impingement it cannot wake up.

On awakening, there is reaction to the impingement according to the preconditioning it has received. A sound awakens the mind, for example, and the mind focuses on that sound, fixes it, investigates it and then identifies it and reacts to it.

At that stage, the kammic contact is established. At that moment too, if there are seven thought impulses, there is completion of the thought moment. For every full thought moment has seven impulses.

However, not all thoughts have the full seven impulsions. Sometimes the thought is dismissed before that. This happens, for example, when the mind is already too weak, such as, when at the point of death.

Every full thought moment goes through seven thought impulsions before another thought arises. The kammic effect takes place only at the moment of the thought is registered, usually at the third or fourth impulsion. It is what we commonly refer to as the intention accompanying the act which is established after the registration of the impulsion at the third or fourth impulsion.

Meditation allows the meditator to perceive all this and by bare attention in insight through mindfulness, he learns to ignore these thoughts even as they arise so that the mind learns to detach itself from the desires (this term includes all reaction, even hatred) that arise as a consequence. The purpose of meditation is to develop wholesome attributes which will supervene the unwholesome thoughts arising as well.

Not all human beings can meditate and only those with the necessary attributes or virtues (paramis) can achieve the path of the holy ones (ariyas).

All humans are born with at least two roots which are the ability to universal or unselfish love (metta) and to charity (karuna). They form the two roots necessary for humans. We can find many examples of such people in life. Those who are interested in saving animals and helping the poor and who run charitable institutions with genuine love for what they are doing rather than for publicity are such examples. Such acts are of lovingkindness and compassion which reflect the two roots which all humans have. These two roots of lovingkindness and charity, are two of the four Illimitable possessed by the Brahmas and are, therefore, also known as the four Brahmaviharas. Through these two roots the desire to help others arise.

A third root required for successful meditation is the belief in the sasana as it allows knowledge of the dhamma without which there can be no "penetration" into the truth of the formations. Coming from a past life makes such persons tihetuka persons, or persons with three roots. Only such persons can benefit from vipassana. Many humanitarians are without it, which is a great pity. They react according to their impulses without being fully aware of the significance of the kammic effect of their acts and so miss out on an important aspect of their good acts which is that of the removal of "self" and its substitution by non-self.

Belief in the dhamma is a requirement because the voidness, or "soullessness", of the formations cannot be realized by the meditator unless he knows the doctrine or the laws regarding dependent origination which is contained in the dhamma. Unless he accepts the sasana he will be without awareness and not see the truth and understand why he has to uproot the desires.

That is why there must be this third root in him to meditate successfully.

Lastly, it is old hack to say that all religions are directed towards an improvement of one's personality and character. Whilst this may be true, how do we see the truth of ourselves and this is the importance of Buddha's preaching of meditation because through it can we see the truth as this book will show. It is not that we should know nothing but what is right. It is that we can do only that which has no ulterior desire or motive at the cost of other people. Only by this can we attain this inner peace.

2

NATURE OF MEDITATION

It is pointless to begin meditation practice without having a clear knowledge of what we want and the nature of the meditation we are hoping to practise in. Before we begin our meditative practice, a clear knowledge of the subject in its entirety is necessary if we do not wish to make a mistake.

Samatha meditation existed before Buddha. The state of Perception and Non-perception is its eighth and the highest jhana. "Nothingness" is not the highest jhana and is only the seventh state. Practised with sila, it is Buddhist in inspiration but it does not lead to emancipation, as we shall see, and it is not the highest state, for there has to be perception to be aware of "nothingness". Only when there is the jhana of perception and non-perception that the highest state is achieved and does not remove defilements which give rise to the desires and their formations.

Though it can give abhinna and the "divine" powers, Buddha had found it to be unsatisfactory. It was because of this that Buddha retraced his steps and introduced mindfulness. By employing Mindfulness of Breathing as his subject, after six years, he found attainment.

There should be no mistaken belief, therefore, that samatha was taught by Buddha as a means for emancipation. There are many points in common but samatha is achievement of powers. Vipassana is the removal of all desires. Both also have cessation of the formations, nirodha, but the cessation in vipassana comes as the formations are stilled through the failure to contact absent desires,whilst that of samatha comes from suppression by ekaggata concentration.

Both samatha, which is the fountainhead of many variations of meditation today, and vipassana have to be understood to know the true nature of meditation. This will become clearer when we study the subjects used and how they are applied in meditation practice.

Once we know the nature of these two types of meditative practice, the other kinds of meditation will become easy to understand as they are mostly limited editions of samatha.

Samatha has intense concentration and there is no mindfulness or understanding of the formations.

On the other hand, vipassana requires insight of the rise and fall of the formations, the workings of our kamma and the Four Noble Truths of the meaning of suffering, the origin of suffering, the cessation of suffering and the way towards the cessation of suffering.

Insight requires mindfulness for such penetration into the truth of the formations by developing awareness of the bases from which the formations arise. Hence the meaning of mindfulness and insight knowledge.

This distinguishes vipassana from all other forms of meditation for no other meditation teaches the examination of the consciousness. Through it we are taught to note how the mind awakens from its sleep, what happens as it awakes and how the beginnings of the thought become full blown. Through it we are also taught to see the truth of ourselves through all aggregates which appear in the rise and fall of the formations.

The result of this is insight knowledge through flashes of realizations called nanas. Whereas the jhanas of samatha are states of concentration, the nanas of vipassana bring about insight knowledge which leads to panna, or wisdom.

Furthermore, the nanas come in a definite series, one leading to the other in complete logic. They come, however, linked with the progress of his virtue. It may be strange but it is true that morality in Buddhism is not subjective but objectively related to the cetasikas of the mind, as will be explained.

Whilst jhanas are temporary states, nanas are not reversible. Once a samatha meditator lapses from the state of concentration, all his defilements return as his impurities are only suppressed and not extinguished.

A nana, on the other hand, is insight knowledge indicative of the level achieved by the meditator. Once gained, they remain, provided, of course, they are of the states where there is no reversibility.

Thus, then the meditator reaches the state of the ariya, there is insight knowledge within him indicative that he has reached that level. From that level, he does not return.

After the udayabhaya nana, for example, as a chulia sottapan, his future destiny is decided permanently, for he has then reached a certain state of perfection. From then on, he continues to the state of the ariyas from which he will never revert.

The state of the ariyas is the final state of vipassana meditation. We will learn that there are four of those states, each with its degree of perfection.

The milestones to this ariya state are marked by the nanas gained. But these nanas can be classified into seven so-called purities. The Visuddhi Magga sets out these seven types of purities up the state of the ariya, of which the arahant is of the fourth and the highest. Visuddhi means purity, Magga means the path. Hence the title of the book Visuddhi Magga.

We will use this traditional pattern of discussion and follow the Visuddhi Magga.

Cleansing means substitution of the unwholesome with the wholesome for one cannot remove without replacing. It also can mean the removal of an impurity through the gaining of a purity. One replaces the other.

During his progress, the vipassana meditator gains the seven Purities, one after the other, by removing their opposites. His progress towards ultimate attainment of the arahant therefore means the removal of all impurities. Thus, at his death, there is no attachment to desire for continued existence and when he dies, the formations cease and do not arise anymore. There will be no further rebirths.

But the termination of his life does not come from a wish not to live on as is the case with us. The lack of desire comes from the extinction all desires in him achieved through the purities. That is the difference. With us, it is only a wish, with him there are no more causes which will give rise to any desire.

There are other ways of marking progress in meditation. Barring hypocrisy, to outsiders, the behaviour of the meditator is a useful way of knowing if there is progress in him, for the outside behaviour reflects the inward change.

For the meditator himself, he knows his own state for he cannot claim to have achieved the nanas in spite of book learning because they have to be actually experienced before their nature can be discovered.

From all this, we can say that the chart of the progress of virtue and the gradual emancipation of the meditator is clearly demarcated in vipassana. There is no vagueness as to the presence of each milestone which is clearly demarcated and marked out. They are defined with great detail. Obviously, these milestones of emancipation put vipassana meditation as the meditation for the development of virtues and the emancipation of the meditator from his defilements and it shows the path to freedom and to purity.

On the other hand, we will find that samatha defines the development of the concentration to the fourth jhana and thereafter, the meditator can enter the immaterial jhanas up to the eighth or he may remain in the rupa state of the fourth jhana to practise his skills for abhinna and the gaining of supranormal powers.

Thus, whilst Buddhists may forego abhinna and practise on the subject of "nothingness" that may gain them rebirth in the Brahma world, it is not insight that he is practising. The difference between the nature of the different types of meditation will become even clearer as we go along.

3

PURPOSE OF VIPASSANA

Vipassana which is known as the path to freedom or the path to purity means freedom from the assavas and purity from the defilements. They are, according to the Abhidhamma, attachment of the desires of greed, illwill and delusion of a permanent ego "atta". Both freedom and purity means the freedom from the serfdom of attachment and freedom means release from the chains of this attachment.

It follows that freedom means freedom from attachment and purity means the eradication of the unwholesome roots of greed, ill will and delusion which are defilements causing the formations which bring about restlessness, agitation, pain and suffering and prevents inner peace and the end of suffering.

It is to understand how this process works and what practice is required that calls for the study of the sasana. The sasana is the teaching of Buddha. Though it concerns itself with the individual and his moral behaviour, this moral behaviour is reflected in the society through the collective will of its members. Thus, the four moral virtues of the Brahmavihara of lovingkindness, charity, and generosity in joining others in their happiness, apply to the society as a whole as well.

It would be wrong to look at meditators and conclude that they are doing nothing better than sitting down and watching his tummy rise and fall.

For that reason, when asked if a certain state would fall to its enemies, Buddha observed that it would not happen because its people were maintaining the five precepts, were orderly and disciplined.

Although every person is born with the three basic roots of greed, illwill and delusion, he also has at least two qualities of metta (or lovingkindness) and karuna (or generosity) and possibly also with the third root of knowledge of the Dhamma.This makes him capable of performing good deeds for their own sake.

Metta and karuna are two of the four virtues of the Brahmavihara and form part of the ten virtues of the Buddha. Metta involves self-sacrifice and karuna allows for generosity and charitable behaviour, both of which develop non-self.

Through these qualities, there is a tendency of virtue in all humans, the strength of which depends upon the degree of greed and illwill and ego in them. The purpose of vipassana practice is to encourage the growth of these virtuous tendencies of good social behaviour at the expense of these defilements.

In fact, if one does not believe in sila, vipassana practice would be worthless to him. Even samatha should be practised with sila. Without it, the development of suparnormal powers does not uproot greed and vanity. In fact, it has a tendency to develop the defilements of pride and vanity through the possession of the supranormal powers. It was this fear that moved Buddha to remark, even when he performed the twin miracles in order to convince the skeptics, that he was ashamed that he had to perform the miracles.

There are lesser variations of meditation which will not be dealt with because it is sufficient to know samatha to understand their limited nature.

The ethics applied to vipassana and the Dhamma possess a religious quality and beliefs that is easily understood even by the simplest minds although it has a philosophy as advanced as one can find. It is a moral philosophy based upon a system of logic of cause and effect so mathematical as to cause a reputed remark by Einstein that Buddha was a mathematical genius.

Buddha's theory the elements and matter, the aggregates and formations, their rise and fall, the consciousness, namarupa, causality and dependent origination are so modern and similar to the present theories of our physicists and psychologist as to be astounding. His conclusion that all matters within the solar system and the galaxies are also governed by the definite laws of causation with its quantum effect is so fantastic that it can only have come from an unusual and inspired mind.

His psychology of paticcasammupada to explain how our intentional acts affect our mental conditioning through cause and effect and how this results in our light and heavy and mixed kamma supplants the concept of sin as morality.

The purpose of vipassana to reach into the mind and remove this unwholesome conditioning by substitution with its opposite is also something unique.

As we react to a situation according to our preconditioning, it follows that a change of behaviour will affect our kamma. If vipassana is practised, logically our minds will be affected. But it must be already preconditioned by sufficient paramis (which is wholesome past practice) to allow the meditator the profit of attainment of purity. For vipassana requires acceptance of the dhamma for the understanding of aggregates and treatment of the formations without which insight wisdom, or panna, will not be obtained.

Vipassana meditation is more than just the practice of concentration. It has a philosophical concept with a moral practice based upon psychology.

Using normal language, we can say that its system of morality is based upon the argument that attachment to the pleasures brought about by the three basic roots of greed, hatred and the delusion of a permanent self, bring feelings of jealousy, hatred, pride and all their derivatives. Attachment to those desires only develops further attachment. We commit wrongs when we give way to those unwholesome acts which will only build up more dependency and demands. Once we uproot these roots of greed, illwill and ego, desires which are unwholesome, they should be lessened if not removed.

In meditation, this is simply done by noting without attachment as these unwholesome feelings rise and fall as formations. Desires have given birth to those formations and they plague his mind with formations such as that of spite, anger, greediness, envy, jealousy, possessiveness and so on, which cause distractions, agitation, sloth and torpor. By noting them in bare attention, as they rise and fall, we condition the mind to detachment from them so that, in this way, together with virtuous behaviour, they are removed and purity of freedom is obtained.

The Brahmavihara has featured prominently and we may see how it can even be applied to the five precepts against killing, taking what is not one's own, indulgence in habitual imbibing of spirituous liquor, telling untruths and non-adulterous relationships.

Through such acts, which are the result of the presence of metta and karuna, sila is strengthened to overcome the defilements of these unwholesome roots and help develop detachment.

Greed, hate and delusion of oneself as a permanent entity of a "self" are the roots of all our ills. Non-hate, non-greed and non-self, cultivated, will replace them and their derivatives with lovingkindness, goodwill, charity and calmness.

The five precepts and the Eightfold noble path reflect the philosophy of Buddhism, provide the sila required to build up paramis and helps vipassana to uproot the unwholesome roots.

The episode of the Deer Park to which Buddha went to meet his first disciples after his attainment, establishes vipassana as the practice for emancipation he found as arahant.

For the ordinary person not interested in the Abhidhamma, the Dhammapada has many stories. Let us, as an example of this method of teaching, take the story of a rich estate owner.

One day, whilst going round for his alms, Buddha met a rich estate owner who was leaving his estate in his carriage for a short journey. On seeing Buddha, he stopped his carriage and, explaining that he had to go out for a while, invited Buddha into his estate so that his wife could perform the dana.

Buddha accordingly went into the estate and, after the wife had performed the dana, started to leave the estate. When he reached the gates, he met the owner returning from his journey. Seeing the Buddha, the man asked to see what his wife had provided for him.

When Buddha showed him his bowl of food, the man was moved to remark that it was such a pity that such good food had been given to a man who did nothing more than to contemplate on his navel when it could be better given to workers of his estate who was performing more useful work.

The man wore old clothes and was using an old cart although he was wealthy. After his meal, his disciples asked Buddha why the wealthy man should have passed those remarks.

Buddha explained that the rich man was rich because he was kind and generous to his workers in his previous life. But he was childless and was unable to make proper use of his wealth because he was mean. He also had no offspring because he had killed a nephew in his care to rob the youth of his wealth in an earlier life and therefore it was in his kamma that he would have no offspring and could never enjoy his wealth.

Here is a common enough story. There are rich men who are unable to enjoy their wealth. There are also such men who have such ungrateful children that they would rob him of his wealth so that they are unable to enjoy their wealth or their old age. This man was wealthy because he treated his workers well. But he did not know how to enjoy his wealth and he had no offspring because he, according to the dhammapada story, had killed and robbed a nephew for his wealth in a previous life.

It is important to know the Abhidhamma to explain the dhamma which include such as the meaning of kamma, the rise and the fall of the formations, namarupa, paticcasamuppada, formations, kamma and the reasons for virtuous behaviour and so on. It is especially important to explain the meaning behind the Dhammapada stories which are simple stories for the education of the average devotee.

Nanas are insight wisdom coming through vipassana meditation. It is knowledge that comes through awareness during meditation. It comes in a flash of sudden awareness of a reality, so that even a simple mind with sufficient paramis can discern what the best university professor cannot find.

Attainment is possible by anyone, young, old, of different intellectual levels, classes and ethnic origins, provided there is already sufficient paramis. For the others, the purpose of vipassana is to provide the build up of such paramis and kamma as is possible for the future.

4

MEANING OF PURITIES

The seven Purities are:

1 Purity of morals (sila visuddhi).
2 Purity of consciousness (citta visuddhi).
3. Purity of views (ditthi visuddhi).
4. Purity in overcoming doubts (kankhavitarana visuddhi).
5. Purity of knowledge and vision of what is and what is not the Path (magga-magga nanadassana visuddhi).
6. Purity of knowledge and vision of the change of lineage (pattipada nanadassana visuddhi).
7. Purity of the knowledge and vision of the whole Path (nanadassana visuddhi).

Purity of Virtue (sila) and purity of the consciousness (citta) are the two main purities which have to be established before the other five purities. Nothing can be achieved without first achieving these two basic purities. Thus any study on meditation must begin with them.

Sila concerns itself with the correct mental and moral rectitude, which helps establish meditation concentration by removing distracting formations from arising out of unwholesome thinking. The terms wholesomeness and unwholesomeness, which appear frequently in the texts have this meaning.

Unwholesomeness is indicated by the arising of formations from the roots of greed, illwill and delusion. Failure to understand that sila has this meaning has led to many a misunderstanding of virtue in Buddhism.

So important is virtue that the Visuddhi Magga practically starts off with a question from a deity and the answer from Buddha as follows:

> "The inner tangle and the outer tangle
> This generation is entangled in a tangle"

And I ask of Gautama this question:

> "Who succeeds in disentangling this tangle?"

to which question Buddha replied:

> "When a wise man, established well in Virtue,
> Develops Consciousness and Understanding,
> Then as a bhikkhu ardent and sagacious,
> He succeeds in disentangling this tangle."

The key words of Virtue, Consciousness and Understanding relate to the three main areas of Buddhist philosophy. First, there is purity of virtue, then comes the virtue of concentration and thirdly, the virtue of understanding which comes through insight.

Virtuous behaviour affects the nature of the mind and is required for meditation for its success as it is necessary to bring wisdom and for peace of mind.

The purpose and the benefits of moral virtue in meditation are as expressed by Buddha to Ananda:

> "The benefit of moral virtue, Ananda," he said, "is the sense of remorse. Monks, should a monk ...desire tranquillity ...higher knowledge, the complete cessation of the asavas (defilements), let him fulfil the moral virtues."

It establishes mental firmness and the right situation for the correct meditation foundation. In other words, the meditator without proper virtue will not be firm and has a great deal of distraction which affects concentration for vipassana.

The reason for moral behaviour should now be clear. It prevents distraction and builds resolve in meditation, and sets up the wholesome background for supplanting unwholesomeness. It starts with the five precepts against killing, lying, taking what is not ours, illicit relationships and indulgence in alcohol and the eightfold Noble Path, it ends with the life of a recluse devoid of any material possessions.

All acts which stem from the roots of greed, illwill and delusion of an "atta", are unwholesome and therefore without sila. Those which help to remove them are sila, that is the morality of Buddhism.

The effects of such acts depend upon the severity, the nature and degree of the intention. Killing a mosquito should not be classified in the same way as killing a human being. Nor is killing with mixed motives or under compulsion the same as killing for joy and entertainment.

The reductio ad absurdum argument where monks are asked the seemingly impossible questions such as whether he would kill a mosquito that may carry the dengue disease, even if it helps social health; or what a farmer should do if he did not use insecticides to preserve his vegetables, are not posed with any honesty of intention and do not warrant replies.

The same logic of intention and unwholesomeness apply to the other four precepts. We do not take what is not ours, or commit adultery, or lie, where there is greed or illwill or vanity involved and where it engenders unwholesome reaction. We can also extend them to apply to drug addiction and when and under what conditions we should tell the truth.

Intention is the criteria for kamma and its resultants, kamma-vipaka, and it is important that we know its weight and how it is mixed, before we can pass judgement. Judgement without knowledge of the Abhidhamma is therefore dangerous and we should be careful not to form judgements readily.

For example, sometimes we hear that since it is wrong to kill we should not consume meat. They even argue that since vegetables have mites, we should not even eat vegetables because we may be killing mites when we wash or cook them. These statements are made without understanding of the Abhidhamma.

In the first place, the practising Buddhist should not choose but take what is provided, if suitable to his health. Attachment to tastes is wrong, so he should take what is given, even if it is meat unless he is a vegetarian. Secondly, buying meat is not the same as killing the animal. Thirdly, the intention of purchasing food is not the same as killing, judged at the time of slaughter.

Buying beef for food from the market is not the same as killing a cow. The intention is not the same. Unless the total condition and act are examined, similarities may bring about wrong conclusions.

The belief that Buddhists cannot take beef is wrong and we should not inconvenience those performing dana by making demands unnecessarily but should take whatever is given. Refusal to have beef is not going to change the history of the cow.

The three requirements fundamental for emancipation does not depend on simplistic arguments but of obtaining the three requirements of Virtue, Concentration and Wisdom all of which depend upon the wholesomeness of intentions and acts. These are the three areas where purity has to be obtained.

Virtue requires daily practice. Consciousness is the base upon which meditation works through applied concentration, of which there are many types and qualities.

Understanding is the target to be achieved through meditation. Wisdom is Panna, which is insight knowledge and it comes through the achievement of the nanas in vipassana practice.

Tangle in the verse means the confusion due to delusion caused by ignorance of the truth. A person disentangles the tangle with wisdom dispelling the cloud of ignorance preventing him from seeing the truth.

This verse is the summary of the beliefs of Buddhism and involves the entire area and purpose of vipassana, the entire philosophy and the Buddhist way of living.

The three roots which comprise of the defilements are lobha, dosa and moha. Every human has these three roots. These three roots have their opposites of alobha, adosa and amoha which are non-greed, non-illwill and non delusion.

Humans are born humans because they have performed alobha and adosa acts in their past lives. They are born into the human plane with at least these two roots and are therefore capable of acts of charity because they can act without greed and illwill. But there is no awareness of amoha.

With these two roots, such persons are "dvihetuka" persons, capable of acts of lovingkindness and charity, provided their greed and hate elements are not too strong. These are acts without lobha and dosa are therefore alobha and adosa acts which do supplant lobha and dosa. But we are born also with the moha, or delusion of self which gives, among other things, the false concept of self and pride.

Without a third root to remove this delusion of self, "atta" cannot be removed. In other words, to obtain purity we have also to be amoha and gain the idea of anatta. Without this awareness in their acts they cannot gain the advantage of realizing that they also help to remove the atta. The cleansing effect upon their delusion and amoha cannot be gained and they continue in their moha through their ignorance, which is a pity.

This third root is acceptance of the sasana and the dhamma which can bring awareness of amoha and so remove atta and bring about amoha and thus develop anatta.

A person born with these three roots are tihetuka persons capable of alobha, adosa and amoha.

When one sees suffering with pity and compassion without anger and is moved to help has a feeling without hatred or illwill, so the feeling is alobha and adosa.

Lovingkindness and charity performed are acts of metta and karuna performed without any thought of gain are without greed or conceit (mana) and so they are both alobha and amoha.

When there is relief to the suffering, there arises a feeling of happiness at the happiness of others. This is sympathetic joy (mudita), arising whenever one feels joy at the change of fortune of others, it is mudita if envy (issa) and jealousy (macchariya) are absent; for then, they are without greed and hate, that is to say, they are alobha and adosa.

Only where there is this realization that there is a voluntary act with awareness which then affects the mind to its advantage. A person without knowledge of the dhamma, when doing such meritorious acts, is unaware of the truth of the voidness and impermanence of "self" and so cannot gain wisdom and remains a person with moha.

Through these acts, greed and anger are subdued by love and generosity. However, there is still delusion that leads to vanity and pride. This is due to moha. With knowledge of the dhamma, the effect of amoha is found in the act.

During meditation this difference arises between the tihetuka and the dvihetuka persons. The tihetuka person who is without this third root of amoha cannot understand that there is the element of atta in his acts. He may even be proud of his charitable acts which he feels is justified without knowing that this pride comes from the delusion of a permanent atta. He thus cannot gain amoha and anatta and this impurity remains, for impurity in Buddhism means unwholesomeness and not perfection in the ordinary sense. The tihetuka person can attain the purity of the state of the ariya because he can remove his atta and gain amoha as well as alobha and adosa.

5

SILA

Viewed as a religion, virtuous behaviour is the most important requirement in Buddha's teaching. But he explains virtuous behaviour in a different way. He did not just refer to it as a group of edicts from a god on high.

His concept of morality and virtuous behaviour is based upon the effect of all intentioned behaviour upon the wholesomeness of the mind, something perceived in meditation. It is unwholesome and therefore unvirtuous if it encourages and develops greed, illwill and delusion that bring about desires causing restlessness and distractions and wholesome when it removes them.

It has everything to do with a flexing consciousness forever reacting to wholesome and unwholesome influences which finally affects a person's future and destiny and nothing to do with a God. Because all our suffering is due to unwholesome desires that comes from the consciousness, we can say that the approach is psychological although the first impression we have is a spiritual and religious approach.

On further study we can notice that the psychological approach is the basis of the reasoning behind the need for moral behaviour but this, with its organization of monkhood and temples, can allow us to call it a religion which employs a psychological approach to explain spiritual values.

For sila is of such a nature as to destroy greed, illwill and ego. So all acts are sila which have characteristics which are wholesome. Thus sila is translated in relation to their effect upon our fundamental characteristics of greed, illwill and ego. Those that help to reduce them are wholesome of sila and those that are not helpful are unwholesome. The terms good and bad and sinful imply a subjective interpretation which is not the case here.

Sila is therefore a unique term to Buddhism. As practised in everyday life, it is behaviour without the elements of greed, illwill and delusion of a permanent self. Such is the case of the Brahmavihara. Through Brahmavihara wholesome consciousness is developed. This is the meaning of sila. It is not the concept of original sin.

Whilst it is true that there is a heaven, as in all the major religions, the heaven of Buddha is which do not have the same meaning. It is not nibbana which is a state of causeless existence but a place of many planes of temporary abodes of the brahmas and devas, the last of which have been translated as gods reborn in those planes according to their levels of wholesomeness.

Nibbana, reserved for those who have reached the highest purity, is the final objective. But, again, nibbana is a concept peculiar to Buddhism. It is not the heavenly plane of existence but a state of consciousness which has come to a standstill when all desires due to the roots of greed, illwill and delusion of a permanent ego have been removed and the formations have ceased.

It is a logical conclusion of the scientific argument that all aggregates are formations which are created through conditions and the combination of events and that they will break up eventually and revert to their elements at which point the aggregate will have ceased to exist; just as a carriage is a concept which is made up only of the sum total of its parts and when it is disintegrated, the carriage will have vanished. Since the consciousness is an energy mass, upon the cessation of the formations, it will also have dissipated into the never ending world of nibbana which is defined as an endless state of silence.

The heaven in Buddhism, is of many planes of existence only, for beings who still have to go through their cycles of lives to finish. Nibbana is reserved for the finality of ultimate deaths. Since it is causeless existence, it has no beginning and end.

From this, we begin to understand the nature of sila. Its purpose is to remove unwholesome. Since greed, illwill and the ego bring about desires and cause restlessness and all the hindrances to successful meditation, the upholding of sila becomes the first of the twin foundations of meditation.

The other of the twins is concentration, for without concentration of an undisturbed and calm nature, the other purities, which can only arise if the meditator is able to see his formations and discern their truth. Something he cannot do if there is no sila and his mind is hindered by the defilements of greed, illwill and ego. Its purpose in meditation is to allow for the purity of correct concentration. Purity of sila therefore, in Buddhist definition, is not purity in the absolute sense. It is purity from defilements due to unwholesome acts.

It has a more precisely defined meaning. It means ethical behaviour that will remove defilements which are the causes of the formations and their rise and fall which bring about the perpetual cycle of births and deaths and all its suffering.

It is intended that with sila, defilements caused by greed, illwill and delusion and their related acts such as stealing and robbing, killing and injury, conceit and vanity, possessiveness, envy, jealousy, spite, gossip, deviousness and so on, will be removed through vipassana.

What are the formations we refer to so often? They are aggregates arising as formations due to desires arising from those three basic roots that appear pleasurable to those ignorant of the truth of their empty and void nature, whose rise and fall are random and without his control, and which leave nothing behind them after their fall.

Their true void and empty nature will be discerned once we understand their three characteristics.

Defining sila in meditation means the actual performance of sila, since registration in the consciousness requires intention in the acts. Knowing their meaning through reading or gossip is useless since there is no act with an accompanying intention as a reaction to the formations.

Seeking to achieve purity is not easy. After all, perfection is never easy to come by. Thus, sila is graded according to each step of progress. Absolute purity of the person comes only with the arahant. In this sense, meditation is not daunting. After all, we can only improve as much as possible.

The path to this purity of sila starts with the simple maintenance of the five precepts and it goes on till we reach the stage when we become recluses or live as monks with the two hundred and twenty seven rules.

Sila is judged by its intentions, both as commissions or omissions. But, by superimposition through opposites. Purity is gained by removal of wrong. The doing of what is right removes what is wrong. Not doing what is wrong establishes what is right. In meditation, however, purity is gained by the practice of abandonment of desires through detachment from the formations.

Proper restraint is part of ethical behaviour. Restraint is the negative aspect of an act. To refrain from doing a cruel act is to do something right. However, to refrain from doing something right is the same as doing something wrong. Restraint is therefore negative aspect of sila, whilst performance is its positive aspect. But, since "the sin of omission is as great as the sin of commission", restraint is not always the correct thing to practise where a positive act is acquired. This can be seen from the application of metta and in acts of charity and goodwill. Where an act consists of mixed kamma, the predominant intention is important.

Buddhists have been subjected to the criticism that they would prefer not to be involved in anything for fear of doing something unwholesome or mixed kamma ensuing from their acts.

This accusation is quite rampant in certain quarters and we need to examine how restraint should be exercised. For it is important in vipassana, that the sila of the meditator and his mindfulness must be maintained always.

Where an act of charity has to be done, the excuse for not doing it because it causes bad kamma is wrong. All acts of charity require some self-sacrifice. Where it is indicated, refusal to do it for fear may be as unwholesome may not be a good reason especially as self-sacrifice is a higher form of metta. Where an act of charity requires taking an action, such as not telling the truth or injuring another animal, the unwholesomeness of the resultant kamma cannot be easily assumed.

There can be mixed resultant kamma. In such case, the predominant intention counts. The conditions and intentions of the decision must all be taken into account, especially where Brahmavihara is involved.

This concerns daily behaviour. In meditation, sila and the defilements are expressed somewhat differently. Briefly, the mind must be concentrated and calm and this happens only with sila. Where defilements of unwholesomeness interfere with the concentration, sloth and torpor, restlessness, agitation, distractions and hindrances result, which will terminate concentration.

The calm and serene, tranquil, pliable and malleable state of the fourth jhana can be obtained through ekaggata concentration. But, where mindfulness is present to note the formations, such unwholesomeness causes the formations that rise and fall continuously in his mind.

Sila reduces distraction, allows the achievement of upekha and mindfulness, through knowledge of the truth of the formations and the practice of detachment and develops purity and progress towards wisdom.

Sila helps the concentration to reach the fourth level before anything useful can be gained. Therefore, purity of concentration is the second purity to be developed before the other purities can come about.

Here we see the important difference between vipassana and samatha. Though both have similarities, there is mindfulness in vipassana where there is none in samatha. Stillness of mind is obtained by suppression of the distractions of the defilements in samatha. Therefore knowledge in the dhamma is unnecessary.

In the case of the vipassana meditator, knowledge of sila and the formations are important. Mindfulness is necessary since the effect of sila is to help remove the defilements through the noting of the formations and their rise and fall.

The formations are the result of a process known as namarupa. What is namarupa? Literally translated 'nama' means the mentality or the mental aspect of something and 'rupa' means the materiality or the material object to be experienced by the mind.

Without nama there can be no awareness of rupa and without the rupa there can be no nama. Only when there is impingement of the mind through one of the six sense bases that the mind will be conscious of and evaluate it according to how it has been preconditioned.

The mind and its mental activities are mental formations. They arise as they do in dreams through desires. Mental images of course, are actually created by the mind itself.

The realization of the formations through namarupa is subject to the laws of preconditioning, upon which their origin is dependent, paticcasamuppada.

Paticcasammupada states that every voluntary act (except an act without kammic effect such as the acts of an arahant or involuntary acts or postures) influences all other act which are related, contiguous or associated and precondition them, thus bringing about kamma.

Every cause has an effect and conversely, every effect has a cause. Nothing happens without a cause and the cause is the condition for the effect as much as it becomes the condition for the cause. Both namarupa and paticcasamuppada is explained separately later.

We begin at this point to see the tremendous effect of vipassana through this argument. We are ourselves the cause of our own destiny. Since all our acts are preconditioned by what we do, we are what we are through what we have done. Vipassana helps us to remove the unwholesome and the resultant wholesomeness will precondition our future.

To change this, we have first to change the pattern of our behaviour by practising what is wholesome. This is the importance of vipassana. It develops mindfulness not only in meditation but also is daily behaviour. He must be mindful at all times of what he is doing, even in speech and behaviour in his everyday life.

We must avoid unconcentrated persons and maintain such as correct speech, behaviour, action, livelihood, mindfulness, concentration and so on; in fact, he must hold to the Eightfold noble path.

But he must not expect too much. His fortunes will not change though he may develop calm and inner peace. For not all the resultant effects of our kamma can be avoided, only the slight ones and such as mixed kamma.

However, there is an important process that is also taking place. Wholesome practice will help bring better paramis for the future. Paramis are meritorious acts performed in the past registered in our present kamma. It requires knowledge in what we are doing. Where a person has performed metta but is ignorant of its effects due to lack of knowledge of the dhamma, he does not have the right paramis for attainment for his acts will lack the necessary knowledge for effect upon moha.

A further reason for meditation is that only humans can meditate and influence his own future because he has volition. Other beings have no such chance and they must live out their present lives according to their kamma. So we should not lose this chance.

Whilst sila helps meditation, meditation in turn also helps the meditator in the recognition of the importance of sila and its practice. Vipassana brings awareness of the formations and their three characteristic marks and that they are anicca, dukkha and anatta.

Realizing that all formations bring suffering and that they are impermanent and void, he loses his doubts, strengthens his sila and begins his attempts to abandon the unwholesome acts which bring about the formations.

Realizing that everything is subject to decay and voidness, he begins to abandon his clinging to his formations and concentrates more strongly in his meditation with greater sila. This is the meaning of sila.

6
NAMARUPA

The first insight knowledge required in vipassana is namarupa-richeda nana. It is awareness that every formation is the resultant of the linking of materiality and mentality. Next comes the paccaya pariggaha nana in which the meditator sees the truth of the voidness and dissolution of the aggregates and that there is no soul or atta directing them. Finally he gains the knowledge for himself that all these are due to ignorance of the four noble truths of the formations which is the samanasana nana.

Only after all these is he ready to enter the cleansing process of the udayabhaya nana state when he will see the continuous rise and fall of the formations.

This importance of knowledge of namarupa and the formations therefore cannot be overemphasised. The explanation in the Abhidhamma sounds difficult but if we use a free translation, it is easy to understand its broad meaning in this way.

Normally the mind is in a state of somnolence called bhavanga. Only through stimulation from one of its sense organs can it be awakened. Stimulated into activity it awakes and begins to evaluate the impingement. But it reacts according to how it evaluates the impingement.

But it evaluates according to how it has been conditioned in the past. It therefore sees the impingement subjectively. Since it is subjective, obviously its subjectivity will change according to its preconditioning.

The stimulation is immediately evaluated through the preconditioned mind. This is the process of namarupa. The evaluation brings about the appropriate response and resultant formations are the result. The preconditioning is known as paticcasamuppada.

Since namarupa brings about reaction according to preconditioning which is partly the result of kamma, in the ultimate sense, understanding namarupa is the prerequisite of our understanding of the process of kamma.

That is to say that paticcasamuppada depends upon the namarupa process; similarly, namarupa is subject to preconditioning. Thus, it is said that through consciousness there are the formations which arise from namarupa. They arise together, for without namarupa there can be no formations. With no mentality there can be no paticcasamuppada.

This process takes place every waking moment of our life. Formations arise according to subjectivity. Therefore we must avoid unsuitable conditions and maintain correct attitudes as reaction to the namarupa depends upon our sila.

His condition of life, which may not be perfect, has been decided by his kamma and he can only act suitably and correctly, as far as possible, according to his condition. Thus, right livelihood is one of the enjoinders of the Eightfold Noble Path. It is thus obviously ridiculous to ask a fisherman with a large family of young children to abandon fishing because he wants to seek peace in a monastery.

In meditative language, when we say that the namarupa process begins as the mind goes into a manodvara state on being impinged upon by the sense bases, it means that, at that stage, the thoughts are free to adapt themselves to the meditator's decisions and are, therefore, capable of being influenced by either proper, improper or mixed motives.

This means that, though they are already conditioned by past kamma and by their immediate and supporting and surrounding circumstances, where they are capable of being subjected to and influenced by the determination of the meditator, he can still influence them by his voluntary acts or restraints such as that which takes place in meditation. They are known as nanakhavika cetana.

This happens only in cases where the kammic effect is not a serious one. Where the kamma is more serious, the resultants (vipaka) have to be worked out and cannot be influenced, no matter what the meditators may do, for their results are already fixed and cannot be changed.

Since not all kamma has fixed and definite resultants, it follows that where the kammic effects are not fixed and can be affected by the kusala or akusala (or mixed) acts of the meditator, it is on them that the meditator hopes to influence by his voluntary efforts. In this way, he can make his acts part of the supporting or the proximate cause or condition for future perceptual volition.

This is the significance of sila and its purpose and effect. Through namarupa in meditation with knowledge of the dhamma a meditator can build up of his wholesomeness and paramis. The formations come in their grosser, subtle nascent forms as they are about to arise. At the higher states, with greater stillness of concentration, the meditator will be able to discern them even in their subtle or the anusaya stage and bring about their non-appearance even as they are about to arise.

These nascent forms are referred to by Buddha in the Mahadina and the Mahasatipattana suttas as the anusayas which are tendencies.

All these formations can result through the contemplation of the eighteen elements (dhatu), that is to say, the six senses, their objects and their six consciousness, or the twelve sense spheres (ayatamas) which is that of the six sense organs and their objects.

In that way, through namarupa, the impermanence and voidness in all formations can be seen. When he realizes that all is voidness and there is no "atta" apart from the effect of namarupa, he knows that everything including the "I" is no more than a collection of the five aggregates, just as a car is no more than a concept formed of a total sum of all its individual parts. So he abandons the "clinging" to the delusion of "atta" and gains wisdom.

7

PATICCASAMMUPADA

Paticcasammupada, or dependent origination, is a psychological process which explains the subjectivity of the mind and how attachment to the unwholesome roots preconditions the mind and all its responses.

There was no such exposition before this. If we bear in mind Pavlov's experiments on conditioned reflexes on animal behaviour we can get some idea of this process.

But paticcasammupada goes deeper. The effect is upon the kamma of the person, affecting consciousness to the point of influencing the person's entire mental makeup and his future. We have to understand its principles to understand the meditative process.

Through paticcasamuppada, our daily indulgence to our desires will develop greater dependency to our desires resulting in the preconditioning of future formations.

With consciousness come the mentality-materiality of namarupa. With namarupa comes contact with the sense bases; with contact comes feeling; with feeling comes craving; with craving comes clinging; with clinging comes rebirth; with birth comes suffering, ageing and death.

Thus, because of ignorance and the lack of wisdom, the formations arise. It is avijja (ignorance) that causes sankhara (formations). With sankhara comes vinanna (consciousness).

With vinanna comes namarupa. With namarupa comes phassa (contact). With phassa comes vedana (feeling). With vedana comes tanha (craving). With tanha comes upadana (clinging). With upadana comes bhava (rebirth). With bhava comes jara and mara (ageing and death).

The concept of paticcasamuppada, therefore, applies to all formations, whether in the cycle of life or individual formations. Thus, not knowing what is right or wrong, in ignorance, we take pleasure and delight in doing things against sila and, thus, develop the conditioning for future responses to pleasures and delight. In ignorance, we take delight when pleasant formations arise. Without realizing that this is due to past conditioning, we react accordingly and enjoy ourselves in ignorance, believing that what we are doing is correct. Mindless that preconditioning to wrongdoing will result in further wrongdoing, we continue to enjoy ourselves.

This argument, applied to the samsara, means that ignorance leads to formations which finally results in clinging, providing the conditions of the kammic causal process (rupadana bhava) which, in its turn, results in the causal process of ageing and death (jara and marana).

Thus jara, which is suffering per se, with its entire aggregates of suffering, pain, affliction, imperfections, impermanence, insubstantiality, unsatisfactoriness and emptiness, found in the five khandas, is conditioned by the bhava.

Bhava itself is caused by clinging (upadana) to the sense desires (kamupadana), false doctrines, views and opinions (dithipadana), rites and rituals which are wrong and not leading to the right path (silabatupada), the false theory of something permanent is us such as the soul or self (attavadupadana).

Upadana itself is conditioned by craving (tanha). Craving is such as for the pleasure of sound (saddatanha); enjoyment of scents (gandatanha); enjoyment of taste and flavours (resatanha); physical contact (pothabbatanha); the pleasure of thoughts and ideas (dhammatanha).

Tanha itself brings about a search for possession or possessiveness and the pleasures derived therefrom (paryasana).

This brings about a desire to acquire (labha); to enjoy and take delight in one's possessions (vinicchaya); excitement in passion, lust or delights (chandaraga); tenacious clinging to one's possessions (ajjihosana); selfish possessiveness (pariggaha); meanness and stinginess (macchariya); possessiveness of one's possessions leading to disputes, quarrels, backbiting, viciousness, lying and even killing (araka).

Since tanha is conditioned by contact (phassa) which, in turn, is conditioned by namarupa which is itself conditioned by consciousness (vinanna), it follows that if there is no consciousness there can be no namarupa.

It is through this relationship of cause and effect with its link to namarupa that allows the meditator to see the insubstantiality and truth of the formations. What he thought was a permanent self is no more than the feeling, perception and the mental activity due to the five aggregates of his body and his preconditioned consciousness. Once aware of this, he loses the belief in the permanent entity of self.

The meditator sees this preconditioning of the namarupa and he then understands that kamma results through namarupa. As insight knowledge develops, he sheds his ignorance and sees the real truth and overcomes all his remaining doubts. He puts away all doubts and is at peace with himself.

Therefore, namarupa itself is simultaneously the source, origin and the condition for the vinanna as well as the result. Without namarupa he would not be able to observe the properties and the phenomena of the the physical phenomena of the four bodily elements of the body (rupa), sensation (vedana), perception (sanna), volitional activity (sankara), consciousness (vinnana). These are the five khandas.

Namarupa and vinanna come together. Without one there cannot be the other. When the formations do not arise the vinanna cannot awaken from bhavanga. Cessation is found and at that point the samsaric cycle is broken. At this point the meditator's life is terminated and he escapes from the cycle of life to enter nibbana.

8

NEED FOR SAMADHI

Samadhi, as with all Buddhist terms, is carefully defined and so has many meanings depending upon its context, the level of concentration we are referring to, the jhana it is in and whether it is in samatha or vipassana concentration we are discussing.

Furthermore, as the concentration must have attributes for it to be used, there is always the underlying presence of sila with its various qualities to provide it with the correct attributes to bring about upekha and to give it the ability to cope with the "cleansing" required in vipassana.

The upholding of sila, first of the seven purities, requires acceptance of the dhamma without which the truth of the formations cannot be penetrated. It is only with the establishing of sila that the type of samadhi can be cultivated.

In the start of meditation, in the first jhana, there is initial and then sustained concentration with the presence of the hindrances of joy and happiness. With ekaggata absorbing initial and sustained concentration he moves into the second jhana, still with the presence of joy and bliss which is reflected in karuna and mudita of the second and third qualities of the brahmavihara.

With the removal of joy of sukha, he moves into the third and with the removal of bliss of piti, he enters the fourth where there is only ekaggata and upekha.

Thus, in that context, samadhi is described according to the state of mind as to whether it is in initial or sustained concentration or ekaggata and whether there are the hindrances of sukha and piti on the consciousness which distracts and restricts the concentration in the lower jhanas.

In relation to the subjects of concentration, there is also the question whether the concentration is in access, or investigative concentration, or if it has developed absorption which will allow it to hold the counterpart sign of the subject for the purpose of surmounting or practise in the skills of abhinna.

From this brief description, we can see how carefully samadhi is defined. Up to the fourth jhana, the factors of concentration are common to both samatha and vipassana. But thereafter, in the quest for inner peace and purities, samadhi in vipassana requires the additional factor and faculty of mindfulness so that another faculty is introduced into its definition.

But that is not all. The mind must be balanced and with the faculty of mindfulness thrown in and another quality emerges which is required to see the formations as they rise from the four foundations of mindfulness.

For this faculty requires also the presence of four other faculties which is common to both meditations. These are the faculties of faith, understanding, energy and effort all of which must be balanced. To have faith without understanding is to believe without knowing why; to have the energy without faith is to have agitation; whilst to have concentration without energy is to have dullness and torpor.

Ultimately, when analysed, only samadhi that is concentrated, calm and balanced is the basic samadhi that is necessary for the exercise in the skills in samatha. To that must be added mindfulness for "cleansing" in vipassana. The rest are incomplete forms.

Mindfulness which acts like a general supervisor or a prime minister of a state was considered by Buddha himself as of universal importance in vipassana meditation. It requires the meditator to keep his mind upon its four foundations, namely, the foundations of his body, his feelings, his mind and the dhamma, as it is in these four foundations that he will observe the working of the dhamma, namarupa, and the aggregates (or khandas) which are the defilements that he has to cleanse himself of.

To see the rise and fall of the formations and their dissolving away, his concentration must be such that his mind is "calm, penlucid, clear, without distraction or blemish, and pliable" enough to see the namarupa working, that is to say, to have the formation itself and to have the mental awareness of it.

Since we know that this can only take place in the fourth jhana where the mind is without sukha and piti, we imagine how detailed the understanding of samadhi must be for one who studies the Abhidhamma.

The meaning here is that the rise of the formations, whatever may be their nature, will not bring about joy or bliss and their opposites of fear and repulsion. Thus it is said that the mind is in equilibrium, calm, penlucid, pliable and so on.

At the beginning of his practice he will have great difficulty in concentration because of the defilements which bring such as elation, joy, agitation, restlessness and even sloth and torpor when he may even fall off to sleep.

His mind will cling on to any formations arising and hold on to any distraction. He will not realise they are attachments due to desires which he finds very pleasing.

Only later, when he develops sufficient knowledge of the formations and the truth of their nature that he will begin to ignore them for what they are. Only then will his mind grow still as he notes them with bare attention. For the moment, be it the smell of good cooking or his daughter's voice, or the ringing of a bell and he will immediately set his mind to thinking of eating, reacting to his daughter's voice or answering the door bell.

This reaction as known as "chasing" and the reaction is distraction.

There are times when he thinks he has sensed a formation, i.e. that he thinks he has heard or seen or felt something only to find, on checking, that there was nothing there. The awareness of the presence of something had no actuality. This is the effect of namarupa. This happens always, for example, in dreams and nightmares. They will also arise in meditation owing to desires. Again, this is the namarupa working because his mind has been so preconditioned.

Soon he will realize all this and his mind will settle down. This happens when he has developed sila and he has reached the point when his concentration will be without sukha and piti. Then will his mind become calm and concentrated and he will maintain his bare attention of noting without reaction and "chasing" and thus will the cleansing process begin.

This can happen only if he detaches himself from his desires which come from ignorance leading to attachment to the roots of greed, illwill and ego. He can do so provided he maintains his sila. This stresses another element in his concentration, the need to still his distractions through the removal of the unwholesome.

This is a good reason why the Brahmavihara subjects have to be practised since they keep out the unwholesome by developing the wholesome.

These four Brahmavihara subjects of lovingkindness, compassion, sympathetic joy and detached calm, encourages wholesome behaviour and, as meditation subjects, give rise to the fourth jhana through upekha, which is the fourth of the four subjects.

With stillness and concentration with mindfulness, he sees the arising of the formations from his sense bases. When they arise attachment and joy and happiness arise. They are two of the hindrances to progress.

Practising the Brahmavihara virtues will assist him to remove sukha and piti from his concentration.

Mindfulness, as an element in his concentration also encourages awareness of the formations which bring about the hindrances. The quality of the concentration, however, also requires that mindfulness, though present, is one without attachment to these formations which give him elation as long as sukha and piti are present.

The formations during the ubayabhaya state include visions and mental creations never before experienced which can be very spiritual and beautiful, and care must be maintained that we do not get carried away by their seeming beauty and attraction. Mindfulness and bare attention require concentration that is detached so that preconditions will be developed that they might not rise again.

Since we have desires that are many and varied in ourselves, such experiences will also be equally exciting and varied which will affect our samadhi.

Our samadhi is distracted as a result of our ability to contact our desires resulting in craving and clinging. Namarupa brings us into contact with the formations which are nimittas so that the mind can learn to detach itself from their presence and thus remove them from our consciousness. Sometimes they may occur in the sequence of a story, so strong is the desire for them.

There was once an instance of the appearance of a spirit who offered to teach a meditator the crystal ball technique and the vision persisted until the meditator firmly rejected all desires to learn this technique.

Visions of saints have even appeared to those who believe that they can be in contact with such spirits. These are but creations of the mind and expose deep-seated desires or fears and appear only in the early stages and the lower levels of meditation. In this way, the subconscious is manifesting its kamma and bad kamma will give rise to unwholesome formations which should be noted and let to fall by themselves.

Such are the realities of meditation concentration. Mindfulness allows contact with the subconscious so that we may be able to deal with them whilst keeping our concentration in line with the faculties and maintaining consciousness is a non-attached state.

The best way to deal with unpleasant or unhappy nimittas is to perform dana. Dana is part of carana (good conduct) and those who wish to meditate should practise it since it gives rise to the correct kamma.

We are aware that unmeritorious acts create bad kamma. The performance of dana for the monks who are seeking enlightenment as one of the followers of the sasana is a meritorious deed which counteracts the unmeritorious acts and can create good kamma.

Dana is the doing of an act of charity. Essentially it is almsgiving to the monks. The Theravada monks are required to give up all worldly possessions. They cannot even cook for themselves and they cannot choose their food. Nor can they even boil water. Their life is hard indeed.

Dana is performance of charity with knowledge of the dhamma. Done with knowledge of the dhamma would influence the concentration by removing some of the unwholesomeness.

Acts without knowledge of the dhamma are not acts performed arising out of realization of the laws so its effect is not complete because the cetana of wisdom is not there. So, also performing dana to a crooked monk would be worthless as one is feeding someone not practising sila.

By supporting him we are perpetuating evil. The highest merit is gained when one performs dana for the benefit of an arahant.

Dana performed is good conduct (carana) carried out which brings merit whose benefit can be transferred to those unfortunate spirits of departed relatives, if required. But dana must be performed wisely.

Charity, such as helping the poor or saving animals, for example, on humanitarian grounds is a good deed but its effect is limited as humanitarian acts are not necessarily done with knowledge of the dhamma and so the important element of intention is not fully employed.

Dana, being part of carana, is part of metta. And metta, karuna, mudita and upekkha, we know, are the virtues of the Brahma and four of the perfections of the Buddha. By their very nature, when practised, they will bring about the meritorious kamma in us as their practice will rid us of hate and illwill, of greed and avarice and selfishness in us and thus of conceit, egoism and ignorance.

In this way we will rid ourselves even of unprofitable tendencies and develop the inclination towards meritorious acts which will give rise to meritorious kamma and so the quality of his concentration and its calmness will be improved.

Because meditation is essentially for the attainment of self-perfection, the practise of the four Brahmaviharas brings about purity through the removal of hate, greed, and delusion which cause the mind to be restless, full of unwholesome desires and distraction which will interrupt concentration.

Metta that comes with affection, unbounded love and benevolence is one of the ten parimittas of the Buddha and is the second principle of the Eightfold Path being that of right view (samma sam-kappa). It is love free from lust, from greed, without illwill and malevolence.

Karuna, which is pity and compassion at the suffering of others including those who are happy without realizing that they are causing pain to others, has as its essence the feeling of pity for others and the desire for the elimination of that cruelty. There is the feeling of alleviation of pain and misery of others and that is why it is also one of the ten paramittas of the Buddha and one constituent of the Eight-fold Path being that of Right Intention.

Mudita itself, the third of the Brahmavihara, carries with it the destruction of envy, jealousy and dislike whereas upekha is a development to be found in meditation.

In upekha, the mind is equalized and impartialised through the realization of the truth. It is not indifference, callousness, or the indifference of the non-perception of the unintelligent. Its proximate cause is the perception of the heritage of kamma. It is equanimity.

In the Brahmavihara it comes with the presence of the other three accompanying virtues of metta, karuna and mudita. It is a state of mind.

Thus, these sila practices are necessary for a quality of concentration.

When interpreting samadhi, we must not ignore the effects and the quality sila gives to it. Without them the samadhi will not possess the qualities required to do its job.

9

MEDITATIVE AWARENESS

What is meditative awareness? Put in another way, what are we looking for in meditation and what can we find? It is according to what we are looking for and the type of meditation we practise that define the awareness required. To many, it is in search of inner happiness. To others, it is a desire to find the ultimate peace in vipassana.

It is through the objective and the kind of vipassana concerned that we can discover the meditative awareness of the meditator and his requirements. Only by looking into his mind and knowing what he hopes to get out of meditation that we can distinguish one type of meditation from another.

Observing a meditator outwardly, we find little to help us understand what he is doing. They all sit cross-legged with eyes shut, hands in front of them and resting on their laps. At times, they are breathing so imperceptibly that they even appear to be asleep.

Once sila and concentration is established, in the fourth jhana, that meditation begins. But it is usual to find more limited forms. For example, meditation itself has been found to be helpful in gaining calm and restfulness for the removal of tension and anxiety.

Doctors advise meditation for concentration, for health, to reduce tension and even for the lowering of blood pressure. This is simple and even the first jhana can be of help.

There is a plethora of meditation techniques and each of them claim theirs to be the best. How then can we decide what is best for us?

The simplest technique, of which the development of concentration, requires holding one's attention upon an object for a certain length of time and that used medically, for the removal of anxiety, is the simplest.

Some speak of transcendentalism, some of the cultivation of the heat energy for health. Transcendentalism, levitation and such as the heat technique also do not require more than the first jhana.

The more difficult to discount are cases where the exponents claim the power of levitation. I know of no such cases personally but the competition in Switzerland early in 1991 that was won by a Mr. Davies of England in a series of hops during deep concentration of balance and power. To me this is not levitation although skill has been developed. But to disagree with their claims can cause a great deal of argument. But levitation as defined in the Pali Canons excludes such hops as levitation.

But when there is claim for divine powers and the ability to read minds, and knowledge of the ability to see things taking place many miles away, explanation usually becomes vague and we do not know the nature of the awareness involved because we do not know if these abilities are innate or if they are developed through meditation.

The ability to direct and to radiate the heat energy in meditation often employed by martial arts experts is another ability used to show off one's superior state. But this could be explained as concentration in the heat element of the first jhana, since the elements cannot give rise to more than the first jhana as we shall see. Stretch your hand out and concentrate on trying to push blood to it. You may be able to do it and see the palm gradually become red with a suffusion of blood. Chinese meditators in the T'ai Chi or the martial arts can do this.

However, we know from the texts that supranormal powers can be obtained but only through proper samatha meditation so that meditative awareness for such claims can easily be examined through knowledge of this meditation which will be described at length later since samatha is an important meditation technique.

There are other techniques such as the Ch'en technique known in Japan as Zen which are Buddhist in inspiration. This meditation was apparently introduced by a saint from India who was a Boddhisatva, one with nine of the ten virtues of Buddha. Through the course of centuries, there has grown a belief that "nothingness" was the ultimate attainment for his followers.

The Ch'en technique and its Japanese counterpart, Zen meditation, speak of "nothingness" as attainment. If this is the seventh jhana of samatha but how it can be achieved without proper training in samatha, again, I do not know.

But "nothingness" is the highest form in Ch'en and Zen. It is Buddhist but the question is if it can lead to emancipation since we cannot deny that it is samatha and not vipassana.

According to Chinese legend, during the state of nothingness, the spirit of the meditator can leave the body for no more than seven days and then return. In samatha, the meditator can maintain nirodha, or cessation of the formations in the highest samatha state for no longer than seven days, during which time there is no movement in his body and he appears to be in a "plastic" state.

This could be the inspiration of the legend of Lee Tok Quai, the beggar saint, whose "soul" returned on the eighth day and had to enter the body of a beggar because his servant had found him in that state and thinking he was dead, had turned his body into a funeral pyre. (The period of seven days presumably is because, though a person can go hungry for more days, seven is the highest limit one can go without water due to evaporation).

Some Tibetan Buddhist monks, who meditate, have demonstrated that they are able to wear wet clothes and dry them whilst sitting in the snow. They do not call their meditation samatha but simply meditation. A rose by any other name is still a rose and this would seem to be the case. Of course, dry cold weather can dry clothes and when body warmth is applied at the same time, they can be dried faster.

Their ability to sit out in the snow, of course, need concentration to keep off the cold. Similarly there are instances of the hermits who can reduce their heart beat or stay alive in confined areas for days, we see aspects of samatha operating in the immaterial jhanas. These meditators are possibly meditators capable of intense and advanced ekaggata concentration.

The nature of awareness in vipassana, however, is well documented and explained in the Pali Canons and the awareness is more complicated and greater because of mindfulness and the fact that where there is more unwholesomeness in the earlier states, the greater and more varied the mental experiences.

For example, in the fourth nana of udayabhaya state, formations that give rise to the bodily elements giving the sensations of flying, levitation, floating, revolving, breaking up of the body, auras and illuminations and such sensations through contact with the body feelings are numerous and common.

To understand what a meditator is doing we have to know what awareness is taking place within him when he is meditating. In a way, through what he is sensing and his awareness we can define his meditation.

But we must know what he expects from his meditation to give him his subject of meditation, and to help him. For the mind cannot concentrate without an object. For without it, he will fall asleep. In this way we will be able to know the type of meditation and what he can expect from it with the subject used. For we know the limitations of each subject.

Therefore, it is equally important to know the nature and limitation of each subject of meditation as it is to know what he expects to gain through meditation.

The reasons for meditation usually come from an instinctive desire to improve ourselves or in the hope of finding some way of escaping some continual misfortune or gaining peace of mind. Sometimes to convince themselves that they can have some advantage over others. At times it may be used to develop their concentration as in the case of martial arts and sports.

Where the purpose is simple, explanation is simple. Where the reason is for the development of spiritual powers, the explanation becomes difficult. Spiritual powers are difficult to prove and even more difficult to explain unless there is already meditation, for the reality of meditation and its awareness is particular to the meditation itself. However, we can say that if supranormal powers are the object, it is subject to dangerous repercussions for the temptation and desire to show off is strong and can have serious repercussions unless sila is maintained at all times.

We also have to be careful that we are not misled. Supranormal powers are not easy to achieve and the achievement of certain powers are exaggerated.

But, no matter by what name they called, be it transcendentalism or something else, it is a form of what we can refer to as samatha and knowledge of the subjects used and the technique of concentration employed will see if this definition is correct.

However, vipassana, which we may refer to as insight meditation, is the only meditation that seeks for purity by the removal of taints in us that encourage attachment to greed, illwill and the ego that result in restlessness, envy, jealousy, possessiveness, false pride, undue humility, spite, viciousness, desire for fame and so on.

It develops the person and provides understanding through a series of insight which is knowledge that comes during meditation in flashes of realization which is emotional rather than intellectual which is obtained through reading books, for instance. Though not at all so dramatic, it is like discovering the power and terror of lightning when we see it strike, something not realizable through reading.

This insight awareness is known as the nanas. We have come across three of them already, the namaruparicheda, paccaya-parigaha and the samasasana nanas. Through them, a yardstick for progress and level of purity is provided.

But to obtain these purities we have to maintain sila which is the base for the wholesomeness required to remove unwholesomeness and we also have to understand the formations, the namarupa and paticcasamuppada and the dhamma to remove the ignorance surrounding us. This is why these subjects have to be first understood before we can understand the Abhidhamma.

From the very beginning the meditator must understand what is meant by attachment or "clinging" to the sense desires, for it is this clinging that give rise to the formations. Desire creates demands for satisfaction. Through the observation of how his cravings give rise to the formations and how they rise and fall in spite of himself, leaving nothing behind, he gains the first knowledge known as namaruparicheda nana.

When he realizes and perceives the clinging, how his cravings give rise to the occurrence of the formations, how namarupa gives rise to consciousness and the perpetual cycle of the rise and fall of the formations, how they rise and fall in spite of himself, leaving nothing permanent behind, he is said to have obtained the first nana.

When he is aware of the volitions emerging from the subconscious into action (nanakhavika cetana) in the rise and fall of the formations, how the formations rise and then fall away even as he notes them in spite of his volition during his meditation, he knows he has gained this wisdom.

He notes how they are already preconditioned by past kammas and how they are conditioned by other surrounding causes and how they can be influenced by supporting and restraining conditions and how mixed kamma (good and bad kamma due to an action with mixed wholesome and unwholesome elements) can arise. He is also aware of what Buddha has said in the Mahadina and the Mahasatipattana Suttas when he emphasized the non-arising of the formations in the meditator who is developed in his practice.

He realizes that namarupa is not causeless, since its formations are not the same nor are they identical. Through this he realizes that their nature and character are different because they result from different causes and conditions; and he sees that the more they are indulged in, the more they become consolidated. He sees that the past influences the present and that the condition for the present will be the conditions for the future.

He becomes aware that it is only through meditation that their arisings can be seen and that, through his own effort and determination, his kamma can be changed.

He notes this by noting how the volitions come about through contact brought about by ignorance and the clinging to the sensations caused by those contacts.

When he becomes conscious of the conditions and the causes of the process of namarupa and his knowledge and consciousness of this process becomes keen, he has developed insight to the second insight knowledge, the pacaya-parigaha nana.

With the establishment of acceptance of the truth by the removal of doubts through further process and the removal of all doubts of the sasana, he attains the third nana that is that of samasasana nana.

Here he achieves the Insight to the truth of anicca, anatta. This means that he understands that all conditioned things come into being and with it comes suffering and decay with its accompanying sorrow, grief, lamentation and finally death and decay leaving nothing behind. He sees this in his formations as he maintains his mindfulness. He sees this in his Mindfulness of Breathing as he watches his rise and fall as he breathes in and breathes out. He also sees the rising of the sign and of the formations and knows the reality of the truth and of the rise and fall, knowing that everything is anicca, dukkha and anatta and that there is to be adosa, alobha and amoha in the end for perfection of purification.

The samasasana nana is achieved when, during meditation, he is able to see both pleasant and unpleasant things and be able to note that formations, both good and evil, are subject to the same laws, their arising and falling being the result of paticcasamuppada conditioned by and the result of craving and desire.

The mind has become calm and malleable and he is ready to enter the fourth jhana. In the fourth jhana, having gained the three purities and the three jhanas, he will begin to develop his insight. To do this the meditator enters the udayabhaya nana for the actual cleansing to begin.

The udayabhaya nana requires not only the fourth nana but, as we have seen, also the knowledge of the first three nanas which allow him to see the formations clearly for what they are. Only then can the cleansing process begin in the udayabhaya nana stage. When this is done, he is an already established meditator and is known as a chulia sottapan.

A sottapan is a noble person. He is a happy person with peace of mind. He will be undisturbed by spite, jealousy, envy, greed and illwill. Though, as yet not a perfect person, he knows what that means. A chulia sottapan is a "Lesser Stream Enterer". Therefore, though not yet a noble one, he is fortunate for he is destined for the higher realms. This, of course, means that he will not be born in a lesser realm but will be born as one of the higher order.

In all this, we see that the awareness in vipassana is difficult to explain without the background of meditative practice. It changes and becomes deeper and deeper. Knowledge of the formations starts with seeing their rise and fall. Without acceptance of the sasana he will not be able to understand them when they arise even though he may perceive them. With this knowledge he begins to see into the truth of how they arise and why they arise. Then he understands that they are different because they arise from different causes. He sees them as they are, void and without substance and he understands the sasana.

From then on come the awareness of the other purities which will become clear when we go on to describe the other purities. For the present we must be satisfied with this summary.

It must also be realized, however, that progress in meditation cannot go further than the paramis will allow him. Since paramis are past meritorious acts, they are part of his kamma. He must accept this. To reach this far is already a very fortunate for the meditator. He has the three roots of the tihetuka person.

If fortunate, he will reach Knowledge of the Vision of the Change-of-lineage which will lead him directly to the path of the ariyas and nibbana.

The ariyas are of four classes, the sottapan, the sakadagami, the anagami and the arahant. The sottapan is the lowest of these ariyas. But only the arahant, the purest of all, enters nibbana upon his immediate death (parinibbana). However, eventual entry into nibbana is assured to all of them.

At the udayabhaya nana state his awareness led him to comprehend the true meaning and nature of kamma and of dependent origination. From then on he begins to understand that the past does not end in the past but leaves behind a kamma that results in a future aggregate.

He realizes that from avijja springs sankhara. From sankhara springs vinanna. From vinanna, rupa arises. From rupa spring the five sense bases (salyutana). From the salyutana come contact (phassa). From contact feeling (vedana) arises. From feeling desire (tanha) arises. From tanha comes attachment (upadana). From upadana comes becoming (bhava).

Because of bhava, there is birth (jati). With jati comes pain, grief, sorrow, lamentation, despair, old age, death and decay (marajarana). Thus, the entire aggregation of ills arise because of kamma.

Thus he moves from one insight wisdom to another till the final nana and purity is achieved.

10

AGGREGATES

The picture of meditation for inner peace is now beginning to get clearer. The formations hold the key to the cleansing process. They mirror the inner and bring about awareness of the existence of the unwholesomeness of the consciousness. Without the formations, the unwholesomeness cannot be discerned and cleansed by noting them with the realization of their true nature and purity.

The five groups of formations, or sankhara, arise from the aggregates known as the khandhas. The khandhas are those of form or materiality, feeling, perception, mental activities and consciousness aggregates. They are the khandhas and are the rupa-, vedana-, sanna-, sankhara- and the vinnana-khandhas.

These aggregates are the result of kamma. They form the preconditioning of all thoughts that arise as the formations. According to their preconditioning, the formations, which are mental objects that arise in the mind when it is awakened from its state of bhavanga when there is contact with one of the six sense bases, take on their nature and character. Through these formations we can understand their preconditioning to which they are subjected.

The sense bases are what we generally call the six sense organs of the ear, nose, eye, tongue, sense of touch and the mind from which sensations arise. They have their faculty of hearing, smelling, vision, taste, feeling of touch and mental formations and their corresponding consciousness.

Through impingement, resultant formations arise by the nama-rupa process, that is to say the process of the mentality-materiality relationship. It is because of this process that we can see the rise and fall of the formations in meditation.

During meditation these formations, which are supportive of another, manifest themselves and they rise and fall according to their kamma which originated them.

They manifest themselves when one becomes, for example, aware of the four elements of air, the heat, the water and the earth elements which manifest themselves in such as the sensation of flying, floating, heat, itchiness, stiffening of the limbs and so on.

How and when are they manifested? When the mind is calm and mindful and when they arise on contact with the mind through the process of namarupa. It is difficult to describe them. They have to be experienced to be clear.

They are what their names imply. Rupakhandha formations are those that arise when the mind contacts the material bases. The other four khandhas of feeling, perception, mental activities and consciousness arise when the mind is in contact with their respective feeling, perception, mind and the consciousness.Their rise and fall confirms the cycle of birth and death in this way.

During meditation, the mind is constantly assailed by these formations coming continuously from these bases. As he sees their rise and fall, he sees the truth of their impermanent and insubstantial nature and he sees the futility of pleasure and abandons the perception of pleasure and permanence. That is their purpose.

As they rise and fall, he sees this as the result of kamma and realizes that they exist outside of his control and that they rise and fall according to their kamma and preconditioning. He is continually confronted by them as they rise even against his will and no sooner as a formation falls, another rise to take its place and he notes that they fall and leave nothing behind.

All he has to do is to maintain his concentration and mindfulness and notes them without attachment and in bare concentration and they will fade away. In doing so he learns not to follow his desires which are the cause of their rebirths.

Through the sense bases the four elements of air, heat, water and earth are perceived. Through the ear door, sounds can be heard even though others may not perceive them. Visions due to the sankhara can appear which have no normal reality. Sensation of touch with things not present is possible. There can even be the sensation of the loss of limbs which has not taken place or one can appear to see into the body the blood gushing through along the channels of the body as if they are real happenings.

Sensations of astral travel, of floating or flying, of illuminations and glows and auras can be common. We can see an example of this meditation experience of a religious woman, when she began to meditate. Even at the third sitting she felt and a glow of light surrounding her as a shield and as if to protect her from harm. This persisted for a while before fading away as she woke from her meditation.

In the next session, there were crisp crackling sounds and she saw beautifully coloured sparks that looked like brilliant Christmas tinsel floating down from the ceiling settling near to her and in the form of a human shape sitting beside her. Not waiting further, she promptly got up and turned off the lights and went upstairs into her room to sleep.

Her example shows and explains the rise and fall of formations very well. Her meditation had only started three sessions earlier and she was able to go into concentration easily enough as to be able to experience formations from her kamma and sankhara.

What she saw were nimittas, or mental images due to contact of the aggregates and not actual spiritual forms. But they are difficult to explain, especially without knowledge of the dhamma.

Loosely, they are the result of mental activity and are formations arising from her kamma. Her visions which are hindrances to meditation, distracted her from concentration so it was interrupted because of attachment.

That the formations were pleasant and experienced so soon after the start of her meditation is due to good kamma because she was religious and had developed calmness referred to by laymen as peace of mind.

The presence of all the six sense doors is necessary for vipassana meditation since the formations have to be sensed through all of them if there is to be the required cleansing of all the formations. Since formations rise from contact of all the six sense doors, they must be all be present before there can be full contact with all these formations. Should there be a deficiency in any of the bases, contact with the formations would not rise from that base.

If that is the case, the unwholesomeness from that deficient base will not arise and therefore cannot be removed. Deficiency of any one of them would render purification impossible. A blind man cannot see and a deaf mute probably cannot speak because he cannot hear.

So also, vipassana meditation would be difficult due to deficiency in any one of the bases.

The six sense doors are the six bases. But they have their six elements and their six faculties of sound, feeling, taste, smell, sight and mental formations and their aggregates of feeling, perception, volition, craving, and applied and sustained thought.

These bases and elements and faculties of sense consciousness are required to contact the formations. They thus play the major part in meditation for the formations are required for the purity of the meditator.

It is through the formations that the meditator sees the namarupa of the rise and fall of his aggregates. Namarupa comes together.

Without one there cannot be the other. One cannot exist without the other. Just as a blind man and a cripple cannot go anywhere without combining their faculties of sight and limbs so also mentality cannot come without materiality.

In this way he understands the emptiness and the voidness of the formations and he realizes that they arise from the kamma. The unwholesomeness of his consciousness is seen as a result of namarupa and he looks for the cause and conditioning for namarupa. Doing so, he realizes that namarupa is not causeless since it is different and unidentifiable.

He sees that the formations come from craving, from clinging and kamma (which makes it different and not identical). And that it, in turn, becomes the condition for the next, related, associated, contingent and subsequent thought. He becomes aware that the existence of every mental formation owes its existence to a past formation and is shaped by it. Thus, the past and the present conditions shape are future thoughts.

This is the theory of paticcasamuppada. So it follows that meditation affects the future by deliberate volitional thought and action. Kamma can thus be influenced during meditation by changing the root condition through the eradication of unwholesome thoughts, provided that the related kamma is not a weighty one which cannot be changed or altered but must take its course and work itself out.

The most interesting and numerous formations come in the udyabhaya nana state when the fourth jhana and mindfulness is established in the meditator so he is to discern the formations clearly. With them come such as bliss, aura, illumination and a false sense of achievement which are some of the ten hindrances of meditation, known as kilesas.

They are hindrances because they are deceptive and encourage attachment or "clinging" and thus hinder the process of abandonment which is required for progress. They are hindrances because they are the result of ignorance and desires and because they give rise to false pleasures. The meditator is deceived by them and clings on to them and thus he does not abandon them and thus his attachment remains and, with them, his ignorance and defilements.

Apart from illuminations and auras, they give the impression of great knowledge and a sharp mind. Sometimes they give a feeling of zest, serenity, bliss and resolve and falsely allow the meditator to think he has achieved those qualities. They can also provide the feeling of exaltation and delight in his achievement and may even allow him to think wrongly he has achieved mindfulness and balance of mind.

But as they are coupled with desires, pleasure and bliss he will suspect that they are illusory. They are in fact aggregates caused by the very ten hindrances to his progress in meditation.

Illumination, for example, is the formation of one of the defilements. It comes as a glow that surrounds the meditator, sometimes lighting up the room and even beyond into the field outside or the sky. This light gives him the feeling of joy or exaltation as if something wonderful has happened to him. It is so wonderful that he may sit there in bliss, clinging on to it not realizing that it is unreal and should not be held on to and is nothing but delusions and he has not arrived at the ariya path.

The feeling of an aura surrounding him is also another formation and another defilement of meditation, so-called because to their shape and glow.

Sometimes his desires are so great that the hindrances become so pleasurable and so deceptive and provide such clarity that he thinks he has become an ariya, his objective and dream.

Sensations of astral travel, reaching into the upper reaches of the azure and deep purple sky, sensing bliss and serenity as he remains in the sky suspended by some supranormal force whilst he looks down on to the distant earth are common instances of such hindrances.

To continue with his progress he has to abandon them for they are the pleasures coming from ignorance and attachment to desires when they are also something insubstantial, impermanent and a delusion.

At times we wonder if those meditators who claim to have seen visions have not seen them as a result of such hindrances. Clinging to them will terminate his meditation progress.

These ten hindrances of meditation known as the kilesas are:

1. Aura, which comes in the sense of an aura;
2. Illumination, that lights up, or surrounds the meditator;
3. Zest, which is the pleasurable interest of insight;
4. Bliss, which is diffusing happiness;
5. Exaltation, which is the feeling of energy, the feeling of being upright and established in the faith;
6. Desire, which is the love of insight and a desire for meditation;
7. Knowledge, through a feeling of the development of a sharp mind;
8. Serenity, which is tranquillity and pleasurable calmness;
9. Resolve, which is taken for faith and resolution;
10. Mindfulness, which is awareness of insight and a balance of mind which is equanimity of insight.

With the knowledge of the rise and fall of the aggregates which the meditator sees as formations, he sees rise and fall of the aggregates with knowledge of the dhamma. This means that he sees the rise and fall with knowledge of the namarupa and paticcasamuppada. So he gains the right insight and realizes that everything is impermanent, that they come and go according to kamma and that when they are gone they leave nothing behind. He sees that there is no one directing them and that there is no such thing as self and that they come as a result of clinging (upadana). Rise and fall can be understood easily if we think of the phrase "come and go".

Thus, seeing and noting them without attachment and in the bare mindfulness, he is detached and does not "cling" to them and they fall and do not rise again.

The progress towards the Path becomes more definite as he moves through the udayabhaya nana state. With the rise of the formations come the ten hindrances and the other defilements that prevent progress. Through their arisings his can see his progress. When he gets rid of them they never arise again and thus he knows that he has rid himself of them.

At the udayabhaya nana, as the knowledge of the namarupa comes free from imperfections and with added strength and firmness, he sees their message even more vividly. This clarity is similar to the clarity of seeing what appears as a thin pencil line to the naked line turning out to be a series of minute dots under a microscope.

From thence on, this clarity of impermanence and pain and suffering develops and when it comes with the knowledge of voidness and the absence of a permanent self, there is realization of a danger facing the entire world. This knowledge of extreme terror is knowledge of the Bhanga nana which nana comes next to the udayabhaya nana.

Bhanga nana with its formations brings about the realization of the falseness of what he sees and which will finally end in nothing. This brings about the formation of extreme fear and despair. He feels like a man caught in the horrors of a jungle with nowhere to turn to.

He realizes the oblivion of everything, the end of the world, so to speak, since all formations are illusions and void of a permanent self. All is lost. He sees only death all round him. He sees the sign of impermanence of all formations around him. He sees the sign of their final breakup and end. This can come in the formations which show that there is nothing but meaningless smoking corpses heaped in a mountain of skeletons with the guard standing there in lonely isolation and there remains nothing else.

This insight shows him the dissipation of all formations to nothing. He realizes that this is the cause of the namarupa arising from contact with the six sense doors over which he has no control. He sees that all the becomings, the generations and destinies provide no refuge or resting place but only pain and suffering, aging, death and decay.

Seeing all this, he sees the vanity, the emptiness and futility of holding on to the concept of a permanent self that does not exist and he sees their voidness. He sees no way out and he abandons all sense of greed for there is no escape from all this inevitable end in nothing. Utterly lost, he gives up all hope and abandons everything.

Another way of expressing this is to say that the meditator, contemplating impermanence abandons the perception of permanence; contemplating pain and suffering he abandons pleasure; contemplating voidness he abandons the perception of self. He, therefore, sees the anicca, dukkha and anatta of things which, of course, is the impermanence, the suffering and the voidness of things.

Suddenly, horrified and broken, he abandons all desires and becomes utterly cold and dispassionate and he looks round dispassionately for a way out. This is a Adinava nana, the knowledge of misery and dispassion. It comes as a result of Bhaya nana. It is Adinava nana because it brings about the formations of depression and disgust. It is knowledge of the truth and disgust of his present situation.

He sees that there will be no terror if there is no arising. If there is no arising, there is no birth, no accumulation of the kamma and therefore no linking with rebirth. He abandons greed and self and becomes dispassionate towards his formations, taking no delight in their false pleasures.

These three knowledge of bhanga, bhaya and adinava, are therefore the awareness of danger, terror and misery. They are different aspects of the same thing and, by interlinking, form a minor group.

Realizing this, he begins to look for a way out through dispassion and abandonment. From this dispassion, he seeks to escape from his worldly condemnation and develops the desire for deliverance from this misery.

Through the desire for deliverance and of escape, he begins to understand with impact, that all the supposed reality is nothing more than formations which he now knows are null and void and do not belong to anyone but are merely formations arising from desires, that he does not control them.

Even as he begins to realize their true nature, he also finds that there is a chance of escape. The awareness of disgust is Nibbida nana; the desire for deliverance is Munchituka nana; awareness that there is an escape is reflected in the analysis known as Pattisankha upekkha nana and are collectively known as knowledge of Reflexion or Sankharupekha nana.

They are the knowledge in the Contemplation on Reflexion because realization comes on looking back on his own life to understand what has happened and what could be done to rectify it. Looking back and seeing danger everywhere, he realizes that all formations are impermanent, painful and empty; that they are all subject to decay and that they contain the three qualities of anicca, dukkha and anatta. Seeing this truth there is sudden alarm followed by fear and sudden dejection.

This fear brings a sense of acceptance of the inevitable. Suddenly, this gives way to a sense of hope as he realizes that there could be a way out and he seizes this chance.

This is explained in the parable of a fisherman who put his hand into his net, thinking that he had found a fish. He pulls it out and, to his horror, he finds that he has caught a snake by the neck instead. This horror is quickly superseded by the realization of terror because it is a snake. All his anticipation is gone. It is dissipated. Thinking that all is lost, he gives way to the inevitable and becomes dispassionate, repulsed by its foulness.

As he becomes dispassionate, he looks quickly around to deliver himself of the snake. There is a desire for deliverance. He quickly swings the snake round and round to weaken it and releases it and flings it away with a feeling of relief. Then he quickly moves away from the place with a sigh of relief, saying to himself, "Thank goodness I have been delivered from the jaws of that huge snake."

So also the meditator, metaphorically, rids himself of that huge snake by ridding himself of attachment to the desires which give rise to the formations.

He escapes his formations as the fisherman escapes death at the jaws of the snake. This he does by the reflection upon their impermanence of the sign as the knowledge arises; realization through reflection on the pain and suffering occurring the formations; realizing the oneself on reflection on their occurrence. That is to say, he sees the sign of impermanence, pain and suffering and the voidness of the formations.

Thus the three nanas in the knowledge on the Contemplation on Reflexion result in this way. He now knows he has no self, friends, property and relations. He sees voidness in the ayatamas, aggregates and their formations, materiality, past present or future.

"Let him look upon the world as a void thus, Mogharaja" said Buddha, "Always be mindful, one may escape death by giving up belief in Self. For King Death cannot see the man who looks this way on the world." (*Suttanipata 1119 Cula Nidessa* (Siam Ed 190) As this awareness of meditation comes, there is cessation of the formations so that there is a calmness due to detachment of formations which have ceased to arise.

He thus becomes calm due to the non-arising of the formations. Thus there is indifference to composite things and he then sees nibbana as absolute peace.

These sixth, seventh and eighth nanas are in the Contemplation on Reflexion. They are also grouped together because they form the sankharupa nana and are sometimes referred to simply as that name. After them comes the santhana nana which is the posture.

We can also group munchitukamyata (or munchituku), pattisankha nanas. They allow for previous experiences to be reviewed and are three aspects of the same thing because the desire for deliverance (munchitukumyata) leads to reflexion (pattisankha), with santhana nana since santhana means posture and together they can be considered as reflexion knowledge that then leads to a posture.

When he reaches this stage, he contemplates and reflects and prepares himself to turn away from the worldly existence towards nibbana. He is then swept towards purity of vision of the change-of-lineage, gotrabhu nana, through the gates into the state of the ariyas as if by tide.

This happens in this way. The sankharupekha nana, which is collectively the ninth nana in this structure, takes place as the meditator further develops in resolve, knowledge of the truth and in equanimity. His knowledge of the rise and fall is strengthened and he sees them precisely and clearly for what they are supposed to be.

He first sees the dissolution, then their three characteristic marks, the terror of dissolution and so on with complete equanimity. He is now even able to see their anusayas, that is, their very stirrings before arising.

It all started at the udayabhaya nana when the formations are understood.

From then on comes the realization of what they are bring about, the realization of danger, utter despondency, desire for detachment from the formations, a search for release, understanding through reflecting on what has happened, tallness of the formations and then arrival at the gates of entry into the realm of the ariyas and, finally, as if with the tide, the meditator crosses the river to land on the other side and becomes an ariya.

11

UDAYABHAYA NANA

Knowledge of the first three nanas of namarupacheda, paccaya pariggaha and samanasana nanas indicate the gaining of purity of sila, consciousness and purity views (sila-, citta-, ditthi- visuddhi). These are the prerequisites for entry into the udayabhaya nana stage, where doubts are overcome by sufficient knowledge and the fourth purity of kankhavitarana visuddhi is obtained.

In it are the ten defilements of meditation (kilesas) which he overcomes which enable him to see more clearly because the defilements are no longer able to confuse him and cloud the truth.

Achieving the udayabhaya nana, be begins to see the way to inner peace clearly. For this nana is insight wisdom to full knowledge of the rise and the final dissolution of all formations, whatever their cause.

He is aware of the correct path. He has the knowledge and the vision of this correct path. He can now seek for the fifth purity of Magga-magga nanadasana visuddhi.

The meditator becomes a chulia sottapan. Though not yet an ariya, he should indeed be a happy person, for he is now assured of being reborn in a happy plane. He is one who has gained the wisdom of udayabhaya nana, or Purification of the Overcoming of Doubt. He is now able to discern the cause and condition of namarupa, the knowledge of kamma and of the rise-and-fall of the formations. Through Purification of the View (ditthi visuddhi), or the Samasana nana, he can see namarupa and paticcasamuppada correctly and so has proper awareness of anicca, dukkha and anatta. Now, he has achieved purity by Overcoming Doubt, he has developed correct views to see through delusion of moha so develop amoha.

Though not yet with perfect clarity, as he is not yet a noble person, he now understands what is ignorance (moha); he is aware that all is conditioned existence and subject to birth and death (anicca) without a permanent self (anatta) being subject to suffering and decay (dukkha); so he will no longer strive for permanence as he no longer has any doubt, so he will be able to develop insight wisdom and understanding (panna) for nibbana.

He is no longer a victim of unresolve and restlessness due to uncertainty, and he will now look for the way into the four noble states of the ariyas, being that of the sottapan, (the Stream Enterer); the sakadagami, the anagami and the arahant, whose passage into nibbana is assured.

From Purity by Overcoming Doubt, he will to gain knowledge of the Vision of what is and what is not the Path. This is the Maggamagga nanadassana visuddhi which will lead him to the sixth purity of Purity of knowledge and vision of the change-of-lineage, the pattipada nanadassana visuddhi that will bring him into the realm of the ariyas.

The entry into the Path comes with the anuloma nana and the gotrabu nana which brings about the temporary cessation of formations as the Path is reached and entry effected.

There are three gateways into the Path, known as the triple gateway and the four separate ariya Paths, each with its own "fruit". As each Path is entered there is the cessation of formations and thus its own awareness which thus identifies each Path. They are named according to the predominance of the factors at entry.

By this time, the vision of the anicca, dukkha and anatta of all formations through their cessation and the impermanence and dissatisfaction of all things conditioned is clear and there is alobha, adosa and amoha. But the perfection is limited and only fully achieved at the state of the arahant which is the final achievement. At which point, there is complete emancipation from lobha, dosa and amoha and thus from all worldly ills and with absolute inner peace.

Vipassana therefore provides the most complete awareness of the truth of all our suffering.

Formations appear most in the udayabhaya state due to the stillness in a well balanced mind because of the defilements. This makes the udayabhaya the most interesting state of all states. But the presence of the formations is evidence of desires at their highest degree. The more the desires, the more the formations. The more the formations, the more the distractions and hindrances.

But this is where cleansing is also more severe. Through mindfulness and noting without attachment, the mind is trained to detach itself from them and this, together with sila, develop calmness and the lessening of the formations and they are slowly reduced through practice (known as bhavana in Pali).

As long as these hindrances remain we will cling to them and so hold on to our desires, there will be no progress. Only when they are overcome by mindfulness can progress be maintained for the concentration will be assailed, confused, distracted and terminated.

At times, there can be a switch over from vipassana to samatha and mindfulness terminated as, for example, the cases when the meditator is noting the impermanence and the pain of decay of the bodily parts when his attention is drawn to the colour of the blood on the bodily part and concentration becomes fixed upon its red colour.

When that happens and he sees the colour instead of sensing the pain, he switches over a colour kasina in samatha meditation instead of maintaining his vipassana practice.

As some meditation subjects can also be employed in both meditations, the difference between these two concentrations should always be clearly maintained so that the nature of the practice does not to change during the middle of a session.

It must now also become obvious that the cleansing process requires detachment from our desires as well as the replacing or supplanting of desires with non-desires, the unwholesome with the wholesome. Or the abandonment of an unwholesome state through acquisition of a wholesome one.

This system of achievement through abandonment of a lower state for a higher one through dissatisfaction is a principle of meditation. This happens in samatha as well where the meditator has to abandon unwanted lower jhanas in order to ascend to the higher ones just as the climber abandons the lower step of a ladder to reach the higher step.

If this process of abandoning continues final purity is gained. If this does not happen, it means that his paramis does not allow him to go further and he will not be able to proceed further.

Abandoning is a process of continued development of the purities till the formations are momentarily stilled in the sankha-rupekha nana state. This is the threshold of the Path where he is, as if caught in a tide, swept through one of the triple gateway into the noble path.

But abandonment at the higher levels is not only of the remaining the grosser faults but of the subtler and finer ones and such as the anusayas, which are formations as they are about to arise, something which meditators of the lower states are not able to observe.

At the state of the arahant, all the actions of the meditator will no longer have any kammic effect because they are now without desire or attachment or any unwholesomeness. His acts are kriya, that is to say, they have no kammic effect.

To recapitulate, sila and samadhi are the two basic foundations of purity from which the other five purities develop. These purities are identified by the achievement of the nanas whose presence, like milestones, help to show the development of purities.

Sila is maintained by observance of the Eightfold Noble Path of Right Concentration, Effort, Mindfulness, View, Intention, Speech, Action and Livelihood.

Samadhi comprises of the first three of concentration, effort and mindfulness. The other five of view, intention, speech, action and livelihood belong to matters of the mind and reflect his sila.

Through sila and samadhi, the meditator will begin to see the three basic roots of greed, illwill and delusion that give rise to the formations due to ignorance of the truth. Proper practise in the Eightfold noble path allows him an opportunity to remove ignorance and dispel the formations which have their beginnings in the subconscious.

Vipassana requires the knowledge of the dhamma for the understanding of the formations and the void nature of namarupa to develop amoha. Purity of consciousness together with purity of views enables him to see the law of causality in the rise and fall of his formations in the udayabhaya nana state and to bring about alobha and adosa as well.

The Patisambhida (187) explains that, in the first purity, he gains knowledge of Insight; in the second the causes of the formations; and in the third, that of the rise (udaya) and the fall (bhaya) of all mental and material formations.

Hence this knowledge is known as the udayabhaya nana which is found during the search for knowledge within the Purity in Overcoming Doubts, or the kank-havitarana visuddhi.

Therefore, the very first knowledge to be acquired in vipassana is the meaning of the namarupa. This knowledge is known as the namaruparicheda nana. It enables him to see the rise and fall of the namarupa.

After awareness of the formations comes awareness as to their causes. This awareness is paccaya pariggaha nana. From this he will see that all formations are subject to the same laws of rise and fall at will with voidness at the end of it all. Thus, with this knowledge comes the samasasana nana. This third knowledge allows him to see the rise (udaya) and the dissolution (bhaya) according to the four noble truths of suffering.

Hence these three knowledge precede the udayabhaya nana state where the meditator sees the rise and fall of the formations for what they really are and becomes fully aware of the void effects of causes under the law of paticcasamuppada.

The udayabhaya is the first of the nine nanas of the udayabhaya, bhanga, bhaya, adina, nibbana, muncituka, pattisankha, sankharupekka and anuloma nanas which lead to the entrance of the Path.

From then on there is also classified, another group of which deals with the actual entry into the path itself. This is the anuloma nana and gottrabu, which is the change-of-lineage of the meditator as he enters the gateway, into the realm of the ariyas.

These nanas come within the fifth and sixth Purities of Maggamagga nanadassana visuddhi and Pattipada-nadassana visuddhi which in turn bring the meditator into the seventh and the last purity of Nanadassana visuddhi.

Nadassana means knowledge and insight; magga-magga means paths; pattipada means gradual progress towards this knowledge of the path. Thus, the whole process of these two nanas is grouped into the sixth pattipada-nadassana visuddhi which leads the meditator into the path.

At this stage there is nothing else to be done. The change-of-lineage is like a final tide that will lift and sweep him into the Path of the ariyas.

Achieving the nanadassana visuddhi is the target of vipassana and the path to ultimate peace.

12

CHANGE-OF-LINEAGE

After the stillness of the formations in sankharupekha nana comes anuloma which immediately precedes gotrabhu nana, the gateway leading into the seventh and the last of the Purities, into the state of the ariyas. The Change-of-lineage marks the border between lokiya plane of the ariyas and lokuttara, that of the ordinary persons.

The Visuddhi Magga takes great pains at giving examples of how this change-of-lineage happens to each meditator. However, there is a vagueness which may have been deliberate to prevent fraudulent claims since the description is hard to understand without the benefit of actual experience.

But before it is set out, it is important to stress that emergence from the entry is defined according to how the meditator has arrived at the Path, as the entry is a triple gateway. Which of the triple gateway is the entry effected is dependent upon whether it emerges as a result of seeing the internal or external formations, or whether the formations are material or immaterial, and whether the predominant aspect at the time of entry was primarily the result of awareness of impermanence, pain, or the voidness of the formations. According to their predominance, the entry is named.

This explains why it is referred to as the triple gateway into the Path. The Visuddhi Magga provides twelve examples to demonstrate how the entry into the gateway is effected:

1. **The Bat** — In this example, the bat, having alighted on a madhuka tree explores its five branches and having found them barren, immediately climbs up a straight

branch, pokes her head through the foliage and looking upwards flies straight off to another tree.

The meaning is as follows. The five branches are the five aggregates as objects of clinging. Finding them to be empty and barren it loses interest in them and abandons them and gains conformity knowledge by climbing straight up and then obtaining change-of-lineage by flying straight up to another tree.

2. **The Black Snake** — This example has been dealt with above in the parable of the fisherman who found a snake instead of the fish he was hoping to catch.
3. **The House** — The owner of a house, ate his meal one evening and climbed into his bed and fell asleep. The house caught fire. He woke up, saw the fire and was frightened. He thought, "It would be good if I could get out without getting burnt". Looking round, he saw a way out. Getting out he quickly went to a safe place and stayed there. His enjoyment of food and sleep are the enjoyments of the five aggregates in ignorance of the truth. Seeing the fire and developing fear is likened to the development of terror on seeing the three characteristic marks of the aggregates. Seeing the way out is the conformity knowledge and getting out of the house is likened to change-of-lineage and staying in a safe place in relief is fruition.
4. **The Oxen** — One night the oxen of a farmer escaped. He went out and recovered them. When morning came he found that he had taken the king's oxen instead. He was frightened of what would happen to him when the king's men found out that he had taken the king's oxen. He immediately abandoned the oxen and quickly escaped to a safe place. The meaning is clear.

   The taking of the escaped oxen is the clinging to the formations in the delusion that "these are mine". Recognizing the truth that the aggregates were never his and are impermanent, painful and non-self, he abandons them in terror and looks for delivery by running away and fruition is found in the safety of the new place.

5. **The Ghoul** — A man went to live with a ghoul. One night, thinking that he was asleep, she went to a place where the dead were exposed and began to eat human flesh. The man, who was not asleep, wondered where she was going to, followed her and found out what she was doing. In sudden fear, realizing that he had better run away before she ate him, escaped to stay in a safe place. The explanation is clear.
6. **The Child** — A mother who was very fond of her own child was sitting in a room on the upper floor of her house when she heard a child crying in the street below. Thinking that someone was beating her child, she went out and picked up the child only to find that she had picked up someone else's child. Quickly, thinking that she might suffer the consequence of the accusation of being a baby thief, she abandoned the child and returned to her room and sat there. Here also the example is clear (7-12).

There are altogether twelve examples given in the Visuddhi Magga. Six have already been set out above. There other six (7 to 12) are similar examples that demonstrate indulgence of desires will never quench those desires but will only strengthen them. The only way out is through their removal as is the case of the formations. This brings about realization that there can only be emancipation of the Path. They are not set out here as their message is similar to the above and repetition would be tedious.

On arrival at the gateway, the meditator will have completed his sixth purity.

What was a despondency, unhappiness, hesitancy, fear, lack of confidence, insecurity and disturbing anxieties has now given way to a mind that is a still and limpid pool of serenity and calm and he will soon experience nibbana. This is the true peace of mind that we all look for.

Buddha explains this by explaining that nibbana comes about only through the stillness of the mental formations which are the result of desires due to detachment from our roots of greed and illwill and delusion and their derivatives.

Once there is no attachment and the formations no longer distract him, he is calm and detached and nothing disturbs him because he is not concerned with greed, or illwill or ego. He realizes the inevitability of death and is not worried because he is no longer attached to life itself. He thus becomes fearless; has no false pride except to do what is proper and correct. He does not look for approbation or cares for condemnation; since he has no illwill, he does not bear grudges, nor is there any sense of vengeance, spite or envy; in fact, he is not bothered at all by those things which bring restlessness, agitation, laziness or dissatisfaction and unhappiness which plague others. He is at peace with himself and has no sense of possessiveness or of possessions.

In the words of the Abhidamma, formations are stilled and he is ready to enter the gateway into nibbana through the change-of-lineage, into the state of the ariyas – a state only he can realise himself and no other.

At the highest level, he will reach parinibbana which is the final nibbana of causeless existence and therefore without a beginning or an end.

It is again emphasised that only a tihetuka person can develop the awareness of delusion of and so gain non-delusion for this requires knowledge of the dhamma to penetrate the truth of non-self and the voidness of the formations without which the seven essential purities, for attainment cannot be achieved. Nothingness does not enable that achievement.

Furthermore, vipassana requires the practice of sila which defines our practice as the nanas define the state of our progress and the knowledge of the dhamma and the realization of the truths of the formations whose presence, our clarity of observation, their nature and their gradual disappearance, signal our progress in the achievements of the purities. This process continues till even the slightest arisings (anusayas) are removed at the state of the arahant.

Let us now take a look at the states of the ariyas in the seventh purity, the Purification by Knowledge and Vision of the whole Path, or the nanadassana visuddhi, so that we may complete our bird's eyeview of the meaning of vipassana and the path to purity.

13
DIFFERENT GATEWAYS

The nine knowledges from the fifth Purity of Knowledge and Vision of the Way, which begins with the udayabhaya nana and ends at sankharupekka nana, lead the meditator automatically to gotrabhu nana and then into Knowledge and Vision of the whole Path which is the seventh purity and the abode of the ariyas.

We may now define the triple gateway into the Path mentioned earlier.

To understand this, we must know that there are seven types of persons who enter this Path and that there are eight noble persons, or ariyas, being those of the sottapana, sakadagami, anagami, and the arahant, four without the fruit and four with the fruit.

During the description of reflection, we have touched upon the sign of impermanence and the voidness of formations. In the description of equanimity about formations, the word nibbana was also mentioned. We should now go back to examine these terms in some detail.

In reflection, there is the sign confirming whether or not he has actually achieved this state and there is a review when he reflects upon the path on which he has come where the milestones are marked in a definite series of insight events.

We know that the signs at entry of the gateways are of three kinds, defining the type of entry and the kind of person making this entry.

The sign is the sign of cessation and it provides a glimpse of the Path. There is first a cessation of the formations before there is the entry. Then there is a sign of attainment of the Path and the sign of its fruit.

He enters through the gateway of voidness when voidness is the predominant quality of his knowledge. This means that he sees that all formations are void and have no self and are subject to their own rise and fall depending upon kamma. "I" belongs to no one and nothing belongs to "I".

When he is conscious that the past makes the present and the present makes the future and the endless cycle goes on without self, without soul, without any permanency and that all materiality is impermanent, soulless and subject to change, pain and suffering and the whole world is conditioned and subject to change and final decay, voidness is the sign of the gateway, entry and the sign of its fruit.

He enters through the gateway of impermanence where this is the predominant quality of his meditation and he sees the impermanency of the formations in the rise-and-fall.

He enters through the gateway of pain where the predominance in his meditation is knowledge of the pain of suffering and the cessation of pain on arrival at the gateway.

All entries occur when there is a cessation of the formations. The difference is in the form of the occurrence of the cessation of the rise and fall. On seeing this sign and reflecting on it and its occurrence he sees there is this non occurrence of the formations.

With this non occurrence of the formations, comes knowledge of the equanimity of formations. This is sankharupekka nana where all formations cease and the consciousness is poised to enter into nibbana.

Often the first entry into nibbana is not complete at the first attempt but is hesitant. The formations do not cease completely and if it does, it does so but briefly, as if it has arrived at nibbana but not quite. This is likened to the story of the crow that flies from the masthead of the ship when it thinks that land is about to be sighted and returning again and again to the ship because of its failure to actually sight land and then leaving the ship when it finally sights land.

The entry by impermanency, or pain or voidness is to say that the entry is through the gateway of anicca or dukkha or anatta. At this stage of entry, the meditator continues to contemplate on anicca, dukkha and anatta which will eventually lead him to one of the triple gateways.

The Triple Gateway

The triple gateway into nibbana can therefore be said to reflect the three characteristic marks of the formations being that of anicca, dukkha and anatta. Anicca is impermanence; dukha is pain and anatta is non-self and voidness. Nibbana is realized according to which of the three factors is predominant when he reaches the gateway. Nibbana, therefore, can be approached in one of three ways.

From the point of view of the signs of entry, the first gateway is through the faculty of seeing formations as limited and circumscribed and entering of consciousness into the signless element. It is signless because the meditator sees impermanence and he is said to acquire signless liberation.

Where there is tranquillity through the rejection of pain and desire; he is said to have entered by the second gateway of desireless liberation. The entry here is by way of the painless and desireless path.

The third gateway is liberation through void liberation. It is void because he sees the anatta of things. This means that he is aware that everything is empty, without a core and without any center. This is entry by the sign of voidness.

Thus, the triple gateway means that there are these three entries and entry is through one of these entries, dependent upon which of the three is the predominant factor of the knowledge of the meditator.

Since all the three characteristic marks are present and the gateway is defined according to which faculty is the most predominant, we can also say that entry is through one of the characteristics of anicca, dukkha or anatta.

Where it is achieved through anicca, it is signless because it comes with the knowledge of impermanence (anicca). In such cases it also comes with faith as the predominant factor. This happens to those who enter through the gateway of faith as the predominant factor. Thus, the signless gateway is entry through faith, or knowledge of anicca.

Where it is achieved through dukkha, it is said to be desireless because it comes with the knowledge of pain (dukkha). Such cases are those who arrive by this gateway are those who come through the jhanas or who have achieved tranquillity through samatha.

Where attainment is also achieved in vipassana as well, such persons are two-way liberated persons as they have been liberated through samatha and vipassana. Such persons are said to have arrived through the gateway of desirelessness or painlessness.

Where the arrival is by way of anatta, it is said to voidness because it comes with the knowledge that every formation is soulless (anatta). Thus, the meditator approaches the Path through the realization that everything is without permanency and that everything is void and without a permanent soul. Such persons are said to have found the gateway through wisdom (panna).

With the knowledge of this classification, it becomes easy to understand the classification of the Noble Ones into seven kinds. Who are these attainers?

Entry to Nibanna is through these three gateways (anicca, dukkha anatta) only and the attainers are of seven kinds grouped in four categories as follows:

1. **The Faith Devotee or One Liberated by Faith** — In this instance the attainer sees all formations to non-existent before they arise. He therefore enters through signlessness. There are two kinds here:
   - On the moment of reaching the 1st path, that of the sottapan, who is known as a faith devotee i.e. he attains the sottapan in his belief of the Dhamma;
   - Thereafter as he progresses up the remaining 3 Paths and achieves their respective fruition he is known as one who has aggained signless deliverance, having abandoned the sign of the formations through the Dhamma.

2. **The Body Witness** — Here the attainer sees pain, suffering and decay in all formations and he knows that it is no use to cling to these formations as desireless aspect faculty is highest. He sees dukka in all formations. He sees paid and impermanence of things and he enters through desireless aspects in all 4 Paths and their fruitions.
3. **The Both Ways Liberated Person** — We have spoken of the 4 jhanas to achieve upekkha (or a calm sustained meditative state) and the continuation in which the arupa or immaterial or concentration on material subjects to attain the 4 arupa states in samatha when such a person then hears the Dhamma and attains the Path through the acceptance of the Dhamma he is liberated by them through samatha and vipassana and known as a two-way liberated person.
4. **The Dhamma Devotee** — The most important thing in vipassana meditation is to achieve insight wisdom and knowledge of the anicca, dukkha and anatta of all formations i.e. that all formations arise subject to decay and ends as void. This insight wisdom comes from the faculty of understanding puts understanding uppermost. There are 3 types here:
   - In the case of the Dhamma devotee he is divided on entry in the 1st Path sottapan and others who enters the highest Paths. In this instance he sees that every formation is void and when they disappear they leave nothing behind (anatta). Seeing this voidness he comes to the understanding that everything is void. At the Path of the sottapan he attains through voidness;
   - Thereafter, in the next 6 instances until he reaches the 4th state he is known as one who has attained to the Vision, i.e. he has seen, realised and experienced with understanding that formations are impermanent, painful and void (anicca, dukkha and anatta) and that cessation of the formation provided genuine balance because he does not feel suffering;

- When he reaches the 4th arahant, he is known as one who is liberated by understanding.

Thus, we can see how the seven ways of arrival at the Path and its fruition are named descriptively, dependent on if it was awareness of impermanence, or pain, or voidness that was predominant and whether in the mind and its faculties at the time of the arrival at the Path.

The Eight Noble Persons in the Four Planes

Since each path has its own respective Fruition, there are eight kinds of Noble Persons in all divided into the four Ariyas of the sottapan, sakadagami, anami and the arahant, each with their respective fruitions:

1. The Sottapan who has found the Path.
2. The Sottapan who has found the Fruit.
3. The Sakadagami who has found the Path.
4. The Sakadagami who has found the Fruit.
5. The Anagami who has found the Path.
6. The Anagami who has found the Fruit.
7. The Arahant who has found the Path.
8. The Arahant who has found the Fruit.

14

ATTAINMENT

Attainment means becoming an ariya. During this entry, one has a glimpse of nibbana in the cessation of the formations. Entry is gotrabu which is by one of three gateways depending upon which is the predominant factor on entry of the three characteristic marks of anicca, dukkha or anatta.

The passage to this gateway is marked by a series of nanas occurring only in meditation which provide insight knowledge. They also act as milestones along our journey.

During the udayabhaya nana state, which sees the beginning of the "cleansing" process, we also begin to see the namarupa as our mind is provoked through our sense organs. The order of these formations are not definite and are all experienced apparently haphazardly, but they arise in accordance to their kamma and the defilements which allow their true nature and their characteristic marks of anicca, dukkha and anatta to be ascertained.

But nanas are gained in a logical and a definite order. This order can expose false claims. Progress, on the other hand, does not come at any definite time table. It depends upon the kamma of the meditator. It may come easily or with difficulty, slowly or speedily or it may not even come at all. If it does not come, it could be because he does not have sufficient paramis, or it may be due to wrong practice.

If he has insufficient paramis then he can practice for his future paramis, bearing in mind that meditation with sila will always keep him in profitable states.

If his lack of progress is due to wrong practice then he should immediately correct it. It is important to maintain the correct practice that requires sila, and develop proper samadhi, both of which are parts of the Eightfold noble path.

Sila stills the mind from distractions to develop proper samadhi with which to see the truth of the formations and the removal of the formations.

Until there is proper concentration and right views without sukha and piti and with upekha, it would be of advantage for samatha practice if he has difficulty in concentration. He could at least establish his concentration up to the fourth jhana in samatha before he switches to vipassana. It is a matter of personal choice and he may switch over at any time and use Mindfulness of Breathing which can take him to the fourth jhana in any event

To be a two-way liberated person, the eighth jhana has to be gained before he becomes as arahant through vipassana.

A meditator who does not achieve abhinna before he attains, is known as a bare-insight attainer.

As the meditator develops wholesomeness, he also abandons the state of loss. As he develops wholesomeness, he abandons fetters, hindrances, defilements and he achieves their opposites. Similarly, he attains freedom from them when he gains their opposites and thus inner peace is found.

Finally, he reaches nibbana when he completely gains his freedom from these defilements and their taints. Hence, the title of the second great book, the Vimuthi Magga, means the Path to Freedom. Unfortunately it comes to us only in its garbled Chinese translation.

The asavas are the taints of the defilements and their derivatives. In order to abandon the unwholesome defilements, the Brahmavihara must be practised.

Purification continues right through to the ariyas states to the final state of the arahant. Thus it does not require absolute purity to become an ariya.

At the first path of the Sottapan, he essentially abandons false view of individuality, uncertainty, adherence to rites and rituals. Since the sottapan is the lowest of the noble ones, not too much can be expected from him. Those who do not enter the monkhood can become sottapans and sakadagami, depending upon his state of purity and how he maintains his eightfold path.

Each level of the ariyas has its own state of purity and they are so many that a schedule has been provided for reference and it would be advisable to look at it.

When he reaches the state of the arahant, he loses all sense of pride, such as his sense of affront when blamed and pleasure when praised. His concept of "I" and even its tendencies or arisings (anusayas) which persist till the very end, are, at last, removed.

Meditation is spiritual. It is difficult to understand without actual meditation experience. The ariya paths and their achievements are even greater mysteries to those who have not meditated. To explain it many ways have been attempted.

By way of an attempt at explanation, we have to understand that nibbana arises when there is a cessation of the formations. What the meditator sees on attainment of the ariya path are but glimpses of it. To achieve it, there has to be no cause to bring about the formations. Therefore, as soon as the defilements of greed, illwill and delusion are abandoned, the conditioning for the arising of the formations will have been eliminated so that they will cease to arise.

Formations are formed and influenced antecedent, proximate, affinitive, contiguous, associated and connect thoughts. When the thoughts are kusala there is cessation of the unwholesome formations.

Upon reaching the sankharupekha state, the formations will cease to arise as there is abandonment, and from this point on, the question of reaching the ariya path is a matter of course, since the meditator has nothing further to do but to let the process continue on its own, for sankharupekka nana is but the first of the three nanas concerned directly with attainment of the Path. For after it, as we know, comes anuloma nana, or conformity and then, gotrabhu nana, or Change-of-Lineage.

Sankharupekha, anuloma and gotrabhu nanas are the three that directly lead the meditator into the gateway where the meditator moves from darkness to light.

This is the culmination of insight practice. It is culmination because it is the final stage and leads to emergence. (Visuddhi Magga page 772, para. 83).

Thus, the meditator comes to the end of his journey. He has gained the knowledge we have dealt with, and the thirty-seven states taking part in the Enlightenment leading to the triple gateway into the Path.

On entry through the gateway, the ordinary puthujhana becomes an ariya.

This entry and emergence is one of the great spiritual mysteries of meditation which cannot be understood unless there is actual experience.

For that reason, even the great book Visuddhi Magga has had to cite the several suttas referred to below to try to explain it.

After conformity, there immediately comes change-of-lineage, leading to emergence. As not to be confused about this insight which leads into emergence, the following suttas cited by the Visuddhi Magga have to be understood.

The Salayatana-vibhanga Sutta (M.iii,220) refers to this as surmounting equanimity by relying on aloofness. The Alagadda Sutta (M.i,139) refers to it as the fading away of greed through dispassion. The Susima Sutta (S.ii, 124) explains it by stating that whereas, previously there is knowledge of the relationship of the states, thereafter there will only be knowledge of nibbana. The Potthapada Sutta (D.i,185) says that whereas previously there is culmination of perception, thereafter there is knowledge. And the Dasuttara Sutta (D.iii,288) says that the emergence is purification by knowledge and vision of the Path as the principle factor of unity.

In the Patisambhida, which is the text most often referred to by most of the authors, it is referred to by its three names of Desire for Deliverance, Contemplation of Reflexion and Equanimity about Formations:

These three are of the same meaning and only the names are different.

The Visuddhi Magga chooses the words of the Rathavinita Sutta and calls it "Purification by Knowledge and Vision of the Way".

This appears as the seventh purity in the scheme of Purity used by the Visuddhi Magga. This scheme is adopted by most writers.

Let us take a practical example of what happens. At the sankharupekka nana state, the meditator goes into a somewhat dreamless somnolence which he will not be aware of till after his awaking later on. At this state there is a sudden he is suddenly aware of a sort of bump and he awakes with a shock, wondering what has happened. He is filled with an excitement that is not the same as when he is suddenly awakened.

He is breathing very fast and looks around as he tries to recollect what has happened and his mind goes back in review of what has taken place. He wonders if he had fallen off to sleep during meditation, which is impossible as it is in the early hours of the morning and he had awakened from sleep to do his meditation and, as usual, was still feeling fresh. Besides, the waking up was without any disorientation as is common with sleep.

In a state of wonderment, he gets up and wanders off from his seat, feeling excited and somewhat lightheaded. The excitement takes a while to wear off and he notices he is still breathing fast.

Did he wake from his sleep or was it gotrabhu, he asks himself. It was as if he had awakened from his sleep, yet it was not. Later, a nimitta takes place which is not the same as the normal nimittas. Is that fruition or was he enjoying the fruition?

The description of this attainment is explained in the Texts in this way.

Change-of-lineage, according to the Visuddhi Magga, is the overcoming of "arising... non-arising..." as it enters cessation, nibbana, thus, it is change-of-lineage (Visuddhi Magga XXII. para.6 page 786).

There is a simile provided in the same paragraph of a man attempting to leap across the stream swinging from a rope and afraid of letting go till the third attempt. On letting go of the rope, he falls on his feet on the other side of the river because he has never done this before. Thus, the change-of-lineage makes nibbana its object whilst conformity removes the murky of defilements that prevent the making of nibbana as its object.

Another simile is that of a man going out into the night to see the moon which is hidden by thick clouds when, suddenly, the wind springs up and dispels the three layers of clouds so that the man is able suddenly to see the moon which is nibbana, either suggesting the three layers of clouds are the three types of gateway to nibbana or of the happening of sankharupekha, anuloma and the gotrabhu nanas.

So far the description is clear. But then the problems arise when we attempt to identify where the Path and where the Fruit. For it is suggested that the attainment and the fruit come within the seven impulses of the same thought moment. But I believe that since there is review at the end of each attainment and review at the end of its fruit, that either there is a confusion as to the meaning of phala, which is the Pali term for fruit, or that there are definitely three different fruits, one for each of the Path.

According to the description of Parayahera Vajiranana Mahathera in his Cambridge thesis published in a book *Buddhist Meditation* published by the Buddhist Missionary Society, Kuala Lumpur, conformity, gotrabhu, the path and its fruition begins and ends with the same thought moment and within its seven impulsions. (See I. – *Mental Process of the Path,* page 411). There is diagram provided by him which makes it clear.

According to him there are the seven javanas (meaning that there are seven thought impulses in the thought moment of entering the Path) of the Path process; three mark the three anuloma moments and assume the gotrabhu moment when it assumes nibbana and the meditator reaches the noble rank.

Where the achievement is fast there are only two anuloma impulsions and three Fruition impulsions. The mind leaves sankhara as its object at the third anuloma and assumes nibbana as its object at the end of the third.

This description is the accepted description by many writers on this subject. The Visuddhi Magga at Chap. XXII para.15 at page 788 has this to say:

"Immediately next to that knowledge, however, there arise either two or three fruition consciousness, which are its result. There must be two conformity consciousness, since one alone does not act as repetition condition. And a single series of impulsions has a maximum of seven (impulsion) consciousness. Consequently, that series which has two conformities and change-of-lineage as third and path consciousness as fourth has three fruition consciousness. That, which has three conformities and change-of-lineage as third and path consciousness as fourth has three fruition consciousness." That is why it was said above "there arise two or three fruition consciousness".

But then, the Visuddhi Magga at the same chapter XXII paras. 19, 20 and 21 says when the meditator comes to the end of the fruition his mind adverts and interrupts the life-continuum for the purpose of reviewing the path. "When that has ceased, seven impulsions of path reviewing arise. After re-entry into the life-continuum, adverting etc., arise again in the same way for the purpose of reviewing fruition, and so on. With the arising of these he reviews the path, he reviews the fruition, he reviews the defilements still remaining and he reviews nibbana".

And it goes on to add that the meditator "reviews the path I have come by". Next he reviews the fruition in this way, "This is the blessing I have obtained".

There is no doubt that the Cambridge thesis draws its inspiration from the Visuddhi Magga. But could it be that "fruit" here means only that which results after the previous thought impulsion and not the fruit of attainment and something which can be enjoyed?

This together with the fact that there the there are eight kinds of ariyas, four with the fruit and four without achieving that fruit would suggest that the fruit and the attainment here does not mean the same fruit, the first being one reflects the achievement and the other being the fruit confirming the attainment.

For the first noble is a person who attains to the Path and the second noble person who attains to the fruition thereof, making it two kinds of ariyas even in the sottapan. This makes it altogether eight noble persons divided into four states of the sottapan, sakadagami, anagami, and the arahant, who have attained without the "fruit" and another four who have attained both the Paths and the fruit.

If both, Path and "fruit" are always obtained at the same thought moment within the seven impulsions, it is hard to understand why there should be emphasis of the eight noble persons unless it is that both the Path and the fruition of that path come in different impulsions at different thought moments.

An impulsion is brief and there are only seven thought impulsions in one thought moment that happens in a flash. Besides, there is also a cessation of nibbana at the Path. How can this happen together unless the cessation is the Path and the awakening from it contains the fruit? That also cannot be.

Surely fruit is used in two different senses here and the fruit of the Path for each Path must be distinct and therefore come at different times. Unless there is another explanation for the presence of the eight noble persons, one for each attainment and another for the fruit of that attainment, we must take it that is the explanation.

Besides, how does one realise whether it is the first of the second or the third or the fourth Path unless each Path is distinguished by a different Fruit and the reviewing of the Path and of the Fruit refers to different objects at different times?

There is a nimitta that occurs after the Path that is different for each Path. Is this nimitta an ordinary nimitta or is it the Fruit?

The texts speak of enjoyment of the fruit after the attainment. Obviously the enjoyment meant in the Texts is the enjoyment of cessation on obtaining the Path. Unless the enjoyment comes in a different nimitta after the cessation of attainment in each Path and is different in each case, how can we distinguish one from the other? If it comes by way of a nimitta, it must take more than just an impulsion of the one thought moment.

Therefore the vision and the fruit must be different. Thus, on page 461 of the thesis *Buddhist Meditation,* referred to above, Parayahera Vajirananam Mahathera, when describing Samapatti or the attainment of the Fruit, states:

> "Those who have attained the Four Noble Paths enjoy in their lifetime the Four Noble Fruits, which are actually called "Samana-phala", the fruits of the samana life, and can only be attained by treading the Path of the Buddha.

> This enjoyment, called "Phala-sammapatti", is entering into the ecstasy in the object of "Nibbana" and remaining in it for a considerable period. Here each of the Noble Persons attains this ecstasy with his own fruit, but the persons in the higher state do not enter upon the lower because when they have reached the higher, and the lower has subsided."

If we accept this text, the term "phala", which means "fruit" must have different meanings. It can refer to the phala of the samatha who enters into cessation as well as phala that comes immediately upon attainment of the Path, apart from other meanings.

For he goes on to quote the Majjhima Nikaya (216) that there are two conditions for attaining the phala, namely, reflecting on nibbana itself or excluding all else so that there is release (ceto-vimuthi) which is then devoid of all nimittas.

This would indicate that here he is referring to the Fruit of achievement in samatha during the rupa state and not that of vipassana. For, he adds on page 463, that "the Fruit never arise in the state of arupa-sammapati, because in the arupa state the seat of the mind (hadaya-vathu) is either inactive, or does not exist at all. So, the arupa jhanas are always mundane."

Thus, if we accept the Mahathera's thesis, we have to be careful when referring to fruition. Though there are eight noble persons in all, the magga and the phala of attainment appears to come within a single thought moment and when we refer to phala of the samanas, the fruition or the enjoyment of it is not exactly the same but comes after.

But, as the phalas are different for each ariya path, obviously there should be distinctions between the eight of them and this is confirmed by the statement that there are eight ariyas in all, two in each state. This is further confirmed by the statement that there is a review for the Path and also a review of the Fruition.

If there are separate reviews of each path and each fruition, can it be possible, in a practical sense, to say that the review of the phala means the phala that comes within the same seven thought moments in a thought impulse? Surely the phala here must means another phala and not the phala come at the same thought moment as the magga. Otherwise, how can there be a separate review for each of them?

And, how can all the maggas have the same "fruit", since, if that were so, it would be difficult to note the difference between each ariya. Surely there must be a separate review for each separate "fruit", especially as the reviews do not come together but separately after each event.

So what does the Visuddhi Magga mean when it refers, in Chap XXII (paras 19 & 20) to review of the path and the fruition beginning with these words, "at the end of the fruition his consciousness enters the life-continuum".

After that, it arises as the mind-door, adverting, interrupts the life-continuum for the purpose of reviewing the path. When that has ceased, seven impulsions of the path reviewing arise. After reentry into the life-continuum, adverting, etc., arise again, in the same way, for the purpose of reviewing fruition, and so on. With these arisings, he reviews the path, the fruition, the defilements abandoned, the defilements still remaining and he reviews nibbana.

This means that the review is a sort of recounting of what has happened to him after both has taken place. At each path, there is a definite improvement since he becomes correspondingly purer. This is verified by the reviews.

Do these reviews mean that there is a separate fruit for each Path, making a total of eight in all? Only those who have reached the Path can answer this question. For it is said that each Path has its own Fruit and the Fruit is different for each Path.

15

THE ARIYAS

This seventh Purity, known as the Purity of knowledge and Vision, is the purity attained only by the ariyas. It refers to the Path of the Stream-enterer (sottapan), the Once-returned (sakadagami), the Non-returned (anagami) and that of the Arahant.

At the entry to the Path, which takes as its object the signless, non-occurrence, or the non-formation, depending upon which of the triple gateway entry is being effected, there is cessation.

Through proximity, continuity, repetition, decisive support, absence and disappearance of the conditions for the formations, the meditator overcomes arising, overcomes occurrence, overcomes despair, enters non-arising and non-occurrence of formations. For a moment, there is a vision of the Path.

Entry, likened to the meditator attempting to swing across to the other side of the stream, who lets go and falls, staggering and shaking on the other side, needless to say, refers to the shock of inexperience as the formations begin again after a lapse. Since the entry to every subsequent Path is a separate entry, gotrabhu is experienced each time. But as there is already previous experience, the shock of entry decreases in its intensity in the subsequent paths respectively. Their identification would become easier to one who experiences them.

After the path comes the fruition. Then there is review as the meditator looks back as he wonders what has happened. There is the occurrence of a vision of the phala, or fruit which is different for every path and there is a review of that phala as well.

On attainment, it is said that the meditator has obtained fulfilment of the states associated with the Path and, with the coupling of the powers and the abandonment of the states to be abandoned and the act of abandoning, with the functions of understanding, there is emergence.

Let us examine the detail meaning of the terms used in describing the conditions of the attainment of the Path:

1. The expression "fulfilment of states associated with the Path" means the states fulfilled which share in the enlightenment is referred to. This is only the tabulation of the thirty-seven states the meditator has gone through to reach the Path. That is to say the states which have helped to bring about the four Foundations of Mindfulness, four Right Endeavours, four Paths to the Power, five Faculties, five Powers, seven Enlightenment Factors and the Eightfold Path.
2. Emergence means the emergence into the path. Upon emergence one enters the Path.
3. Coupling of the powers refers to the coupling of the serenity power of samatha and insight power of vipassana for the attainment of the Path by the two-ways liberated meditator. This happens where the samatha meditator, through the predominance of his power of serenity in his samatha, attains the eight jhanas to reach the eighth jhana before switching to vipassana to obtain arahantship. Since insight power is in excess at the time of emergence to the Path, both these powers of serenity and insight must be coupled together with the coupling of the other four powers required for attainment.
4. The "abandoning of the states to be abandoned and the act of the abandoning" for attainment are set out in the Schedule. It is more of a reference note than anything else. We have gone through these states. Each lower state is abandoned as a higher state is achieved and this takes place even in the states of nobility. When we look

at the Schedule, we note that the grosser feelings are removed first and then the subtler till, finally, even their anusayas.

Often, we come across descriptions of the state of the meditator which describe his achievement by the abandoning of unwholesome thoughts or states. This is the same as a statement of his achievements to show his progress, for by abandoning one he attains its opposite. Thus when we say he abandons agitation, it is the same as to say that he has achieved calm.

5. The functions of 'understanding' mean that understanding of the meditator has now to reach its height and he is able to penetrate the truths at each of the four paths and see the four functions, is of full understanding, abandoning, realizing and developing.

   Penetrating the four truths and their four functions are as follows:

   - Suffering means oppression, means being formed, means pain and torment, means change; and that is its Truth;
   - Origin means accumulation (of kamma), means source, means bondage, means impediment; and that is its Truth;
   - Cessation means escape, means seclusion, means not being formed, means deathlessness; and that is its Truth;
   - Path means outlet, means cause, means realizing (seeing) means dominance, and that is its Truth.

Thus, the sun lights up, dispels darkness, makes visible and allays the cold, so too the truth has its four functions. Whether we agree or not with this style of description, the realization is the psychological and ethical conclusion of vipassana meditation which is:

> That we know the meaning Suffering; that we know the origin of Suffering; that we know the cessation of Suffering; that achieving the Path is the way out of Suffering In this way, through insight, the meditator has experienced the taste of the noble fruit, attained cessation and has achieved the worthiness to receive gifts first as a sottapan, then as a sạkadagami, then an anagami, and finally an arahant.

The sottapan has attained the qualities listed in the Schedule. But this is only a small satisfaction. So he continues to cleanse himself of his defilements till he reaches the status of the arahant.

Who can attain cessation, nirodha?

Only the anagami and the arahant who have the eight jhana attainments can obtain it. No barẹ insight noble ones even can attain it. For cessation often come to one with the two powers of insight and serenity.

For these he must, at least, have the base of nothingness and he must have tranquillized the three formations verbally, bodily and mentally plus the power of concentration and mastery of adverting, attaining, resolving, emerging and reviewing the jhannic states. And he must have the sixteen kinds of exercise of knowledge of the arahant.

The sottapan has only ten and the once-returned sakadagami has twelve. The anagami has fourteen whilst the arahant, having gone through the exercises of the sottapan and sakadagami and the anagami with the Paths and Fruits, has sixteen.

However, the anagami, with fourteen kinds of exercises, does not have greed, and therefore has serenity as a power and he too, can attain cessation. Thus, fourteen is the minimum and sixteen is the maximum required. The Pathana Sutta (PM 902) thus, refers to anagamis returning from cessation to illustrate this point.

In answer to the question of a deity as to who can succeed in the disentangling of this tangle, came the following words from Buddha:

"When a wise man, established well in Virtue,
Develops Consciousness and Understanding.
Then as a bhikkhu ardent and sagacious,
He succeeds in disentangling this tangle."

This then explains the opening verse of the Visuddhi Magga. By the time he reaches this stage he need no longer ask this question for he would already know the answers. He will already know all there is to know.

Even the question of whether there is a god or not becomes academic as well. For this question is the result of ego and desire for salvation and he has cut off all desires. Further, his practise for purity also does not depend upon an answer to that question. God if there is one, is a matter that is no longer a matter of concern for him.

PART II

PEAKS OF POWER

Power of mind over matter through subjects of meditation

16

MEDITATION REALITY

The experience of meditation is entirely mental. It is also subjective to the conditioning of the mind. In a way, it is a world of dreams where reality and the fantasy is one and the same and time is, in this sense, not measured. We perceive what we want to perceive and that there is no past, present or future but a series of realisations that become history almost immediately. Through it we note there is no reality outside of our minds, no future or past but a series of events flashing by this is the significance of the reality of meditation.

This is because the reality is in the mental formations he perceives in meditation. He sees how thoughts arise from his subconscious and how they are subjected to the desires and attachment which give them their nature and shape. Through them he sees the truth that they can be adjusted or removed through the removal of their causes. By practice, he can shut off contact with his senses leaving only the mentality contact open. Through this contact he develops his mind.

Instead of physical representations and images before which devotees prostrate themselves, the visitor to a meditation centre sees, instead, meditators sitting, cross-legged, silently, with eyes closed, apparently, in deep reverie or fast asleep. But the meditator seems at peace with himself for he looks calm, detached, and untroubled. Nothing appears to be taking place. However, the reality is not what it appears.

Though he appears to be sleeping, there is plenty going on behind those closed eyes. For he sees the never-ending rise and fall of formations from which he will discern the truth and control his mind. It is not mind control. It is more than that, for the mind is allowed its freedom to roam. It is not astro travel or transcendentalism. For mind control is only a part of the practice of meditation.

What he sees begins with the results of contact with his elements and ends with the discovery, eventually, of the truth of the formations. That is the reality of meditation. Through intense training of his concentration in samatha he can, not only control his mind but also exercise the power of mind over matter in samatha, or he can reach into the realm of calm and peace and discover for himself the reality of existence itself in vipassana.

For inner peace comes when he eradicates the unwholesome attributes of his mind, whose constantly flexing and everchanging consciousness, is the center of all human behaviour. That is truth that he will discover in his meditation.

Meditation brings about different states of concentration at the different stages, depending upon the nature of meditation and different subjects used. Different mental attributes and defilements are found and are involved at every stage.

Since concentration requires subjects and since different subjects giver different results, care must be taken of the subjects used. For example, in both samatha and vipassana meditation, the fourth jhana must first be obtained before one can go further. In the fourth jhana the mental state is ready for the meditator to practise on the ten kasina subjects to gain supranormal powers (abhinna). Here he is in rupa (or material) state.

To proceed further to the fifth state beyond, he must abandon the rupa state to enter into the arupa (or immaterial) state. Here he must use immaterial subject such as space etc going up step by step.

So he must first enter the fourth state before he can employ one of the kasina subjects. Thereafter he can use the first of the arupa subjects, to enter the arupa state. No other subject will do. So also, we have to be careful to remember that samatha and vipassana meditation requires different meditation technique to give rise to different results.

In samatha, for example, the factors of concentration and their powers of surmounting are more important than the hindrances and the obstacles to progress as the obstacles can be overcome by suppression. The mind, concentrating on the counterpart sign of the subject, excludes all that which is not related to the sign. All his mental factors are concentrated in ekaggata concentration on the sign of his subject and in the practice of the skills.

It is this concentration of the that obliterates outside contact through suppression, unlike vipassana which seeks to contact his mental formations and to remove attachment to the desires that give rise to the formations that distinguishes the two.

When he moves to the immaterial plane, his concentration shifts from materiality to the immaterial one of the subjects of space, consciousness and non-conscious, nothingness and perception and non-perception.

When he is confined in enclosed space, is the meditator in the nothingness state or the state of non-perception? His metabolic rate is slowed down to such imperceptible levels that he is able to survive with so little movement of air in the box. According to the Texts, he can remain in a sort of suspended animation for no more than seven days in the eighth state after which he must wake up thereafter or he will not wake up at all. Is he in such a state?

So much for the Texts. A Chinese legend of Chinese meditator whose spirit had left his body when concentrating on nothingness. During his absence, his servant, thinking that he was dead, put it to the funeral pyre. His spirit, returning on the eighth day was confronted with this misfortune and it entered the nearest available object. This happened to be that of the body of a beggar. Hence he became known as one of the eight Chinese immortals, Lee Tock Quai, the Beggar Saint. Thus he became a "lohan" in the fourth state. The term "lohan" could have been the Chinese translation of the arahant.

However, the legend seems to be samatha in inspiration in view of the concept of a "soul" leaving the body but the term "lohan" seems to be due to confusion with arahant of vipassana.

The history of Zen, which is Ch'en in Chinese, has it that Buddhism was introduced into China by a boddhisatva from India who taught "nothingness" to be the ultimate achievement of Buddhism. This, we know was pre-Buddhist and the practice is samatha. But, somehow, it has become Buddhist and became Zen Buddhism in Japan.

We know that the concept of "nothingness" is samatha and is only the seventh state. That it is now known as Buddhist meditation has added to the confusion since many Buddhists hold this view today.

It could be that the "boddhisatva" was Fah Hsien, the monk who had been sent to India, where he remained for thirteen years and translated the Vimuthi Magga into Chinese before he returned to China. Who else from India could have known enough Buddhism and Chinese to have been able to teach Buddhism to the Chinese. It is this translation of the Vimuthi Magga that remains with us today, the original in Pali, being lost.

The meditation of Zen is dissimilar to vipassana. Though Zen can be practised with sila, it does not have the purification of the consciousness but of "nothingness". Nor does it have mindfulness.

Both have their peaks of power, but one provides the power of concentration whilst the other develops clarity and calmness of mind.

What really happens during meditation cannot yet be examined by instruments. The reality can only be found through actual experience of meditation. The only one to know is one who has experienced them. That is why a friend for guidance at the beginning of meditation has to be one who has had experience in meditation.

There are myriads of formations that rise and fall due to the impurities which are due his state of mind. The lower his state the more the distractions. He needs to overcome them and their hindrances, which impede his progress, before he can reach a higher state. But as he goes on and reaches the higher states, however, the less are their distractions. Each state is gained through knowledge of a nana or other. Knowledge of each nana reflects a different state of mind.

Because the attributes and the defilements are different in every state, through them we can know his progress and the state he is in. Even the state of purity can be discovered through the mental attributes found in his consciousness. This assists the friend to help the meditator. At a certain state, the meditator has to overcome the formations that seem to arise from everywhere, his bodily parts, his feelings, his mind and the dhamma, from which is he is to observe how they rise and fall in their nature and their voidness on their disappearance.

They arise due to contact which arise from desires. Thus, during meditation, when he itches and feels ants crawling all over him, when there are no ants; or when he feels hot and perspires profusely although it is cool; or when he thinks he sees visions, or taste food, or hears distant voices appearing as if from distant lands of from some other place in the sky; or feels himself floating or flying, which are of his mental making, he knows that they are the elements or nimittas due to contact with his senses.

Such contact may even result in the awareness of rigidity or vision of the bones of his body, blood coursing through his body as if his arteries are made of transparent plastic tubes, travelling into the sky like superman, blowing up into a floating balloon or swivel like a compass to find a point. He may even see spirits appearing before him, offering him the powers he has been dreaming of.

All these are insubstantial things, the result of formations arising from his mindfulness bases. They reflect the state of his mind and what it contains. He sees for reality something that is not there.

He hears sounds and sees sights that are not there. They come from the deep-seated desires and fears through contact with his mind or dhamma.

Desires for beautiful things may appear as formations of beautiful spirits and fragrant beings and he might even sense an imagined fragrance in the air.

This experience shows that he has achieved the ability to see the rise and the fall of formations and see their meaning. It indicates contact with his sense bases. With their presence come the hindrances mentioned earlier of such as bliss, aura and illuminations, haloes, intense joy and pleasure, visions of most beauteous spirits, which bring pride and a feeling of superiority.

They agitate and excite and attachment leads to "clinging" which will effectively terminate concentration and must therefore be overcome.

The meditation reality here is that of the udayabhaya nana state and he must overcome the hindrances to gain udayabhaya nana and this requires awareness of the three characteristic marks of the formations which are those of anicca, dukkha and anatta.

Thus, the presence of the constituents of the various defilements bringing about "clinging" requires the presence in balance of the factors of mindfulness, of faith, energy, concentration and understanding; the lack of which would terminate meditation. So the meditator has to practise more sila.

Feelings of anger and its associates such as envy and illwill, as much as desire due to greed for the beautiful will result in the attributes of agitation and distraction which will terminate concentration.

The thought formations arise in this way. The mind is in a state of bhavanga akin to sleep in life's continuum. Unless it is awaked through contact it will not stir into any movement. When there is contact through one of the sense doors, it moves into a state between sleep and wakefulness. This is the state of manodvara.

In this state the thought is subject to evaluation by the consciousness and a decision reached whether it is worthwhile noticing the impingement or not.

The anusayas, or tendencies that come before the thoughts become full blown also arise at this state, but it is not discernible to the new meditator but only to advanced ones. These anusayas can be understood if we refer to occasions when people have been heard to say, "I could feel anger rising within me but I was able to suppress it before it came over me".

The impingement creates a thought impulse which has seven thought moments before it falls away to be taken by another thought impulse.

Where the impingement is to be ignored, it falls away before the full seven moments and is immediately forgotten without any further effect.

This is explained in the parable of the two men who heard the sound of a falling mango. One of them who is not interested, notes its fall and the fact that it is a mango and ignores it, promptly falling off to continue his sleep. The other, knowing that his mistress is waiting for the mango, wakes from his sleep, picks up the mango and goes to his mistress with it. The mistress in his case being his desires.

This parable is used to explain the formations and the attachment to them as if they are his mistress.

The meditator, one who has reached the ariya state, can dissipate these thoughts even as their tendencies arise. They can deal with the subtle defilements through and their tendencies.

This is not yet the case of the new meditator, who still has his mistresses in the form of desires who distract and disturb him but from which he is unable to detach himself due to his desire for them. He has still to cope with the grosser characteristics of his defilements before he can rid himself of their subtle nature.

It does not matter which sense organ has "awakened" the mind and what object comes as the consequent formation. As long as there is impingement, the mind is immediately awakened and the whole process of namarupa and paticcasamupada begins, and the formations are penetrated for the truth of their nature.

This is the reality. Wisdom in insight meditation is the knowledge discovered of a truth, nana which finally leads to understanding. The mental requirements for nana to be obtained and the reality of nanas has far higher requirements than any other meditation.

Not all meditation subjects have the same effects since they do not contain the same capabilities. They all bring different effects as they have different characteristics that vary in effect on how they are used, not all providing for the same level of concentration or degree of progress. Concentration moves from one jhana to the next till the fourth jhana is gained and the subject used must provide the capacity of surmounting one jhana to the next till the fourth. Where a jhana cannot cause to appana and provide the power of surmounting, there can be no surmounting and the concentration remains at the upacara stage.

One cannot skip but must proceed from one jhana to the next, gaining the factors and mental constituents for the next jhana before the succeeding one can be obtained. This continues to the fourth. So also in the case of nanas, one must obtain the earlier nanas before there are mental attributes for the next nana to be obtained. That is why there must be the third root and sufficient paramis before the ariya states can be gained.

To obtain the fourth or udayabhaya nana, for example, one must already have the attributes of the earlier three nanas to have the constituents for the udayabhaya nana which is the fourth nana. Sometimes this is expressed as the attainment of purities one after the other in systematic order.

For this reason, knowledge of the reality and the attributes of the mind is important to understand attainments. It is only after the wisdom of the earlier nana is obtained before he can claim to have found the wisdom of the higher nana. Nor can achievement of a higher jhana or nana be obtained with a subject incapable of producing the attributes of that jhana or nana.

The reality of samatha and vipassana meditation is not exactly the same. One has no abhinna but has the panna to see nibbana whilst the other has abhinna but no panna and cannot see nibbana. Many choose samatha because one can feel and see the exciting results. These powers are desirable and the meditator is impressed by the claims of supranormal powers by others and, believing them to be true, think they can also obtain it if they become disciples. Unfortunately, it is not only difficult without past practice and any success is improbable so they turn away from meditation and its true meaning, unfortunately.

Often, the abilities to sense vibrations, mental telepathy and such as extrasensory perceptions are mistaken for true abhinna powers. This is not so.

Abhinna has greater powers than such inherent characteristics. But practise requires the fourth jhana where the mental attributes will allow for required practise in the skills.

Concentration of the fourth jhana has a concentration that is purified, bright, unblemished, rid of defilements and is malleable, wieldy, steady, and "amenja" (which is imperturbability normally used of the concentration of the immaterial jhanas together with the fourth jhana) so that it is firm and clear enough to hold on to a counterpart sign it has brought about through appana and malleable enough that it can be used for the practice of the skills directed to the achievement of supranormal powers.

Most of all, they should be warned that samatha is dangerous if not accompanied by sila, for it can cause pride, conceit and unwholesome desires that often accompany such achievement.

Meditation, practised for the wrong reasons and objectives bring unwholesome characteristics that will lead to bad kamma. Remember the story of Dr. Faustus who sold his soul to the devil. It is worthwhile to know the pitfalls and limitations of the various meditation techniques offered before indulging in them.

In fact, they should be careful not to be influenced by claims such as astral travel and the ability to read minds to allow themselves to become disciples to the wrong persons for wrong reasons because it might affect their kamma adversely. Most of all they should see if the claims are not exaggerations of nimittas or formations caused by contact through their body or feelings.

All meditation first requires the fourth jhana but not all the subjects can bring the counterpart sign to provide the power of surmounting to the fourth jhana so where claims are made but by the use of wrong subjects, we must be careful of such claims since we know that all subjects can give rise to the fourth jhana.

In the beginning of concentration, there are only the attributes of vikara concentration where the counterpart sign may arise. At that moment, sloth and torpor is eliminated and full attention of the mind is directed towards the object of concentration. Then comes vitakka, which is sustained mental application in the sense of investigation in the exercise of being engaged in the subject. At this stage, doubt is removed so concentration is sustained. Here there is piti which gives zest and sukha which provides radiant and pleasurable feelings in opposition to illwill.

When it appears, illwill is diminished. Vitakka can be slight or immature (khuddaka piti), growing (or khanika piti), absorbing (okkantika piti), thrilling (ubbega piti), intensive or fully developed (pharana piti). In this jhana, it has the last meaning because it has to be developed.

When these attributes have arisen, the concentration is known to be in the first jhana.

Initial concentration is likened to the visitor at a museum. First he notices an object. Then, as his interest aroused, zest and pleasure suffuses his mind. In enthusiasm and joy he begins to concentrate on it.

Soon he finds his concentration fixed on the subject as he settles down to examine it. At this point there are the constituents of initial and sustained concentration, and the initial enthusiasm slowly subsides and this is the first jhana.

Since the initial concentration flows into the second continuously, the fourfold system refers to these two states as one and calls it the first jhana.

This is not so in the fivefold system, the first jhana is where there are only the attributes of initial concentration, or vicara, and, where there are both initial and sustained concentration, it is known as the second jhana. This is the only difference between the fourfold system and the fivefold system of definition. Buddha himself used the fourfold system.

His concentration intensifies and begins to fix only on the subject where there is vitakka. This sustained concentration in turn grows into the one-pointed concentration of ekaggata as he moves into the subsequent jhana even where there is still sukha and piti which is joy and bliss.

With ekaggata concentration, the initial joy of discovery is also eliminated till there is only the feeling of pleasure in the third. Joy is the attribute of sukha which exists in the second jhana. When this subsides leaving only the pleasure of piti, the concentration is said to be in the third jhana.

Sukha was removed since zest gives rise to restlessness and stands in the way of sustained concentration. Piti is suffusing radiant pleasurable feelings. It is also a distraction to intense concentration. So it has to be removed as the concentration and when this is done the meditator moves into the fourth jhana which is now detached from them and is therefore calm and unattached to joy and pleasure. This is upekha. When this happens, the concentration is ekaggata without distraction and agitation and calmness without distraction is upekha. This is the fourth jhana.

Ekaggata and upekha are necessary before there can be absolute concentration for practice in the skills for achievement of abhinna powers. Without these attributes a steady and firm concentration, no true abhinna can be achieved.

Besides paramis, only practise in the fourth jhana through the use of the ten kasinas can give rise to such powers. Claims of abhinna powers through any other subject cannot be correct. This concentration is also the basic concentration for vipassana. The fourth jhana or its equivalent is necessary for insight. But here, the element of mindfulness is required which is distraction for samatha.

Thus, the mental requirements for vipassana and the nanas which provide wisdom and purity of the consciousness of the meditator require more attributes than that required for samatha.

Whereas it is only concentration that is emphasized in samatha, in vipassana we need to know other mental attributes of the consciousness as well because mindfulness is required.

The development up to the fourth jhana is for the establishing of concentration. They are both similar to that point. Thereafter, the way forward divides into two paths, the path of samatha and the path of vipassana. In samatha, there is only one-pointedness (ekaggata).

Ridding himself of the initial concentration of vicara, the meditator rids himself of the attributes of sloth and torpor associated with wrong thinking and samma sankappa, or Right Thinking, is gained. Then, by ridding himself of initial concentration, doubt is removed and faith is established and sustained concentration arises.

Sukha which is joy comes with hatred and illwill. Without hatred, there can be no joy or delight. Both are opposites of the same feeling.

With the ridding of hate and illwill, joy and therefore sukha is removed. With this removal, detachment is encouraged and upekha is developed.

Piti is pleasure which is the diffusion of zest and comes with the fading of happiness. Distraction and agitation are removed when zest is lowered. With the abandoning of piti, there remains only concentration and equanimity.

Therefore the attributes of concentration are different in each state.

There is elimination in some and replacement in others. Ekaggata arises out of vicara and vitakka, whereas upekha arises out of the absence of the mental attributes of sukha and piti.

Abhinna is direct knowledge. It is the development of mental powers through practise in the skills in the fourth jhana.

When attempting to describe these powers in common language, the inability to find suitable words defeats us. But is the text to be translated literally in the light of present knowledge? For example, the Texts refers to the ability to enter others' minds. Can we translate it as mental telepathy or as something more than that. For this ability enables the meditator to look into the past and the future of others as well.

Again, when the texts talk of astral travel, which enables the meditator to travel through to other lands and planes, there is also the inference of entering the time dimension and the planes of existence, so it is not just a mental formation.

Then, can we translate the ability to become many and from many, back into one, or to disappear to mean something more than the power of mass hypnotism?

After all, everything comes from the heat waves of the sun. And all sound or visual waves are but energy waves in different forms and wavelengths. We already know that not all energy waves are felt by the human senses except those that fall within perceptible range. Are other forms of energy waves not perceivable by human senses possible?

All direct knowledge happens in the material sphere. It is the consciousness and its energy that does it all. Can the powers be misunderstood because of the grand language at a time when science was relatively unknown? Or do they describe energy wave forms we still don't quite understand?

Just as invisible steam has the same components as steam, and steam to water and water to ice, yet stemming from the same substance though different in form, can it be said that abhinna concerns the projection of the mind into realm of other sense vibrations from other forms of energy waves that cannot be sensed by our normal senses?

Just as the television takes in energy in other forms that can be translated into vision and sound, are there other energy forms which the mind trained in abhinna can perceive and develop which normal minds cannot?

Can it be that there are other forms of energy taking different vibrations which only a human mind, trained in such things, can sense, just as the television and the cameras can translate electrical energy from space stations into sight and sound, or a dog with its higher sound range can hear his master coming home long before the others.

17

STARTING MEDITATION

Meditation is a serious practice. Unless there is motivation there will be no persistence and determination. Furthermore, the mystical nature of the subject can easily lead to misrepresentation. Therefore he needs a good friend and proper books, such as the Visuddhi Magga and some of the suttas from the Tipitaka, to be by his side. The Visuddhi Magga, originally written for monks and samanas, is one of the most authoritative texts available but it is difficult to understand unless one has meditated for some time. Of all the suttas, the best for the purpose of starting meditation is the Mahasattipathana Sutta because it deals with Mindfulness.

A good friend is as essential as the books, to start him off. He should be from one of the established vipassana meditation centers, such as one recognised by the Mahasi Center. Such centres normally have sayadaws specially sent there to teach meditation. A sayadaw is the best person to help the new meditator. Where a sayadaw is not available, someone from there knowledgeable enough to give proper guidance and to be able to give proper interpretation of experiences encountered during meditation, would do. Especially as the meditator will be venturing into an unknown world from which there will arise formations that can be easily misinterpreted, deceiving or frightening.

The first duty of such a friend is to decide if an aspirant is a suitable person to meditate. A drunkard, a person crossed in love, an emotionally unstable or mentally unbalanced person, and one who is not sound and in possession of all his faculties are unsuitable persons.

The next duty the friend has to do is to provide both a particular and a generally useful subject for meditation.

A particular subject is one used for meditation itself and is chosen depending upon the predominant characteristics of the meditator. One with lust or strong desires, for example, can be usefully provided with a foulness subject, or mindfulness of death, to encourage detachment from the temptation of such desires and lust through disgust.

A generally useful subject is a subject upon which the meditator may generally use even when he is not meditating. The best of such subjects of general application is the Brahmavihara, known variously as the Four Divine Abidings or Illimitables. They perhaps form the central theme of sila in Buddhism and encourage selflessness, generosity, self-sacrifice and remove pride and conceit, all of which go to thoughtful and generous behaviour towards others and help in establishing alobha, adosa and anatta, the essential qualities to be obtained.

How often do we find ourselves being frustrated and angry with our neighbours, for example. This produces distraction. At such moments, the Brahmavihara subjects at once help to make us realise that anger solves nothing and we at once look towards some other kind of response that is not revengeful or spiteful or petty.

To provide the subjects, the friend must be able to judge not only the temperament of the meditator but the characteristics of the meditation subjects and what jhanas they can provide. A heavy responsibility lies on a good friend to make certain which subjects are suitable for the meditator, and he not only must be able to judge the character of the meditator but he must know the exact nature of each subject and its abilities to give rise to the jhanas.It is one of the areas where a little knowledge is a dangerous thing.

Having provided the meditator with a particular and a generally suitable meditation subject, (the Mindfulness of Breathing and the Brahmavihara are suggested) he has to make certain that correct approach to the subject and practice are applied.

Topping this list of "good friends", of course, is Buddha himself since he was not only fully enlightened but was also a self-taught Buddha. Thus Buddha said to Ananda, "it is owing to my being a good friend to them that living beings subject to birth are freed from birth" (S.i.88).

Since Buddha is no longer with us it is obvious that we can no longer look to him as a good friend. So, next down the list is one of his disciples. Again, since they are no longer with us we have to look further down.

These, in order of preference, begin with those most completely versed in the dhamma such as the ariyas and theravada monks in monasteries. If they are not to be found, someone less qualified such as a practitioner holding the right precepts and practice and who has attained the jhanas, or one who knows the three pitakas, or even two pitakas, or one pitaka, will do.

Be careful however of temples which practise samatha, by whatever name it is called. Many of them are not beyond advertising themselves in the hope of gaining contribution, something that a vipassana monk would disdain from doing.

The beginner is armed with meditation books such as the Visuddhi Magga and some of the suttas from the Tipitaka that are easily obtainable from the accepted centers and as such books on the Mindfulness of Breathing and satipathana that are less likely to be misled.

A good friend is only a guide. When he is established in his practice, he can go off on his own as Ananda was advised by the Buddha. But, in the beginning, the guide is necessary to explain the formations that can be very unnerving as this example will show.

Two friends were meditating in the jungle. During the night they heard the call of the crow pheasant that is a series of "gongs". One of them, seeing the image of a ghost before him, was caught in a sudden fright and jumped from his place with a yell of fear, which also terrified his friend, and they both fled from the scene, seized with terror.

If they had someone of experience with them, he could have explained to them that the ghost was a mental formation, a nimitta, and would have disappeared had he kept his cool. Unfortunately, there was no such friend and they were more adventurous than experienced.

Formations come in all shapes and sizes and never in the same order. They are not easy to understand. Only someone with sufficiently wide experience can understand and explain to them correctly, interpreting them as they should be interpreted. With one who is inexperienced it may be difficult to do so and misunderstanding may be the result unless there is someone there with sufficient meditative experience to interpret.

Practice has to be regular and systematic. Having been given a subject and understood its nature, the meditator should now seek out a secluded and friendly place for his practice. Before he begins meditation, he should have cleaned and fed himself at least an hour before meditation and begin his practice so that he will not be distracted with his hunger or digestion.

He must, as the texts say, keep his bases clean. That is to say, he needs to have both physical and mental cleanliness, by which is meant that he also needs to maintain his virtue and avoid distracting and unconcentrated persons.

The illustration of the oil lamp makes this clear. For the light to burn steadily, the oil and the wick must be clean. The oil and the wick are the physical bases. The light is the mental consciousness. If the oil is dirty, the light and the flame will flicker and be unsteady. If the person is dirty, there will be distractions and concentration will not be steady.

The practice of meditation is set out more fully discussed in Mindfulness of Breathing subject.

In summary, he must sit on a hard platform to maintain a steadiness during concentration, cross-legged or in semi-lotus or full lotus position, depending on which position he feels more comfortable. If he should find this difficult in the beginning, he can sit on a low cushion which he can remove later when he becomes more comfortable.

It is wrong to torture himself to sit in any orthodox position. Vipassana needs no torture. It will not help in vipassana. The most important is to have a steady stance comfortable enough not to be distracted.

The best place is a quiet area in a practising monastery or one that is proper for meditation.

The Mahasi Center normally sends one of its senior monks to centers such as the Malaysian Buddhist Meditation Center in Penang and in certain states in Australia and the United States during certain periods, and during their residence at the Center, meditators may register themselves at the center for training.

Meditators are required to hold eight precepts during their practice during residence in such centers when food is prepared for them and proper guidance provided.

Mindfulness at all times required is beneficial and there should be no distraction and unnecessary conversation or discussion.

In meditation, the meditator should not overeat, should wait for some time after his meal to rid himself of after meal sloth and torpor, clean himself properly before he sits to meditate.

The sitting posture must essentially be comfortable and he must not slouch and should maintain an erect position and look straight ahead with his hands in front of him, on his lap, preferably with palms together at all times.

He sits with his eyes closed unless it is to grasp the learning object of the kasina object in samatha when he can slightly open and close his eyes for the purpose of building the after-image from which the conceptual image will come. The erect, comfortable sitting position is important because he cannot be sloppy and slouch and he must sit loose because he wants no constrictions or tightness about himself so that he may be mindful of the formations.

The meditator can always practice at home or in groups provided there is proper guidance. Meditation is a very personal matter, so also its speed and progress which depend upon the kamma of the meditator.

He is not practising samatha, so exercises are not necessary. He should not try to slow his heart rate or do any such thing but should try to keep normality to concentrate on mindfulness with emphasis on improvement by removing the influence of the basic roots of greed, illwill and delusion.

Society cannot change if the individuals in the society do not change. The individual does not change unless his sense of values and his value system are changed. To me, this is a fundamental point that is often overlooked when political systems and philosophies are discussed so that when there is a revolt, it comes often as a shock such as has taken place in Soviet Russia today as racism raises its ugly head after seventy years of Soviet rule and the people reject the constraints of Communism.

Does it matter what system is introduced if the members of that society remain essentially without any change of their values and value system?

At the present rate of indulgent materialism and permissiveness, can it not happen that we will finally destroy the very society whose health has contributed to our own wellbeing? If the answer is maybe, then insight meditation, which emphasizes on the elimination of desires rather than on their indulgence, might provide a partial solution.

During meditation, manifestations will assert themselves in the form of formations. They reflect his state of cleanliness, generally arising first with contact of the elements.

At times formations will arise from the physical elements and then the mental base. The mental formations, for example, arise when he has visions appearing without any special sequence.

Sometimes, they may appear in a sequence unfolding before his eyes. These could be of past events that have made an impression in his subconscious. When these formations appear, the meditator must not react but merely note them as they appear, whether desirable or repulsive. Where they are frightening apparitions, he must realise that he is a human, of a higher plane, especially if he is holding precepts and these are nimittas coming through his fears or hopes and they cannot hurt him.

In fact, some monks deliberately indulge in forest and graveyard practice in the hope of confronting such apparitions which are mental formations of deep-seated desires and fears coming from a past. They manifest themselves as part of the purification process.

Where the formations appear as desirable, they are nevertheless one of the ten hindrances to meditative progress and should be ignored.

In meditation, jhanas come as the states of concentration, nanas, on the other hand, mark development in knowledge and are sensed as sudden flashes of awareness.

The realization of nanas has often been compared to the experience of lightning and thunder; to experience is to know.

The meditator, as he notes the formations and they fall away as fast as they have arisen, leaving nothing behind, will become aware that they never repeat themselves or return again.

To summarise, the meditator begins meditation by:

1. Choosing a clean quiet life.
2. Maintaining the Five Precepts.
3. Finding a "good friend".
4. Eating moderately so as not to be sleepy.
5. Keeping himself clean for meditation.
6. Seeking a quiet place to meditate undisturbed.
7. Taking up a meditation subject.
8 Sitting on a clean hard base or floor.
9. Sitting upright and taking up a lotus or a half-lotus (cross-legged position, if possible).
10. Holding both hands in front of him in his lap with palms upwards.
11. Closes his eyes.
12. Breathing in and out easily and quietly.
13. Keeping concentration on his breathing.
14. Starting off with at least twenty minutes' practice per session which should be increased to at least an hour as soon as possible.

18

PERFECTION IS OF THE MIND

In Buddhist philosophy, one does not talk of the "soul", or "atta", as its doctrines relate to purity, not of a soul, but of the mind and its consciousness. The meaning of perfection is purity of the mind from the desires of greed, illwill and the false concept of a permanent ego. So also is the idea of "cleansing", which is that of the mind.

Inner peace, therefore, is that of the mind and its purity. Moral terms are also meaningless unless it is defined in that way.

That being the case, it is easy to understand that inner peace is not only peace of mind in the ordinary sense but a peace that is accompanied with a mind that is not full of doubts, desires, ambition, greed, jealousy, spite and so on.

For the doctrine is that it is the distracting formations from the roots of greed, illwill and the ego that cause distractions, restlessness, dissatisfaction and unhappiness. Unless there is wholesome behaviour, right concentration, right practice, right consciousness and so on as defined in the Eightfold noble path, there can be no inner peace.

This is the reason for proper and wholesome behaviour. The Eightfold noble path are the eight requirements for correct thinking, livelihood and behaviour. They form the basis of sila.

Sila, or virtuous behaviour, is required for the removal of the unwholesome formations that are noted in meditation. This is the reality of meditation. It is the eradication of these formations through sila that is the target of meditation and which ultimately result in nibbana.

This logic, extended to life itself make it easy to understand the meaning of cycle of life. It is attachment to desires that give rise to the birth of the formations. Thus, attachment to life also brings about rebirth of the consciousness in another body. Once there is detachment to life itself through the eradication of the desires and there is no more attachment, or upadana, the rebirth-relinking process will end and the endless cycle of rebirths will be terminated. At the point of the final thought moment, the consciousness will cease to function and parinibbana is obtained and he reaches nibbana.

This is the ultimate aim of vipassana. It means perfection of the mind which requires abandonment of unwholesome desires. Upholding the Eightfold noble path of right view, right intention, right speech, right action, right livelihood, right efforts, right mindfulness and right concentration, as the basis of good behaviour is required. It starts with the simple rules of the five moral precepts and explains their requirement.

It is a gradual process of achievement. The extent of which depends how our consciousness, its faculties and its mental attributes have been developed. This is kamma. Each person has his own kamma with its resultant characteristics.

Perhaps it is worthwhile to give an illustration here of what this means in ordinary situations. Not everyone has the same characteristics and sense of values or value system. There are those who refuse to listen because they have already made up their minds. They have mental blockages and will continue to do what is obviously wrong because they think they know better. These are the people with strong egos and little faith. In this sense we can say that they have insufficient understanding and their sense of greed, illwill and delusion is strong and their kamma is such that they will be unable to utilise this chance to improve themselves and they are not able to reach the more profitable states. The dhamma has little meaning to them.

On the other hand there are those who will never do anything that comes from greed, illwill or ego. They are those who are virtuous in practice. They will accept the dhamma without questioning if they can gain anything for themselves. They accept it because they believe it is correct. That is all. Among them we can find the arahant who is one in the highest human plane. He is one who is said to have done everything that requires to be done and that there is nothing remaining to be done by him.

The meaning of this expression means is that there is nothing more that he can do to attain purity. He has gained full knowledge of the dhamma and, therefore, understands the namarupa and paticcasammupada and has seen their effects upon the consciousness with knowledge of the dhamma.

In the cases of the Brahmans, Alara and Udaka, they reached the seventh and eighth states respectively of samatha respectively and they went to the Brahma world because of their sila. They were in the highest human planes. But they did not have the knowledge of the dhamma, so, in spite of their high states, final entry to nibbana was denied them. Such persons can easily reach the highest plain of purity once they learn of the Dhamma and realise how there consciousness are affected by their thoughts and actions. That was why Buddha expressed regret that they had passed away before this Enlightenment and before he would teach them the Dhamma.

Knowledge in the dhamma is required to provide amoha. That is a reality of the process of "cleansing". Where everything else has been done, and all other purities such as sila and consciousness have been gained, listening to pure dhamma itself could end moha and nibbana obtained. Hence Buddha's expression of regret when, on enquiry after them on his attainment, he found that they had died before his attainment and therefore had had no opportunity to listen to his dhamma through which they could have attained nibbana.

Buddhism has different planes of existence which reflect the purities of living beings. Through these planes, the purity system and levels of achievement of Buddhism are explained. Even in the human plane there are those who are in more fortunate states than others. Thus some are born beautiful and intelligent whilst others are born in unfortunate circumstances and are dirty and stupid.

This does not mean that there is no hope for them. Even Buddha was born many times in very bad conditions before he bacame Gautama, a Prince, who found enlightenment. Kamma must be understood with reference to these states, and purity itself has many stages. If we may not gain nibbana now, we can, at least, hope that we will go into the more profitable states rather than the more unfortunate ones.

For example, Alara and Udakha entered the Brahma planes and Sakkha, the King of the Heavens, is a deva though he is by no means a perfect person and is supposed to have some five hundred wives.

It may be easier to understand these levels of existence if we use the term "cleanliness" instead of "purity". In this way, we can say that the states of existence reflect different stages of cleanliness with only one absolute, nibbana. Even hell itself is a place of temporary abode, measured by its various levels of hideousness and suffering.

There is no other absolute, only nibbana. Even heaven and hell are temporary abodes. We can even be born as animals or in the lower kingdoms dependent upon our states of purity. These are only temporary states in which our kamma is worked out. Whether these are or are not metaphorical states are not, in my mind, very relevant. They only give expression to the sense of destiny and states of purity.

Instances, such as illustrated by the story of King Bibimsara, who gave his four wives their freedom of choice and handed over his kingdom to his brother to take up the life of a samana, are but illustrations to explain a point two thousand five hundred years ago.

So also the story of the most beautiful Queen Quema, who, because of her past paramis, virtue and attachment for the beauty of a king's garden, married a king but became a dung beetle in the selfsame garden she married into, because of her extreme attachment to the palace grounds.

Kamma is the cause of human destiny. Where a person has bad kamma, he may even reject what is to his own advantage even when good fortunes is thrust upon him. This is exampled in a story of an unfortunate merchant who married a beautiful and devoted wife, whom he found so obnoxious that he could not even sleep in the same bed with her. He finally got rid of her by inducing her to climb up a fig tree so that he could surround its trunk with thorns to prevent her from descending and pursuing him.

That she was obnoxious to him was not her misfortune but his. For whilst she was up the tree, a passing king found her and rescued her. Then, he was so taken by her beauty and graciousness that he married her and she became a queen. One day, whilst on a procession, she was confronted by a street labourer who approached her and begged her to help him out of his misery. It was her former husband who had become so impecunious that he was now a labourer toiling by the roadside.

Nibbana is the highest state attained only by the purest and most deserving. Let us see how it is generally defined and examine the mental attributes required for its attainment. "Nibbana" is defined by the Oxford Dictionary as "the extinction of the individuality and absorption into the supreme spirit as the Buddhist highest good". That definition does not quite explain the Buddhist meaning.

"Nibbana", explained Sariputta, the wandering mystic, "is the extinction of lust, hatred and delusion".

"Nibbana" comes from "ni" and "vana" which means a state without lust or craving. In the Samyutta (i) 31, Buddha referred to the world being inflamed with the fires of lust, hatred and delusion and when this fire is burnt out, nibbana, the coolness, is obtained. This, of course, refers to the meaning of "ni" which, in "nibbati" means to blow out.

Buddha also explained it as a state of being with "neither coming or going nor standing; neither death nor birth". "It is", he explained, "without establishment, without procession, without bias; that is the end of sorrow, nibbana".

This is repeated in the same Udana Sutta (80) to mean "nibbana is without change because it has no dependence on the law of causality. Thus, there is calmness with satisfaction, and, therefore, without desire.

Since there is no desire there is no activity and therefore no kamma. Since there is no coming or going there is no birth and death. Since there is no birth or death there is no this world or that world or any world. Since that is so there is an end to sorrow".

Just as a river is constantly flowing so it is the same river but with different waters, until it becomes still and therefore without movement and no end or beginning, so also the consciousness which constantly flows and flexes without end till it is suddenly stilled and so reaches nibbana without beginning and without end.

Below nibbana are the thirty two planes of existence for all living things. It is said that we reach those planes dependent upon our kamma. Of all these planes, it is in the human plane that there is volition and therefore the human can have advantage through meditation.

Through meditation, kamma is affected. What is kamma and how does it affect us? Kamma has many meanings dependent upon the context it is used. But these meanings have the same idea though how it can be affected can be separately defined.

Firstly, our past acts decide our present life through its resultant effects. Those, who believe that kamma is fate and that they cannot change the kamma uses kamma with this meaning. But they are wrong because there are many kinds of kamma and effects of some of them, such as the light ones and mixed kamma, can be avoided by right action.

Since meditation provides right action and the opportunity of gaining panna and it can change or affect later kamma. With paramis we can even attain. Without it we can reach profitable states because we have volition that can affect kamma. It is most unfortunate if we will not take advantage of this opportunity to enhance our paramis and avoid the states of loss.

Thirdly, kamma can be explained in many ways, for there are nuances to its meaning. In one sense, it explains the concept of crime and punishment. Thus, we are in the planes according to our kamma. We are what we are because of our kamma. We are in severe states of loss because of our kamma.

The effects of heavy kamma due to severe wrongful acts are, however, unavoidable and can take effect immediately or inevitably in one of the lives to come. In this way we can say it is fated since we can never hope to avoid it. Thus, Devatatta, who finally decided to apologise to Buddha, was swallowed up by the sands of a nearby river bank when he went to wash himself after his journey to clean himself before presenting himself to Buddha because that was in his kamma.

Yet, it is not fate, as light or mixed kamma can be affected by the present acts.

The theory of a permanent soul as a separate entity from consciousness and not subject to constant change, is foreign to the theory of Buddhism which requires the acceptance that the consciousness is the heart of all subjective truths.

Even sila has its effects and can only be understood in relation to the mind and states of consciousness. For that reason, all meditative practices relate to the development of the consciousness and different mental faculties and attributes.

Even faith, which is commonly regarded as a belief, is interpreted according to its effects upon the mind. Thus, it is explained, without faith we will have doubt. Doubt weakens conviction so that conviction is lost. When conviction is lost, we also lose determination and become lazy and are overcome either with sloth and torpor or become restless and agitated with doubt and uncertainty and, finally, lose concentration and our practice is terminated.

The necessity for correct practice does not come from religious beliefs but from the need to have the proper concentration for the removal of the defilements which restlessness, agitation, sloth and torpor arise from the lack of faith and determination. It is because concentration is so important to meditation and its nature and mental attributes vary in different states of meditation and levels of purity, concentration is so closely defined.

At the lowest level, there is development of concentration only for a limited purpose, such as is found in the Yehudi Menuhin school of music, or tennis schools and mind control institutions. There is no spiritual enlightenment and so mental attributes involved are irrelevant as well as the faculties of enlightenment.

Chanting and incantations in religions which believe that there can be salvation through those means, only bring about hypnotic trances with the resultant creation of visions due to desires for such visions. Sometimes, there is even transic power attributed to the assistance of a god.

There is hypnotic concentration without any conscious direction, the states arising and visions created being no more than also due to concentrated desires. This explains why trances are often only obtained by weak-minded persons who sees gods of his own beliefs.

These practices employ the simplest techniques. Through hypnotic persuasion, through incantations or chantings, the meditator, gaining more and more self assurance, develop superhuman efforts.

Students taught to focus their minds upon an object, accompanied by hypnotic inducement through repetition of words, develop a strong desire for certain objectives and, through self-will create in their minds, the desired objectives. Should the subject happen to be a kasina, absorption concentration is created and the nimitta is created and a sense of achievement is the result.

Sitting in the snow naked to dry clothes is a good example where both mind control and the laws of physical science are both employed. The meditator sits and is able to stand the cold. The cold dry air and his body heat both help to dry the clothes. Lo and behold, the audience is impressed.

Such ability as the transfer of heat to the various parts of the body for curative purposes, has also been demonstrated, but whether this is only the sensation of heat as an element of the body has not been proven, so also the objectivity or otherwise of that sensation.

Then there again a search for a still higher spiritual objective, such as the transcendental meditation, levitation and such other forms.

This explains the development of the inherent abhinna powers from which incidents and pictures of far away places can be discerned and times when physical punishment can be inflicted without feeling of pain or injury, where the application of force is not too strong.

Are these feelings the result of abhinna or only the sensations of our own elements, such as the air element which can cause the sense of transcendentalism and levitation?

A study of these various forms of meditation and their descriptions, however, fit samatha. From this we can assume that the best of them are samatha in inspiration. This belief is augmented by descriptions of their meditative practice, and the subjects employed in meditation.

That they are used without mindfulness of the rise and fall and the mental factors present, confirms their relationship to samatha.

Where we hear of successful confinement without exposure to air for a number of hours, or even day, with no ill effects, we marvel at the success and wonder if it is the result of the seventh or the eighth state samatha when, it is said, that a plastic state can be achieved.

There are also some schools of meditation which claim that their followers will achieve the ability to read people's minds or develop such powers as to be able to influence others to their will. We do not doubt that to be possible, but to what extent? Some meditators also claim levitation which can come through lightness caused by concentrated coordination of the body such as is done by ballet dancers who have to be lifted into the air. But which claims are the result of meditation or physical skills, or inborn tendencies to feel thoughts and presence I cannot say unless such claims are thoroughly examined.

Medical experiments in the United States in Framington have shown that the theta waves are increased in meditation. The theta waves are those found in the threshold of sleep, not the waves delta waves of sleep. So there is no sleep but a state proximate to sleep. Beta waves, which increase the heart beat, are also reduced, so that a period of calm takes place.

Freedom from stress is therefore reduced because the beta waves are cut down, but he is conscious and able to perform without excitement since the delta waves which indicate sleep are not present.

All these tend to show that the consciousness is developed in a certain way whilst there is a state of unawareness. However, the Framington experiments do not distinguish between samatha and vipassana meditation.

No experiment has yet been performed on vipassana meditators and we do not know if there is any difference and if such differences can be measured.

Meditation, even at the lowest levels, can bring about calmness and concentration. It can influence such as worry and unrest. It can even result in the power of mind over matter as is shown in transcendental meditation and "levitation". At the highest level it is vipassana that can help in our kamma.

But this is not to depreciate lower forms of meditation. They all have limited effects, some better than others. But applied wrongly they can have adverse effects on our kamma and therefore, whatever meditation is pursued, sila and the Brahmavihara subjects should always be practised.

It loses its good effect, for example, if the practitioners claim that their meditation is of such power and quality that it can influence world events through concerted practice because the wave vibrations engendered can permeate throughout the world to bring about peace. In making this false claim they distort the aim of meditation and forget the effect of their claim upon the kamma.

During meditation, the entire process of the subconscious appears to be opened up and its workings are exposed through the formations.

Thus, we can speak generally in layman terms of the dark recesses of the mind, wherein lurk deep-seated fears and hopes, loves and resentments, guilt and spite, which cause depression, hauntings, suicidal tendencies and nightmares that manifest themselves in sleep when the mind is without guard. In meditative terms, formations due to the desires will manifest themselves when the mind is still and calm in the fourth jhana and the faculties and mindfulness are balanced.

Because purification is a matter of the mind and its attributes, we have to understand what these attributes are and how they can be acquired and abandoned.

Generally, a person acquires in one of two ways. He acquires through gaining the wholesome or through abandoning the unwholesome. This is the meaning of "cleansing". The consciousness is left completely open to the formations and it is improved through one of these two processes. The practice of sila encourages this process.

Because one encourages the exposure of the subconscious to the formations coming from within the mentality, vipassana meditation can upset an unbalanced mind through the nimittas arising. It can cause hallucinations which the meditator cannot cope with and there have been such accounts of psychotic disorientation among meditators who have been known to run about naked in the meditation halls, because they are unsuitable or mentally unbalanced, such as alcoholics and those crossed in love who have been allowed to practise meditation.

Because purity is also cleanliness, cleansing in vipassana means the removal of the unwholesome with the wholesome. This is the function of sila.

This is the essential function of sila and the five enjoinders against killing, stealing, lying, imbibing in spirituous liquor and adultery. Lack of concentration on this function has led to the repetitious recitation of these enjoinders without proper understanding of their inner reason, resulting in a great deal of false and unnecessary argument. Killing itself, for example, is nothing. It is the intention that goes behind the killing that is important.

Restraint from killing itself can be a sila act for it means the giving up of uncharitable feeling and illwill, and gaining the opposites of charity and lovingkindness. Thus, bringing about wholesome kamma.

The enjoiners against killing, stealing, lying, intoxication and illicit sexual relations are discouraged for similar reasons for they are the products of greed, illwill and delusion and their related feelings of possessiveness, jealousy, envy, spite, self-righteousness, revenge, self aggrandizement that bring about corresponding illwill, hatred and revenge which are unwholesome and attachment to them prevents the development of wholesomeness.

Restraints from committal of those acts are sila because they encourage their opposite effects. So also are the ten practices of Brahmavihara which encourage positive acts of goodwill, charity, generosity and reduce the importance of self and personal glory and so help to overcome greed, illwill and ego.

Now, would it be wrong to accept this unless our mental makeup inclines us towards their opposites? In this, we can also see the meaning of kamma. But we also recognize it as related to intentions, or cetana, and the mind and not to a preordained soul.

Our kamma is therefore created and shaped by cetana. During meditation, formations arise which allow us to recognize their unwholesome preconditioning, through which realization we can dispel them by noting their three characteristic marks with the assistance of sila.

The removal of desires is not by permissive indulgence which will only fan them but the removal of their roots by supplanting them with their opposite and through removal by realizing their three characteristic marks of impermanence, suffering and voidness in all formations.

This cleansing process is also logically explained. First, the grosser characteristics of the defilements are removed and, as the mind becomes clearer in the higher states, their taints or anusayas are removed with pride and conceit being the last to go when arahantship is gained.

We normally talk of a person's character as if there is a permanent entity with certain characteristics. But there is no evidence that there is such an entity no matter how hard we stretch our imagination. But there is such a thing as a mind and a consciousness through which we perceive and gain experience.

Psychologists talk of genes, Darwinians of adaptability and natural selectivity, Pavlovians of conditioned reflexes. Where physical characteristics are concerned genes are easy to understand. But when it comes to scale of values and how the value system is achieved between various individuals, genes do not appear to be total answers.

Darwinians speak of natural selectivity, but, if there were entirely true, how is it that there appears to be different answers for the same conditions such as the colour designs and different behaviourial patterns under similar conditions of the different fauna? Nor is the Pavlovian theory suitable for complex behaviourial patterns of different individuals in mental adjustments and preferences.

On this basis, the concept of a flexing and fleeting series of formations of a consciousness with three basic roots subjected to preconditioning, falls between the two arguments. It accepts the genes do create beings as seeds do trees. But it holds that there is a consciousness which learns from experience which shapes the consciousness itself. Thus, Buddhism is both philosophical and psychological, concerned with the mental process, using arguments reminiscent of pure Aristotelian logic.

Because of the intricacies of the kamma which are the resultants and of intentional acts which are both cause and effect of immediately antecedent, contiguous, related, supportive or proximate causes which may result in heavy, mixed and light kamma, only those with predisposition will even try to understand it.

But its argument is entirely simple and logical. The only things that appear to be spiritual and superstitious lie in the explanations contained in the Dhammapada with its planes of material form and formless beings existing in the spiritual and material planes.

Other than that, its argument is neither mystical nor dependent upon superstitions but upon exposition of the mental process, even the planes of existence which can be explained as the various states of purity of the mind .

19

POWERS OF THE SUBJECTS

Though the meditator appears to be sleeping, plenty is taking place within his mind for meditation is a mental occupation and everything takes place in the mind. Though he appears calm and unperturbed outwardly, his consciousness is active and shaping itself according to how he sets his mind and the subjects used.

We have already learnt that meditation starts with the cultivation of concentration and the gaining of the jhanas up to the fourth jhana before any skills can be obtained. All the forty subjects can give rise to the first jhana which has initial and sustained concentration and joy and bliss.

But not all of them have the power to provide appana concentration and for surmounting the first jhana to enter the second or any further jhana. That is to say, they can give rise to upacara concentration, which is investigative concentration, without the establishment of firmness of appana to "seize" and hold the counterpart sign to surmount the jhana.

As every jhana advances in purity, the surmounting requires the removal of sukha in the second and piti in the third jhana respectively till the fourth is reached with the presence of only ekaggata and upekha. This requires faith which provides firmness and determination.

So, another way of examining the progress is to see what attributes have been suppressed by the meditator. Where the subjects have inner essences, factors for surmounting are absent.

For this reason, the ten kasinas, which are totality subjects, are said to be the only subjects capable of providing the factors for the surmounting up to the fourth jhana, for they have no inner essences.

The only other subject that can also give rise to the four jhanas is Mindfulness of Breathing. But it is a recollection and not a totality subject and can give rise to abhinna and training in it is of no benefit for this purpose.

It is in the fourth jhana that the meditator can practise for the skills or ignore them for entry into the four immaterial jhanas. To enter the higher jhanas he must abandon the lower jhana so that, to enter the immaterial states he must first have obtained the fourth jhana before he can abandon it to obtain the factors of immateriality for entry into them. Such is the nature of meditation.

Everytime there is an attempt to attain a higher jhana, the lower jhanas have to be abandoned just as a climber has to leave the lower rung of a ladder to climb to the higher ones.

Even in vipassana, there also has to be abandoning. Thus the meditator is said to have abandoned an unwholesome defilement and gained its opposite. This process can also be put in the opposite way. In these instances, the meditator can also be said to have acquired wholesome virtues which have supplanted their unwholesome opposites.

As it is attachment to unwholesome desires which make us slaves, assistance for their abandonment in the cleansing process of vipassana is the purpose of the subjects.

In that way, the foulness subjects are to shock us into rejection of desires and lust by making us realise the ever present death and decay in all human and loved objects, whilst the Recollections of the Buddha and so on are to encourage us to wholesome behaviour through examples.

All these subjects for vipassana, however, require the application of the faculty of mindfulness into the concentration so that it can supervise them and make certain that all are in balance and ready for the rise and fall of the formations.

Of all these subjects, the best is Mindfulness of Breathing. Known as anapanasati, it is a Recollection introduced by Buddha. In itself it can give rise to counterpart sign and all the four jhanas and, though not useful for samatha, it can allow for mindfulness and the noting of the formations and their eradication, something that the kasinas cannot provide.

The power provided by the subjects in vipassana lies in their ability to direct awareness to the true nature of namarupa and persists throughout his meditation and varies with the three characteristic marks of anicca, dukha and anatta in the formations. They help to effect cleansing of the consciousness.

That is the reason why we should concentrate on such as the foulness subjects. But Mindfulness of Breathing is not foul, nor is it a Recollection of sila behaviour. It is just noting the rise and the fall of breathing. Yet, through it we note the formations rise and fall like out breathing, rising and then falling away as they like in spite of all our attempts to control them and falling away to nothing, leaving nothing behind.

The achievement of the cleansing process which ultimately ends in placing the lay practitioner into the realm of the ariyas, or "holy ones", is identified by the acquisition of nanas, or insight wisdom, which breaks through the crust of false pleasures and delights. These are the peaks of power which mark his progress towards the Path.

The beautiful and wondrous visions, bliss, illumination and auras are examples which bring joy and happiness and even flatter the pride and vanities of the meditator, are the mental formations found in vipassana. But they are not the achievements but are hindrances of vipassana.

It is the purity from these occurrences that is the achievement. For purity gives the meditator the power of understanding, the detachment from the torments of jealousy, hate, envy, dissatisfaction and acquisitiveness and which releases him from suffering and despair.

But all this demonstrates the effects of the subjects and the power of the mind to conquer even our innermost unwholesome desires through mindfulness after the fourth jhana is obtained and we are in the udayabhaya nana state, where detachment and freedom from greed, illwill and delusion with their resultant selfishness, acquisitiveness and possessiveness, illwill, jealousy and spite, vanity, pride and boastfulness through the development of virtues as reflected by the brahmavihara, is possible.

One thinks of metta towards all beings in all forms, but, one begins first with a single person, stretching one's practice to encompass this person without attachment or desire. Later, when there is already sufficient practice, one includes a hated one as well. In this way, slowly, the practice is developed so that the neighbourhood of the temple will be full of love and well-being, both in the form and formless world.

Metta directly conflicts with hate and illwill and all those feelings associated with illwill. As with metta, so also with karuna and mudita. They both replace their opposites with their virtue.

Karuna requires the doing of deeds of generosity. It is charity without any ulterior motive. It is charity without the intention of fame or recognition but charity with the pure intention of giving help and assistance to someone else out of a feeling of generosity. Therefore it is cultivation of non-greed and so, is conducive of the destruction of greed.

Mudita comes when one has the feeling of genuine happiness at the relief of misery and suffering of another being. One feels genuinely happy when one sees some other being escaping misery or being relieved of some suffering or agony. This rather generous and rare quality is the development of the awareness of non-self. By developing the awareness of the suffering and the pain of others, the awareness of non-self is developed. By cultivating in oneself consideration for others, the thought of self is diminished.

The basis of morality in these four subjects is in selflessness, feeling for others in generosity and kindness which result in calmness of concentration without the agitation, distraction, sloth and torpor in meditation preventing its interruption and termination.

The ultimate achievement of vipassana is emancipation from all our suffering. Though samatha does not provide this, nevertheless, one who holds to the Brahmavihara during its practice can attain the Brahma planes as the name of that plane signifies.

The meditator who holds to his Brahmavihara who has achieved the first jhana will reach the plane of Brahma companionship in their assembly, or retinue (brahma-parisajja), or ministers

(Brahma-purohita) or even that of the great Brahmas (Maha Brahma), depending on his level of practice.

Those in the second jhana will reach the planes of the Brahmas of minor lustre (parittabha), or infinite lustre (appamanabha) or that of the radiant Brahmas (abhassara) whose bodies emit rays like flashes of lightning.

Those in the third jhana will reach the planes of the Brahmas of minor illumination (parittasubbha), of infinite illumination (appamanasubha) or that of a mass of illumination (subhakinha).

Those in the fourth jhana enter the planes of the great fruits of the realm of unconscious beings (asannathala), and the Five Pure abodes of the Immobile (aviha), Serene (atappa), Beautiful (sudassa), Exquisite (sudassi), and the Supreme (akanittha).

The five pure abodes are also the realm of the anagamis. They are those who have reached the path of the non-returners. The categorizing of the anagamis here, amongst the jhana meditators, demonstrates the inter-twining that sometimes occur between samatha and vipassana meditation.

This shows the extreme importance of practice of Brahmavihara, no matter what the meditation is. Apart from that and the kasinas and Brahmavihara, there are other subjects for meditation that either reflect the positive examples of virtuous behaviour such as the Recollections and the Asubha, or foulness, subjects which encourage good through restraint from wrongful acts.

Asubha subjects relate to foulness. The ten foulness or asubha subjects relate to different forms of corpses which is the swollen, discoloured, festering, fissured, mangled, dismembered, cut and dismembered, bleeding, worm-infested and skeletons.

They are insight subjects, meant to dissuade lust and such heavy forms of greed for human beauty and so on. Yet, though they are vipassana subjects, the meditator must remember to keep his concentration on their nature rather than on their colour. Should his concentration be held on its colour, it becomes a colour kasina upon which the fourth jhana can be obtained.

He practises insight if he keeps his concentration on the foulness and the rotting state of the corpse, noting its repulsiveness, its disgusting state and sees the disgust and the impermanence of life, its painful characteristics and the reality behind it all; recalling that it used to glitter with adornment and beautification and seeing the reality of the decay and the rot in its present state.

They drive home the message by powerfully and are for those given to lust and sexual desires. But they only bring about the first jhana. When using it, the meditator looks at a corpse and quickly notes its location, situation, its mental image, its posture, its shape, direction and its various parts, quickly obtains the learning-image so that he can produce its counterpart or conceptual image afterwards in the quiet of his own room.

Mindfulness of the body is another recollection subject introduced by Buddha for the realization of the unsatisfactoriness, painfulness and suffering of an impermanent, fragile and transitory body. In this subject, the body is divided into thirty-two parts, They are such as one's hairs, urine, bile, sweat and so on. Awareness of their ugliness and filth thus prepares him for the ultimate rejection of his pride and greed for himself.

Known as the kayagata sati bhavanga, it contains the four primary elements of fire, water heat and air which are themselves also subjects of the formations.

20

CONCENTRATION REQUISITES

The first requirement for emancipation is virtue. We have dealt with it at length and may now deal with concentration which is the other basic purity to be established before there can be Panna.

Samadhi takes its term from samadhana, from which the term samadhi is also derived. Samadhi in meditation requires the presence and employment of mental attributes specific to the kind and states of concentration and the consciousness.

Concentration can be defined in different ways. It can be defined in its first four jhanas as follows.

The normal way is to describe it as it occurs in sequence as initial and sustained concentration and as access and absorption concentration.

As one begins concentration, one enters into the initial state when there is happiness and bliss which contains distraction and therefore interferes with sustained concentration. It becomes sustained, for example, when joy and bliss are removed in the calm without distractions in the fourth jhana. For concentration to be of use, there has to be sustained concentration.

It is said to be in access and in absorption concentration when the counterpart image has to be held for surmounting or for the skills in abhinna. Thus, the meditator is in access concentration when the concentration is in an investigative state before it seizes upon the counterpart sign to hold it firmly in absorption concentration in the counterpart sign.

In samatha, it is the jhanas and the supranormal normal skills that are obtained through ekaggata and upekha and practice on the counterpart sign. In vipassana it is the nanas, or insight, that is gained with mindfulness through which there is the realization of the truth. Everytime a nana is experienced there is the presence of an awareness and there are reviews that indicate the progress and the nature of purity gained. Both meditation techniques employ different mental attributes with different results.

These differences is another way of knowing the type of meditation and the states achieved by the meditator in that meditation.

Samadhi of samatha and vipassana stem from the same roots but their achievements are different and their final aims are different. Both require the ekaggata and the upekha of the fourth jhana but from then on they differ. Since sila can also be employed in samatha, the mental attributes are similar only up to a point, from then on vipassana requires the presence of mindfulness and knowledge of the dhamma to provide the capacity to gain the nanas. Since the nanas will bring about different mental states, the different attributes must also be different in each state.

In the conversation between the Elders, Sariputta and Maha Kotthita in the Majjima Nikaya and in the Vibhanga, a clearer picture is given as to the constituents of ekaggata which is said to have five parts and that it contains vicara, vitakka, piti, sukha and citassekaggata. The meditator first enters vitakka concentration, then applies concentration. This application is vicara concentration. Then, piti is absorbed and so is sukha, till all the five parts are present in the fourth jhana. Thus, from the factors present we can know the state of the concentration.

In samatha, ekaggata is obtained through non-interference of the factors of distraction and agitation and sloth and torpor through the suppression of greed, illwill and delusion. Through suppression, these factors become dormant and are absent from the concentration which then becomes ekaggata.

What are the factors that can lead to absorption of the counterpart sign for the practice of the skills.

Where there is need to develop the counterpart sign, the after image, or the parikamma nimitta must first be created from which there will arise the patibhaga nimitta, or learning sign. It is from the learning sign that the counterpart sign, or the ubhaga nimitta, is developed.

Required for these signs are the factors which give rise to parikamma-samadhi or preliminary concentration. Here, it is access concentration, or upacara samadhi, that is required. This concentration is the preliminary investigation of a subject from which appana samadhi, or absorption concentration, is achieved. Thus we can say that from upachara samadhi there will come appana which will allow the counterpart sign to be held for practice.

But, though the attributes must be present for the development of the counterpart sign, there must also be factors in such subjects for the counterpart sign to arise, otherwise there will be no counterpart sign to concentrate on. That is why it is important to know what subjects have the factors that can give rise to the counterpart sign.

For the counterpart sign to appear, upacara concentration must first be established and when appana appears, the sign is grasp with firmness and resolve.

When the counterpart sign first appears and appana has not arisen, the meditator will try to keep it whilst awaiting for appana, which will only appear when the samadhi is unwavering and there is present factors necessary for training on the counterpart sign.

Training in the skills in abhinna requires these factors. Without these factors, the counterpart or conceptual image cannot be held firmly enough to practise on. Thus, though the counterpart sign can arise in upacara, it is only the preliminary for appana.

Access concentration is the access or entry into a concentration leading to absorption. Access is like entering into a city and meeting the guard at the gates and taking a peep inside the city gates. The access is shaky, as a child is shaky on its feet when it first begins to stand. It is full of distractions and thus, is said to have 'blemishes'. There are still impurities of the sense desires so it has "defilements".

Absorption, or appana concentration, however is different. It is sustained and applied concentration, applied on the same object with a view to investigation and the mind is continually engaged in this exercise.

During absorption concentration, the mind is slowly steadied and held on course so that the distractions are lessened and the "blemishes" of the object become less and its defilements too become less and the concentration is "purified and is penlucid". That is why it is said that the counterpart sign is a symbol of the real image that is pure, clean, and without blemishes and defects.

It is precisely this that makes it imperative that the samatha meditator know what subjects he has to use for his meditation, since only the ten kasinas can give rise to the counterpart signs and no other.

Those subjects that can only lead to upacara concentration can never be used for the practice of skills simply because counterpart signs and therefore appana concentration is impossible. Except for Mindfulness of Breathing which, although it can give rise to the fourth jhana and the counterpart sign, is a Recollection and the counterpart sign is uncertain.

Upekha of the Brahmavihara is found in the fourth state arising after the first three jhanas and has no counterpart sign.

Only those subjects which have the factors of surmounting to the fourth jhana in appana can be used to advantage. These, as we know are only the kasinas, except Mindfulness of Breathing.

In the training of the skills, the samatha meditator has, first of all, to look at the subject of his meditation. For the mark of the subject as a preliminary exercise. This mark is that known as the parikamma-nimitta. From this, he develops a learning sign, which is a mental replica of the original and so contains every visible aspect of the original sign. This is the patibhaga nimitta.

Finally, from the patibhagaha nimitta he creates in his mind, the counterpart sign, or the ubhaga nimitta, which is symbolic and appears in its essential and pure form without the blemishes and irregularities, upon which he practises his skills.

The language used to describe the practice is quaint but sufficiently interesting to repeat. It describes the appearance of the counterpart sign and appana concentration,as indication that the mind is tranquillized and now malleable enough to be trained in the ten ways required for the ten skills, without which he cannot obtain abhinna and the supranormal powers. How the ten skills are practised will be set out when we deal with the subjects and abhinna.

In vipassana, however, the factors for investigation required in appana are not necessary. What is required is a tranquilized and a malleable mind, clean and without blemishes in which there are the factors of penetration and reviewing the achievements obtained with mindfulness present together with the four faculties to gain wisdom through the dhamma, by penetration into the truth of the formations.

Whatever the language used, the message is quite clear. Concentration for vipassana requires knowledge of the dhamma for the factors of penetration into the truth of the formations, without which there can be no panna. The requirements and attributes for its concentration are therefore fundamentally different from that of samatha and definitely more complex.

The reason for the presence of the factors of penetration into the truth, and the importance of knowledge and acceptance of the dhamma for vipassana, comes back to the fact that we require alobha, adosa and amoha to gain our freedom from the shackles of the desires arising from lobha, dosa and moha. This freedom can be obtained through awareness of the three characteristics of formations which are anicca, dukha and anatta, and how all aggregates, when they break up into their elements, are subject to decay and there is nothing left other than a void and there is no such thing as a permanent entity.

For the damma to have effect on the consciousness, acceptance of the sasana is required not only to supply the volition but also to provide the faith and the determination factors for firm, undistracted and a pliable concentration, so that the mind can be responsive enough for development in any way suitable for skills in samatha or for vipassana penetration into the formations.

Here we must remind readers that, although there can be the counterpart sign of Mindfulness of Breathing in the fourth jhana, it does not lead to abhinna and the counterpart sign can come to different meditators in various forms. There is no one definite sign. It is further described under the meditation subjects.

There are common factors present whether it is samatha or vipassana. Sila is one of them. It is necessary as it provides the factors of faith and determination and the removal of the defilements which distract and prevent concentration such as agitation, restlessness and sloth and torpor.

Vipassana needs the factors of sila to develop the base for the penetration of the truth, starting with the five moral precepts and the Noble Eight-fold path. Because of this, the arahant must have Right Livelihood, which is one of the requirements of the Eightfold path, due to the requirements of his high state. Right livelihood requires, amongst other things, the giving up of all worldly possessions, including the ties of his family and all his personal belongings except for the bare necessities as he has to have no attachment to belongings at all. He has to "go forth" so to speak, out of his house into that of a monastery or a temple or to a place where the following conditions exist and depend on dana for his food:

1. Where there is discipline of mental faculties as prescribed by the Patimmokka;
2. Where there is discipline of bodily faculties and where he has given up all his worldly impediments and nothing is owned except bare necessities;
3. Where his livelihood requires living in the right way;
4. Where there is constant practice and conduct within the Noble Eight-fold path.

There were only the Buddhist monasteries in the time of Buddha. Since such conditions were difficult to find outside these places, it becomes obvious why it has been said that an arahant must seek refuge among the order of the sangha within seven days of his attainment or die in the face of hostile conditions. For, when the meditator has reached the state of the arahant, he must for necessity, seek refuge in a place of seclusion such as a monastery, for he would not be able to survive in his state outside of it.

It was only in such places that the monk can free himself of all the five impediments that still attach him to life. They are such as his disciples and his books. To be emancipated, he no longer requires any attachment whatsoever, so he needs to be free even from his life, wife and his friends.

Because Buddhist meditators must hold their sila, he needs the following:

1. A suitable place for an abode. He needs easy access to food e.g. a friendly neighbourhood.
2. To guard his speech which must be mindful and proper and not be aimless and unsuitable.
3. He must always be mindful and concentrated in what he does.
4. He must avoid persons of unconcentrated and aimless talk and not given to rowdy or disturbing behaviour.
5. He must take the proper food.
6. He must stay at a place where the climate is suitable to him.
7. He must always maintain suitable postures for his meditation e.g. walking, standing, sitting or lying down.

These are the seven requirements of proper living, association and cultivation necessary to cultivate the right attitudes of mind so as to avoid their opposites, which are the unsuitables.

He is required to avoid distraction during meditation so as to gain appana required concentration at all times on the subject so that the learning sign will not be lost and the counterpart sign can arise.

Further, he is required to maintain the following requirements:

1. He must make his basis clean – That is to say, he has to be clean both physically and mentally, to gain proper and steady concentration. For when the basis is unclean it is, as stated before, like the oil lamp with a dirty wick and oil, any one or both of which will prevent a constant and a purified light. Should the meditator be unclean, his meditation will also be unsteady and disturbed. His consciousness and mental concomitants be unclean and so, purification cannot be achieved.
2. He must balance the faculties of faith, understanding, energy and concentration with mindfulness in attendance always.

   Since mindfulness is not required in samatha, we can assume that the text here refers to the jhanas applied to vipassana.

The Visuddhi Magga sets out five similes explaining appana concentration, two of which are reproduced here because they make the meaning quite clear and the rest are ignored because they repeat the same idea.

The first compares it to the man who is mindful enough to unwind a cobweb without breaking it. The second is that of the bee, which is mindful enough not to overshoot the flower as he approaches it for pollen or mistimes its approach and descends too late.

3. Skill in the sign – This sign is the counterpart sign, the practice and description of which are fully described in the subjects of meditation.

Mindfulness of Breathing have counterpart signs but they vary and are different, not only on different occasions but with different meditators. For its counterpart sign is an inner state and may come as a torrent, or as a star, or a cluster of gems, a braided string, a wreath, a stretched cobweb, a puff of smoke, a lotus flower, a fluttering, a rubber bladder being inflated with air and so on and so forth – to each his own sign.

The sign occurs when one is concentrated at a certain point and notes the breath as it goes in or out. One does not follow the breath in or out, up or down but notes it at a certain point. So one does not anticipate the breath, nor does one chase after it, just as one notes the point at which the saw blade works on the wood but does not follow the saw blade before or after it passes over the wood.

If one follows it, the sign is lost. It is also lost because of another characteristic, as one moves into the higher states it becomes so subtle that it can become so subtle as to become imperceptible. In such an instance, as we are told in the parable of the herdsman who has lost his cattle, one waits at that place where it was lost for its return, which it must do just, as the cattle will have to return to the water-hole for their drink when they are thirsty.

Thus, when the sign is lost, the meditator fixes his attention on the spot he last lost the sign, and waits for it, quietly and patiently, to reappear to note it again.

How does one note it? At first it is the actual breath. Some note it at the nostrils, some elsewhere such as at his stomach as he watches the rise and fall of his breath. Then it is the counterpart sign which comes and then goes away, returning again probably in another form.

How does one breathe? Some breathe heavily, some lightly, varying their breaths fast or slow, or deep or shallow. It all depends on how he prefers it, according to his inclination, so long as it is not distracting and interferes with the concentration.

It is wrong to insist that all meditators should adopt only one style of breathing, whether it be hard and furious or slow and long drawn. It is mindfulness that he should be concentrating on, not his style of breathing.

4. He exerts his mind on the occasions it should be exerted, and
5. He should restrain his mind on the occasions it should be restrained.

In both these instances of (4) and (5), the meditator pays attention on the investigation enlightenment factor, and develops the happiness enlightenment factor.

In short, the meditator builds his energy and happiness (pleasurable) factors and he:

- asks questions
- makes the basis clean
- balances the faculties
- avoids persons without understanding
- cultivates persons with understanding
- reviews the field for the exercise of profound knowledge
- keeps resolute upon investigation of status.

This is repeated as we examine the attainment of eleven factors that lead to the arising of the energy of enlightenment, which comes when the meditator moves from a lower meditative state to the next higher one. These come both in vipassana and in the attainment of the arupa states in samatha meditation, since the meditator must abandon the lower states in both meditations as unsatisfactory before he can ascend to the higher one – abandoning even the abhinna powers obtained in the fourth jhana that he may reach the arupa jhanas. So the factors are common to both because of abandoning.

He, thus, does the following:

- reviews the fearfulness of the status of loss,
- sees benefit in obtaining the mundane and supramundane achievements depending upon energy,
- reviews the course of the journey to be travelled in this way, the path taken by Buddha, Pacceka Buddha and the great disciples which only the non-idler can take,
- being a credit to the giving of alms by encouraging the givers through correct conduct and behaviour,
- reviews the greatness of Buddha, thinking of his praise of the energetic, and remembering that dispensation is only helpful if it is honoured by correct practice, and not otherwise,
- reviews the greatness of the heritage of the Good Dhamma that cannot be acquired by an idler,
- removes stiffness and torpor by attention to perception of flight, change of postures, frequenting the open air, etc.,
- avoids idle persons,
- cultivates the company of energetic persons,
- reviews the Right Endeavors,
- maintains resoluteness upon that energy.

And he develops the eleven factors that lead to the arising of the happiness of enlightenment which are the recollections of:

- the Buddha,
- the Dhamma,
- the Sangha,
- virtue,
- generosity,
- deities,
- recollection of peace,
- avoidance of rough persons,
- cultivation of refined persons,
- reviewing encouraging discourses,
- resoluteness upon that happiness.

In restraining his mind, he cultivates three of the seven enlightenment factors – serenity, concentration and equanimity factors which are defined as follows:

Serenity (or tranquillity) of 7 factors – these are composed as follows:

- using superior food,
- living in a good climate,
- maintaining a pleasant posture,
- keeping the middle path,
- cultivation of persons tranquil in body,
- resoluteness upon that tranquillity.
- Concentration with its 11 factors.

These factors lead to the following:

- skill in the sign,
- making the basis clean,
- balancing the faculties,
- restraining the mind on occasion,
- exerting the mind on occasion,
- encouraging the listless mind by means of faith and sense of urgency,
- looking on with equanimity at what is occurring rightly,
- avoidance of unconcentrated persons,
- cultivation of concentrated persons,
- reviewing the jhanas and liberations,
- resoluteness upon that concentration.

The five factors leading to equanimity enlightenment are:

- maintenance of neutrality towards living beings,
- maintenance of neutrality towards formations,
- avoidance of persons who show favouritism towards beings and formations,
- cultivation of persons who maintain neutrality towards persons and formations,
- resoluteness upon that equanimity.

6. How does he encourage his mind when he should? When his mind is listless and sluggish he should review the eight grounds for a sense of urgency: birth, aging, sickness, death, suffering of the state of loss of the past noted in the round of rebirths, the future rounds of rebirths and the suffering for nutriment.
7. Looking upon the mind with equanimity.
8. Avoidance of uncultivated persons.
9. Cultivation of concentrated persons.
10. Resoluteness upon that state.

The reason for this concentration is it that requires the greatest balance of the five faculties of mindfulness, energy, etc. and the meditator has to employ all factors required with the utmost sensitivity.

We have emphasized that to gain the higher jhanas there must be abandonment of the lower states and surmounting. Why is this so?

The opinion here is that there are four or five thought impulsions for surmounting thought impulsions on the same object in which the first four or five are the stronger impulsions of the initial thought (vitakka), sustained thought (vicara), bliss (piti) happiness (sukha) and then one-pointedness of unity of thought (ekaggata) which are those of the preliminary or access concentration. This is prior to the attainment of absorption itself.

The factors and meaning of access and absorption concentration are set out in detail to emphasize the need for ethical behaviour required for uninterrupted and full concentration. It is also a constant requirement for sila to build up the preconditioning required for such uninterrupted or undisturbed concentration. Only in this way can purity of concentration be obtained.

In order to be able to meditate with success, he must also keep his basis clean, find for himself a suitable place for meditation, maintain correct attitudes, have friends who are concentrated and properly behaved, eat in a proper manner suitable for his meditation, keep in mind the example of Buddha and his great disciples, have proper discourses and be firm and resolute in his practice.

This is the main purpose of sila. A mind of hate and greed develops an unwholesome kamma, restlessness, sloth and torpor. Such hindrances are encountered by every meditator and they hinder progress because they prevent purity of concentration, since their defilements interrupt proper concentration.

They are grouped into viz:

1. Sensual passion.
2. Illwill.
3. Sloth and torpor.
4. Flurry and worry.
5. Perplexity.
6. Ignorance with the ten kilesas (torments) of greed, hate, dullness, conceit, error, perplexity, sloth, distraction, impudence and fearlessness of consequence.

By cleanliness, it is meant both physical and mental cleanliness. He must perform profitable acts and hold to wholesome thoughts in speech and act.

Any preconditioning that will bring concentration without distraction, agitation, doubt, sloth and torpor are wholesome acts; that which encourage them such as desire, illwill and wrong views are unwholesome.

Unwholesome deeds are those that lead to the ten duccantas, such as murder, destructive desires, ill-treatment, harsh speech, envy, jealousy, adultery, bewilderment and perplexity, sloth and torpor, shamelessness (ahirika), recklessness of consequences (anotta), distraction (uddhacca), selfishness, worry and conceit.

The meditator must be mindful also of the delusion of his ego that brings about pride, conceit and boastfulness and be aware of false pride and false modesty.

He must remember greed is desire that includes possessiveness, envy and lust. He also has to bear in mind that hate, in all its forms, cause misery of one form or another to others. They are unwholesome factors which result in hindrances, fetters and torments in meditation which block progress.

Gross fetters are the first to go and only in the final ariya state that the taints or anusayas of those gross feelings can be discerned and removed. That is why, the last of the subtle tendencies of pride and conceit remain, only to be removed by the arahant.

At this state, he is no longer concerned if there is a soul for he will no longer have greed for an entity.

At that state, he will have shattered the darkness and moved from darkness to light.

21

ATTRIBUTES IN MEDITATION

The Abhidhamma is full of terms referring to mental attributes, faculties, attributes, concomitants, powers, abilities, functions and resultant states, hindrances, torments, fetters, defilements and so on which make the texts more like psychological tomes rather than religious texts. But their importance is such that Buddha himself advised that those who do not understand the Abhidhamma should not attempt to teach the dhamma.

A typical description of an effort required for meditation, for example, is described in this way. There are four efforts required in meditation. The four efforts are for the prevention the arising of unwholesome thoughts; the prevention of unwholesome thoughts that have arisen from establishing themselves; the promotion of wholesome thoughts, and their development once they have arisen. These four efforts are known as the sammapadhanas and so on.

Again, in explaining the requirement of certain faculties for proper concentration, the wording provided by the Abhidhamma is as follows. There are five faculties required in samadhi. They must however, come with their powers for without their powers they will have no ability to achieve what is required. The faculties required are the faculty of faith, energy, concentration and wisdom. Their powers are known as (bala). Therefore their powers are those of mindfulness, faith, energy, concentration and wisdom, known respectively as saddha-bala viriya-bala, samadhi-bala and panna-bala that have to be balanced. These faculties must not only be present but they must be balanced between themselves as with the faculty of mindfulness which act as the Prime Minister (primus inter pares). The explanation for their balance is also given at length.

Even mindfulness is explained psychologically. First, all its efforts and faculties should be anchored at all times at "their four stations", being the four areas where contact can be made and formations arise.

They are known as:

1. The satipathana of contemplation of the body (kayanupassana),
2. Of the feelings (vedananupassana),
3. Of the mind (cittanupassana),
4. Of the dhamma or the law or conditions or mind objects (dhammanupassana).

Mindfulness is so important in vipassana that they are explained in detail:

1. **Mindfulness of the body (kayanupassana)** – This is mindfulness of the aggregates of the physical phenomena. In vipassana, the first knowledge required is that of namarupa nana. Without this attribute, he will not be able to discern the rise and fall of the formations.

   Having obtained the fourth jhana, the meditator maintains his mindfulness to learn the truth about the formations by noting the rise and fall of the formations. This can also be described as the rise and fall of the aggregates. Through the namarupa nana, the process of mentality-materiality, takes place in this way. He hears the opening of one of his sense doors and as he notes the formations rising from it, even as he notes them, they end and the sense door closes. Thus, he notes them as they rise one by one and then close till only one is kept open.

   In Mindfulness of Breathing, he notes the aggregates of breathing and soon notices the cause and the actual appearance of breathing in and out notes the 'sign' and sees that breathing has its beginning and its end and notices its true nature.

Even as he walks, stands, sits or lies down, he is also conscious of the rise and the actual dissolution of the aggregates of the physical phenomena of his body just as in the case of his breathing.

As he perceives the appearance and the dissolution and the breakup (or dissolution) of the aggregate of the body and the cause, insight knowledge begins, the first of which is the namarupa nana, through which he gains the second knowledge of paccaya pariggaha nana and so on, from nana to nana systematically.

The second nana is awareness of the dissolution voidness and emptiness of the aggregates. Gaining this knowledge, he now understands that there is no soul or superior force directing his rise and fall of formations, and realise that all his formations are due to ignorance of the Four Truths which is that craving for pleasure of the senses. Kamma, which is the resultant of cause, bring about a constant cycle of rebirths and that it is this which is the mentality nutriment essential for the phenomena; that the citta (mind), being the motivating force for all living beings, supported by this nutriment, bring about the formations just as their absence can lead to dissolution of the aggregates.

This third knowledge which is that of sammanasana nana is the actual perception of the sign of change or the disappearance or the deterioration of the physical phenomena.

So the awareness of the rise of the formations is namarupa nana, the unsatisfactory appearance of the phenomena is indicative of paccaya pariggaha nana, that of realizing the sign of change, the disappearance or deterioration of the physical phenomena and that their falsity is due to ignorance of the four ariyan truths in sammanasana.

In this way, it can easily be understood why belief in the dhamma is essential for knowledge of the truth of the characteristic marks of the formations, and knowledge of the Abhidhamma is necessary to explain it.

Through these attributes, the yogi begins to experience the four elements of his body and their behaviour according to their own nature.

Thus, pathavi-dhatu (earth or solid with attribute of hardness element) gives the impression of hardness or stiffness; apo-dhatu (water with attribute of fluidity and cohesion) gives the impression of fluidity and softness; tejo-dhatu (fire with the attribute of heat or cold) gives the impression of heat; vayo-dhatu (air with the attribute of motion) gives the impression of transmigration or such astral sensations, whether he is then noting his posture or observing the repulsiveness of parts of his body.

Thus, he learns that his body comprises only of the 4 elements in various combinations.

2. **Mindfulness of the true nature of the feelings (vedanupassana)** – In this second station of mindfulness, the meditator is mindful of his feelings and observes the pleasant or unpleasant, or neither the pleasant nor unpleasant feelings associated with his sensual desires. His knowledge allows him also to realize their impermanence, unsatisfactory nature and their soullessness and thus, perceives their rise and fall. He remains detached from craving and wrong views and is mindful without clinging to the five aggregates or khandhas just as he has done with the bodily mindfulness.
3. **Mindfulness of the true nature of the mind (cittanupassana)** – Likewise, the yogi maintains mindfulness on his mind and observes its formations and anicca, dukha and anatta. He knows when his mind is accompanied by Raga or not. Raga means pleasure in or craving for something good or bad, weak, medium or strong.

He also knows when his mind is with or without anger (dosa), when it is with or without bewilderment (moha). He is also incapable of knowing the Four Noble Truths, incapable of adopting a correct attitude, when it has nuchanana,that is only capable of evil counsel in all matters and blind to the nature of an unmeritorious deed (akusala), when it is distracted vikkhitta citta or amahaggata citta (or in an undeveloped state), or when it is inferior as uttara citta or anuttara (superior), or if it is in the sensuous world (kamavacara citta), or in a concentrated state (samahita), or liberated (vimutha citta) or in an unconcentrated (asamahita) or unliberated state (avimutha).

Thus, he perceives the actual arising and dissolution of the mind, the cause, therefore, and its soullessness and remains detached from craving, wrong views and clinging to the five khandhas.

4. He perceives the true nature of Dhamma (Dhammanupassana) which are:

   The five hindrances (Nivarana). He keeps his mind steadfastly on these hindrances which are obstacles in one's spiritual progress, that is, hindrances to the doing of kusala deeds, achievement of the Jhanas, the four Path insights by:

   - Kamachanda: all forms of craving (tanha) and desire (lobha).
   - Byapada: illwill, harbouring evil desires to ill-treat or destroy others and to bring others to trouble.
   - Thina-middha: sloth and torpor, feeling of indolence in particular, for doing good and meritorious deeds
   - Uddhacca-kukkacca: distraction (agitatera) and worry, with a mentality that cannot concentrate but is flitting about and worrying over past acts and omissions
   - Vicikiccha: doubts and wavering of the mind.

   He keeps his mind on these five mental hindrances, or nivarana, of sensuous desires, illwill, sloth and torpor, distraction, agitation and perplexity inimical to jhana, and notes when they are or are not, or are about to arise and he makes it a point to have them discarded when they arise and so that they do not arise again, in that way to uproot them.

Thus, he also makes a conscious effort to uproot them in his subconscious as soon as he is aware that they are about to arise, even at this stage, noting them he notes their dukkha and their anatta; thus cause them to fade away by noting their characteristics and their true nature. Thus, he makes certain his mindfulness as in all the other cases, is for gaining (upassana) and further mindfulness and he remains aloof from the five khandas which are progressively deteriorating.

The five Khandas. He keeps his mind steadfastly the 5 khandas of:

- Rupakkhanda – aggregate of the bodily phenomena,
- Vedanakkhanda – aggregate of feeling or sensation,
- Sannakkhanda – aggregate of perception,
- Sankarakhanda – aggregate of mental formations (volition and action other than Vedana and sanna),
- Vinnanakhanda – aggregate of the consciousness.

These five khandas are known as the upadanakhandas which the meditator also steadfastly notes with bare attention, as he knows they are just mental and physical phenomena which are subject to anicca, dukkha and anatta. He does not "cling" to them and merely notes their arising and fading away as fast as they have arisen, their place taken yet by another arising thought.

The 12 sense bases (ayatama). The six sense bases of the eye, ear, nose, body, mind and mental bases come with their respective consciousness so that there are twelve ayatamas altogether which are responsible for the ten fetters (sambojjhanga) being those of:

- sensual craving (kamaraga). This is craving for the sensual feelings of the senses.
- Anger, disappointment, fear, grief and resentment (patigha). Thus, if we are detached from greed and hate (lobha and dosa) we would not have these feelings.

- pride (mana). This comes from the delusion of self (atta).
- belief in the illusion of a permanent self or soul (sakkayaditthi). Again, the belief in atta prevents the meditator from seeing the impermanency of things.
- doubt, scepticism, wavering (vicikicca) which also gives to scepticism is due to ignorance (avijja) of the truth of the true the rise and fall of the aggregates and the impermanency of things.
- wrong beliefs (silabhataparamasa) which means the refusal to accept the ariya path of the eight Enlightenments as the path for the relief of suffering (dukkha).
- craving to become a Brahman with a mind and a body or with a mind and no body (bhavanga).
- envy or jealousy (issa). This is a reflection of greed that brings about envy and hate which brings about illwill and jealousy.
- meanness and stinginess (macchariya).
- ignorance (avijja). This means ignorance of the four truths of suffering. These samyojjanas or the fetters which arise through the ayatamas or senses bases and their consciousness.

The meditator keeps his mind steadfastly on the dhamma when they arise and does no more than to note them when they arise or he knows they are about to arise and after they have arisen. He perceives the cause of their arising and their actual dissolution as they take place and he remains detached and is mindful only on gaining more mindfulness and for vipassana

The seven bojjhangas. Bojjhanga means a mental factor of enlightenment.

- The description of the bojjhanga is an insight enlightenment factor.
- All states of enlightenment have this factor in them. The bojjhanga is this enlightenment factor.

- All the faculties need the faculty of power directed to enlightenment or it would otherwise be meaningless. For example, mindfulness will only be effective if it has the power to supervise to bring about enlightenment.

The bojjhangas are classified into:

- Sati-sambojjhanga, which is the constant mindfulness factor which enables the meditator to comprehend the Ariya truths;
- Dhammavicaya-sambojjhanga, which is the investigative knowledge of the phenomena of the dhamma factor;
- Passaddhi-sambojjhanga, which is the serenity or tranquillity factor in his practice;
- Samadhi-sambojjhanga, which is the factor of concentration;
- Upekkha-sambojjhanga, which is the factor of equanimity;
- Piti-sambojjhanga, which is the delight factor he must feel in satisfaction of his search;
- Viriya-sambojjhanga, which is the effort factor in his practice;

Ariya factors. These are some special mental attributes in the mind of the ariya.

Through concentration and awareness of the principle of cause and effect, there is the removal of defilements and their taints and all their tendencies, known as asavas, at the entry into all the four ariya paths (bhavato abbhavangang dhammato gotrabhu savantiti asava).

He knows when an asava is about to arise or when it is completely developed because of anasikara and dhammavicaya, the latter of which means the complete knowledge of the true nature of the five khandas. In this sense also, he knows the true nature of their anicca, dukkha and anatta.

These four asavas are sense desires (kamasavo), becoming (bhavasavo in the kama, rupa and arupa bhavo in the bhavanga), error, ignorance.

They exist with the four graspings or holding on (idam-saccabhini-veso) of sense desires, error, rites, rituals and ceremonies and concept of the soul. The last of the asavas are removed at the state of the arahant because it is only then that can discern the taints of the four truths and end suffering by entry into the path of the arahant.

22
CONSCIOUSNESS PROPERTIES

The consciousness and not the soul, is the centre of all mental life of Buddhist teaching. Knowledge of how all our activities affect our consciousness is essential to the understanding of the philosophy and teaching of the Abidhamma.

Mental attributes and properties of the consciousness in all its states are described in so much detail by the Abidhamma that it would be only fair that we list them out with equal detail. In this chapter we are dealing with the mental properties required by the consciousness to reach the various states of meditation and what it requires to act in those states.

In all consciousness, there are these seven mental properties, known as cetasikas, which are common to every thought, whatever it may be, wholesome or unwholesome, without which there can be no thought at all. There must first be contact (phassa), from which feeling (vedana) arises followed by perception (sanna), then by volition (cetana) after which there is identification on the individuality of the object (ekaggata), psychic life and attention.

At that point there is reaction according to preconditioning and the mental properties that will come will depend upon whether the thought arising is moral or immoral. It is immoral if it relates to the three basic roots of dosa, lobha and moha. In such a case, all the thirteen mental properties, or cetasikas, connected with unvirtuous thoughts arise.

They are:

1. Delusion, false belief (moha),
2. Impudence (ahirika),

3. Recklessness of consequence, shameless (anottappa),
4. Distraction (uddhacca),
5. Greed (lobha),
6. Error (ditthi),
7. Conceit (mana),
8. Hate (dosa),
9. Envy (issa),
10. Selfishness (macchariya),
11. Worry (kukkucca),
12. Sloth (thina) and torpor (middha),
13. Perplexity, doubt or uncertainty (vicikicca).

These cetasikas induce sloth and torpor, idleness and restlessness of mind due to their desires and wrong views that interrupt concentration in meditation thus causing distractions and even termination.

Where the resulting reaction is moral, kusala mental properties such as mindfulness – required for vipassana; disinterestedness – required for calm (upekha); lack of illwill (adosa) found in the Brahmavihara; balance of mind; composure (cittapassadhi); buoyancy of mental properties (lahuta); buoyancy of mind and pliancy of mental properties and mind, are present.

All these cetasikas are found in the fourth Jhana. Otherwise, the mind would not be fit for further work.

They are listed as follows:

1. Faith (saddha),
2. Mindfulness (sati),
3. Prudence,
4. Discretion (ottappa),
5. Disinterestedness (alobha),
6. Amity (adosa),
7. Balance of mind (tatramajahattata),
8. Composure of mental properties,
9. Composure of minds (cittapassadhi),
10. Buoyancy of mental properties (lahuta),
11. Buoyancy of mind,

12. Pliancy of mental properties (mudita),
13. Pliancy of mind,
14. Fitness of work of mental properties,
15. Mental fitness of work,
16. Proficiency of mental properties (pugunnata),
17. Proficiency of mind,
18. Rectitude of mental properties,
19. Rectitude of mind.

The effects of preconditioning on the consciousness when a formation arises are as follows. When impingement is sensed, contact arises. Along with it comes feeling, perception, volition and then identification of the individuality of the object. If, at that moment, should an akusala thought arise, such as that connected to greed, hate or illwill, desires arise along with the cetasikas that bring distraction, terminating concentration.

Where, on the other hand, kusala thoughts are present, there is concentration which remains in sustained application and meditation continues to flow smoothly.

In meditation, akusala thoughts come with any or all of the four common properties of dullness, impudence, recklessness and distraction, associated with the akusala thoughts of greed, illwill and conceit, and their concomitants of envy, selfishness and worry. Wrong views are present with its sloth, torpor and perplexity.

They come, as it were, with the following; the four asavas of sense desires, of becoming, in error, and ignorance; the four ties of covetousness, illwill, practice of rites and rituals, dogmas; four graspings (of sense desires, error, rites and ritualism, belief in atta or a permanency of self; the six hindrances (illwill, sloth and torpor, flurry and worry, perplexity, ignorance); the seven forms of latent bias (sensual passion, lust after life, aversion, conceit, error, perplexity, ignorance); and the ten fetters set out in the suttanta of lust after life in the kamaloka, rupaloka, arupaloka, aversion, conceit, error, practice in rites and rituals, perplexity, distraction, ignorance; the ten fetters of the Abhidhamma (sensual passion, lust after life, aversion, conceit, error, practice of rites and rituals, perplexity, envy, selfishness, ignorance); the ten torments of greed, hate, dullness, conceit, error, perplexity, sloth, distraction, fearlessness of consequence, shamelessness.

In short, purity of the mind requires the removal of all of those defilements to bring about the factors for undistracted concentration. They all come from the requirements of adosa, alobha, amoha.

The concentration must not have the attributes of dullness and distraction, sloth or torpor. It has to be "purified, penlucid, unblemished, undefiled, malleable, pliable, firm and imperturbable", and "the meditator must be in a state without pain and pleasure, a state of equanimity and absolute purity of mindfulness" (Samanaphala Sutta 232 and 234).

That is the meaning of that statement by Buddha when describing the fourth jhana.

The Compendium Part 1 (2) which divides the four rupaloka (or material) moral consciousness into five instead of four jhanas (by splitting the vitakka and vicara application into two jhanas), classifies the four jhanas as states of moral consciousness. Dealing with the moral aspects of the jhanas, it holds that ekaggata cannot be obtained if there is distraction and that upekha requires the absence of the feeling of desire and anticipation of pleasure and joy. It is only a matter of description.

In the Anguttara Nikaya (8, 11 Text IV) in the Book of Eights, Buddha also refers to the four jhana system, instead of the five of the Compendium in the following way when speaking to Veranga, the Brahman:

> "Verily, Brahman, aloof from sense desires, aloof from evil ideas, I entered an abode in the first sensing (jhana) wherein applied and sustained thought works, which is born of solitude and is full of zest and ease", etc. He then adds, "By putting away ease and putting away ill, by the passing away of the happiness and misery I was want to feel, I entered an abode in the fourth jhana, a state of utter purity of mindfulness and disinterestedness, free of ill and ease".

Thus, the requirements of the various cetasikas are required for the fourth jhana as a prerequisite for attainment, even in insight which require mindfulness and awareness of the dhamma.

Sila is required for the requisites of firmness, calmness and pliability of mind, and acceptance of the sasana establishes the basis of undisturbed and undistracted concentration to see the truth of the formations, without which there can be no panna and thus ultimate freedom.

23
HINDRANCES

Hindrances are mental defilements which block progress of meditation. Known as the kilesas they encourage joy, bliss and distract the concentration of the meditator and so prevent the maintenance of the calmness and continuity of upekha necessary to hold on the fourth jhana to bring about the removal of the formations necessary for meditation progress. It should be obvious that these hindrances are hindrances because they encourage attachment to desires and prevent the development of alobha, adosa and amoha.

Apart from them, there are many others such as fetters and torments with different names but which perform the same function.

But, first, let us take a look at the ten defilements known as torments because they torment the meditator. They are the torments of hate, greed, dullness, conceit, error, doubt or perplexity, sloth and torpor, distraction, impudence, shamelessness of consequence.

They all stem from the three roots of hate, greed and delusion. If we are ignorant of the truth, we would be shameless, impudent and in error. If we think we have a permanent soul, we would be conceited and would be too lazy to make effort to change, and would suffer from sloth and torpor.

If we are dull and full of doubt, it is because we suffer from delusion and are ignorant of the truth and are full of conceit through ignorance, and do not care to change.

Next, we can have a look at the ten fetters set out in the Abhidhamma and the Suttanta.

They are conceit, error, practice of rites and rituals, doubt or perplexity, distraction, aversion, sensual desires (or passion), lust after life (in the Suttanta these are more correctly enumerated as the three lusts for kamaloka, rupaloka, and arupaloka) and envy.

These fetters all variously bring about the fourteen immoral mental properties or cetasikas of the mind:

1. Delusion, false belief (moha),
2. Impudence (ahirika),
3. Recklessness of consequence (anotappa),
4. Distraction (uddhacca),
5. Greed (lobha),
6. Error (ditthi),
7. Conceit (mana),
8. Hate (dosa),
9. Envy (issa),
10. Selfishness (maccahariya),
11. Worry (kukkucca),
12. Sloth (thina),
13. Torpor (middha),
14. Perplexity, doubt or uncertainty (vicikicca).

They fetter the meditator by their properties and impede his progress.

Their opposites are the nineteen moral or "beautiful" mental moral cetasikas which result through their removal and they accompany kusala thoughts:

1. Faith (saddha),
2. Mindfulness (sati),
3. Prudence (sahiri),
4. Discretion (attappa),
5. Disinterestedness (alobha),
6. Anxiety (adosa),
7. Balance of mind (tatramagghattata),
8. Composure of mental properties (kayapasadhi),
9. Composure of mind (cittapasaddadhi),
10. Buoyancy of mental properties (lahuta),
11. Buoyancy of mind,

12. Pliancy of mental properties (mudita),
13. Pliancy of mind,
14. Fitness of work of mental properties (kamannata),
15. Fitness of work of mind,
16. Proficiency of mental properties (pagunata),
17. Proficiency of mind,
18. Rectitude of mental properties (ujukata),
19. Rectitude of mind.

Apart from these nineteen kusala properties, there are three of right speech, action and livelihood; two of illimitable Brahmavihara pity (from karuna), appreciation (from mudita) and reason (pannindriya) makes twenty-five profitable mental properties in all.

The listing of the mental properties into kusala and akusala categories, the defining of the hindrances and fetters, the common and the specific properties of the mentality present as the mind operates, assists us to define with greater clarity how specific properties occur, which define our states of the mind, concentration and karma.

When the mind awakens, the following common properties must always arise:

1. Common or Universal Properties:
    - contact (phassa)
    - feeling (vedana)
    - perception (sanna)
    - volition (cetana)
    - individuality of object (ekaggata)
    - psychic life (jivitindriya)
    - attention (ananasikara)
2. Particular Properties:
    - Initial application (vitakka)
    - sustained application (vicara)
    - deciding (adhmoka)
    - effort (viriya)
    - pleasurable interest (piti)
    - donation, desire-to-do (chandra)

Common properties are those common to all thoughts. They appear within the first seven concomitants operating in all the nine consciousness which take place when the mind awakens to the impingement of the sense organs.

They are particular properties when limited to the consciousness requiring those qualities and accordingly the moral or immoral qualities of the act concerned.

Thus, the common properties are the first to be present and required when the mind awakes to the impingement of the sense base. For example, the mind, on being awakened from bhavanga, immediately senses the contact as being hurtful, repulsive, or pleasurable and desirable, as the case may be. They do not require any application of the mind and thus, do not require further properties necessary for the application of the mind.

At application, due to this contact, the particular properties arise dependent upon the evaluation, nature and quality of the thought and whether it be wholesome or unwholesome.

What particular properties arise depends upon our practice and how the mind has been preconditioned.

We can, now, see how the thought process is interwoven in practice and how the principles of paticcasammupada works through preconditioning of the mind, whose in-built response to any impingement brings on resultant mental properties in our thoughts according to this preconditioning.

As this preconditioning, which is karma, can be affected by meditative practice, meditation is necessary to influence their change.

As a thought sensation arises, the mind reacts to it with volition. If there is no interest in it and no attachment, it is rejected, even as it arises and is recognized, and there is nothing more to it.

However, he may react to it. If he does, the volition and his reaction are the result of his preconditioning. Any alteration of the preconditioning will result in a change in the preconditioning and therefore the resultant reaction.

If the sensations come from the five physical senses, they do not require any application attention, and so he reacts to them according to whether they are desirable or undesirable. If he does not react, he will see them rise and fall as another thought rise to take its place. If they arise from the dhamma, then the karma resultant takes effect.

Unwholesome thoughts not only lack of concentration, dullness, sloth and torpor. Since the thoughts are unwholesome, attachment affects the karma adversely, bringing about more unwholesomeness just as a drug addict only develops further attachment trying to satisfy his addiction with more drugs.

Conversely, with wholesome volition he supplants preconditioning to unwholesome thinking with non-greed, non-hate or without delusion which bring about the wholesome cetasikas, bringing detachment and calm concentration in meditation. By not reacting to the desires (which, of course, covers feelings of repulsion and hatred since they are all attachments), upekha is maintained and this allows him to note the process of namarupa. By which, he will realize that what arises will surely fall away to avoid its place to be taken up by another thought.

He becomes aware that the object is noted by the mind and that what the mind sees is only the subjective image of the object the awareness of which is through the sense organs.

The mindfulness of the meditator allows him to be aware of the void and empty nature of these formations, realizing that they manifest themselves due to preconditioning of the mind.

Being mindful of the five precepts, in his daily life, he withholds from acts of greed, hate, pride and conceit and so desists from deception, lies, indulgence in spirituous liquor, taking what is not his and committing such as adulterous relationships.

As his behaviour changes, so will his character and consciousness, since each thought and the resultant thought have their separate preconditioning and its concomitants and influence by its past, contiguous, adjacent, related and associated thoughts.

In meditation, akusala thoughts bring about distraction and terminate the meditation by distraction, sloth and torpor, excitement or agitation and so on. Without the akusala factors, and where there is kusala, there is calmness, and concentration is not interrupted so that it can continue from state to state.

The kamaloka states bring distraction, restlessness, remorse and thus, lack of concentration and balance of the faculties which require calmness. Thus, lust (raga), for example, causes restlessness and there is greed for possession, jealousy and strong desires for fulfillment.

Illwill brings about desires to cause hurt and pain. Ignorance of the truth develops pride, egotism and so on. Greed and wrong views will produce seven of the defilements of concentration, whilst illwill provides the other three, making ten defilements in all. These ten defilements of meditation which prevent purity can only be removed with sila; therefore making it the basis of the purities and enlightenment.

24

CLASSIFICATION OF SUBJECTS

The forty meditation subjects listed in the Visuddhi Magga are the main subjects. Their classification does not cover their derivatives because the derivatives have the same characteristics as the main subjects and are therefore unnecessary.

They are all the subjects that are used in both samatha and vipassana practice and this makes it strong evidence that both techniques are not strange to samanas and monks who would probably have practised both at one time or another; though, of course, not all samatha subjects, especially the kasina subjects, need be practised by those who are aiming for the peace and purity of the mind through vipassana.

This would probably account for the fact that some religious Buddhist sects still practise samatha today.

The controversy as to whether samatha should be attempted at all by vipassana meditators is therefore unnecessary and is to be regretted since we ought to know the differences between the two and recognise that samatha has its uses, especially in the development of concentration up to the fourth jhana. It is suggested by the author that there is common ground and similarity in samatha and vipassana practice up the fourth jhana which is requested in both practices. It is only after that, that the practices branch out to different paths.

Not all the subjects can provide the four jhanas and, of the forty subjects, only ten are true samatha subjects. These are the kasina subjects. They can, each of them, separately, give rise to absorption concentration up to the fourth jhana.

Kasinas are totalities. That is to say that they have no inner essences; and, as Totalities, practising skills in all of them, can provide abhinna. In fact they are the only subjects that give rise to true abhina, or supranormal powers which have to be abandoned later to reach true emancipation provided by vipassana.

Only these ten subjects can give rise to the fourth jhana. Mindfulness of Breathing is the only exception. It is the only other subject that can give rise to all the four jhanas, but it is not a kasina subject and is not useful for the practice for abhinna. Thus, since the fourth jhana is required in all cases to reach the higher stages, those who are not interested in samatha need only to practise on mindfulness of breathing as his subject.

Other subjects have limited abilities, such as the Brahmavihara where upekha in the fourth jhana is the result of the other three jhanas obtained in the other three of its virtues of metta, karuna and mudita.

Some subjects cannot give rise even to any absorption in appana and so cannot surmount to any jhana, so they can give rise only to access in the first jhana.

The forty subjects are grouped as follows:

1. Ten kasinas.
2. Ten kinds of foulness.
3. Ten Recollections.
4. Four Divine Abidings.
5. Four Immaterial states.
5. One perception.
6. One defining.

They are categorised in several ways:

1. Firstly, they can be classified as to their suitability to the temperament of the meditator.
2. Secondly, they are classified as to enumeration.
3. Thirdly, as to those that can bring access or absorption concentration which is necessary for samatha, practise on the counterpart sign.

4. Fourthly, they are classified as to the jhanas they can effect.
5. Fifthly, they are classified as to whether they can bring about the jhanas which have or do not have the surmounting factors.
6. Sixthly, they are classified into subjects which need or need not be extended in meditation practice.

7-9. Seventhly, Eighthly, and Ninthly, they are classified as to conditions, plane, apprehension, and condition.

We shall now describe these classifications in detail:

1. They are categorised according to suitability to temperament as follows. The ten kinds of foulness (asubha) subjects and mindfulness of the body (making eleven in all) are suitable for a person of greedy temperament. Greed means greed for sense desires such as lust and so on.
   - Contemplation of foulness (asubha) is concentration on corpses to realise that foulness, decay and putrefaction is the way for all flesh. Thus, it is very suitable as a subject for a person of greedy or lustful temperament since greed would be in the meditator's nature that is to be removed from him as a defilement.
   - The four Brahmavihara and the four colour kasinas are suitable for one with hate temperament which includes illwill, envy and those easily provoked to anger and so on.
   - Mindfulness of Breathing is most suitable for a person of deluded or speculative temperament. Of all the subjects, this is the only meditative subject by which the meditator determines the time of his death and even to decide it.
   - The six states of Recollections of Buddha, Dhamma, Sangka, Virtue and recollections of generosity and deities are suitable for one of greedy and faithful temperament (whose characteristics are similar to that of greed except that it is a profitable state instead of the unprofitable state of greed).

- Mindfulness of Death, Recollection of peace, the Defining of the Four Elements, of Perception of the repulsiveness of nutriment, are suitable for intelligent temperament.
- The kasinas and the Immaterial states are suitable for all kinds of temperament whilst the kasinas are also suitable for one of speculative temperament and for deluded temperament.
- We must remember that the choice of meditation subject is based upon which root of greed, illwill and delusion is predominant and that it comes in different descending orders in every person.
- The purpose of the meditation subject is to deal with the predominant defilement only. For example, the foulness subjects are for the purpose of abandoning greed or lust; loving kindness for abandoning illwill or hate; Mindfulness of Breathing for the purpose of removing speculative and deluded thought; Perception of Impermanence for the purpose of eliminating conceit (atta).

2. They are enumerated as follows:
    - Ten kasinas are totalities of earth, water, fire, air, blue, yellow, red, white, light and limited space kasina;
    - Ten foulness are foulness, asubha subjects being bloated, livid, festering, cut-up, gnawed, scattered, hacked and scattered, bleeding, corpses and skeleton;
    - Ten recollections are of the Buddha, dhamma, sangka, virtue, generosity, deities, Mindfulness of Death, Body, Breathing and Recollection of peace;
    - Four Brahmavhara subjects are the Divine Abidings of metta, karuna, mudita and upekha. Four Immaterial states are the arupa subjects of base of boundless space, consciousness, nothingness, neither perception nor non-perception;
    - Perception of repulsiveness in nutriment;
    - Defining of the four element of heat, air, water and earth.

3. They are also classified as to those which can or cannot produce absorption concentration as follows:
   - The Eight Recollections (excluding Mindfulness of Breathing and Body) and repulsiveness of nutriment and the defining of the four Elements can produce access, or upachara, all the others can produce absorption (appana) as well.
   - Of those which can produce absorption concentration, only the ten kasinas and the Mindfulness of Breathing can produce all the four jhanas whilst the first three Divine Abidings, or Brahmavihara, can bring about three jhanas and the fourth Abiding brings about the fourth jhana.
   - The four Immaterial states, of course, can bring the fourth jhana since they have to surmount the fourth jhana to reach their own immaterial states. As they also have their own immaterial states, they each bring about the jhanas in their respective states as well.
4. They are classified as to their jhanas and their surmounting factors.
5. They are classified according to whether they have surmounting factors or not.

   Surmounting is of two kinds. One is the surmounting of the factors and, the other is the surmounting of the object.

   To understand this, we have to keep in mind that in the first jhana there is reasoning and investigation, zest or joy, bliss or happiness. Thus, one has to surmount the factors of the first jhana before surmounting the first jhana.

   In the four Brahmavihara subjects, the meditator must surmount the factors of reasoning and investigation in the same object as that of metta to reach the second jhana in the same subject. When he has surmounted the factor of zest or joy in that subject, he would be able to enter the third jhana also in the same subject. Then, having surmounted the factors of bliss or happiness in the subject, he will be able to reach the serenity of uppekha with its ekaggata in the fourth.

The Brahaviharas have no counterpart signs as they are really subjects related to states which become more and more subtle till the upekha is reached. At that stage, the subject becomes almost imperceptible though the mind can be taken up with a kasina or mindfulness in its four stations of vipassana.

In the case of surmounting the objects in the four immaterial states, one must surmount the objects in the immaterial states one after another in successive sequence as well. Achievement in the four immaterial states require abandoning of the earlier states, one after the other, for the final state to be achieved.

This suggests that meditators cannot claim that they can enter the state of nothingness without first entering and then abandoning the jhanas of space and consciousness first.

This is the same as in the case of the kasinas. The meditator has to reach successively the fourth jhana in each kasina in turn, if he wishes to practice in all of them in the skills, respectively working backwards, forwards, and so on, in every kasina till he has achieved the ten skills in each of them, before he can gain full direct knowledge and the supranormal powers.

Practise also includes exercise in extension of the kasinas. Extension means extending and contracting, enlarging and shrinking of the counterpart sign. Without extension there can be no exercising or training in the skills.

This is not so easy without sufficient paramis. The rest of the subjects need not be extended as these would be of no benefit to anyone since abhinna cannot be obtained through them.

6. They are classified as to whether they are with or without counterpart signs.

What is extended? It is the counterpart sign. Only twenty-two meditation subjects have counterpart signs. They are the ten kasinas, ten foulnesses subjects, Mindfulness of Breathing and Mindfulness of the Body.

The counterpart signs of Mindfulness of the Body and the ten kinds of foulness have definite locations and extension of these signs are of no benefit, as can be seen in their detailed description. Training in them for kasina is of little use.

As for the Immaterial states, space is the removal of the kasinas; consciousness consists of an individual essence; non-consciousness is mere non-existence of consciousness; whilst perception and non-perception again is only an individual essence.

Similarly to the rest of the subjects, they do not have counterpart signs. Twelve of those with no counterpart signs have individual essences, being eight of the ten Recollections, Perception of the repulsiveness in nutriment, the Defining of the elements, bases consisting of boundless Consciousness, and neither Perception nor Non-perception.

7. They are classified into 'planes'.

All forty meditation subjects are to be found in the human plane. Twelve do not occur on the Brahma plane being the ten foulnesses, mindfulness of the body and perception of repulsiveness in nutriment. This is obvious since spirits do not possess physical forms, unlike those of human plane. On the other hand the immaterial states can occur in humans when they are in the immaterial or arupa states.

8. They are classified according to apprehension.

Apprehension means how the subjects can be apprehended by the sense of sight, touch and hearsay.

The eight kasinas (excluding the air kasina), and ten foulnesses are apprehended by sight and at the beginning stages they are apprehended by the eye. Mindfulness of Breathing must be apprehended by feel or touch.

The air kasina must be apprehended by sight, feel or touch. The five parts of the body ending with the skin must be by touch, the rest by hearsay.

The divine state of equanimity and the four Immaterial states are the five states that cannot be apprehended by the beginner, the other thirty-five are.

9. They are classified as to conditions.

Thus nine kasinas, except the air kasina, are conditions for the Immaterial states. All ten kasinas are conditions for direct knowledge (abhinna).

The first three Divine Abidings are conditions for the fourth. Each lower Immaterial state is a condition for the higher one. The base for neither Perception nor Non-perception is a condition for cessation attainment.

From this classification, it is clear that claims of achievement must be measured against the subjects used and what they can bring, bearing in mind that the lower jhanas can be conditions for the attainment of the higher ones.

A detailed study of the meditation subjects makes one realize that knowledge of the subjects is important to know what the meditator can hope to achieve by way of which subjects.

Further, since they are meditation subjects, their effects can only be realised during meditation and it is difficult to know their nature and qualities, which are so well-defined, without actual meditation. But once experienced, their truths will be known. That is the reason why teachers encourage meditation before explanations are given.

There is a totality in the system and extreme logic and an almost mathematical precision in their definition which is unique. Everything takes place in the mind with its ever flexing consciousness through the cetana, or voluntary intention, which builds a kamma that influences the man's own future.

Knowledge of these classifications, their nature, characteristics, factors and limitations of each meditation subject is necessary before meditation can be properly taught.

An example will show what is meant by this. The elements are subjects which can give rise to no appana. Therefore they have no surmounting factors. They are also material subjects. Thus, in spite of the experience of formations, no matter how superb, the meditator is only in the first jhana. Since there are no counterpart signs, skills in abhinna cannot be practised, nor is he in an immaterial state, so any claim to those achievements are due to lack of knowledge of the formations and the meaning of the skills.

When the elements are contacted, various formations can arise. Beginners, who do not have knowledge in the subjects and their effects, find these sensations unique and sometimes erroneously believe that the formations are representations of supranormal powers, so attractive are they.

Again, should the meditator fall asleep and wake up whilst using one of these subjects, there is no doubt that it is not the gotrabhu, as such subjects can only give rise to the first jhana.

25

THE FOUR ELEMENTS

The human body is composed of four elements from which formations will arise during meditation. These elements are those of apo, vayo, tejo, and pathavi which is respectively that of the elements of fire, air, water and earth elements which are experienced as heat, floating, liquid and rigidity sensations and their derivatives.

These subjects have inner essences and do not have the factors of absorption and surmounting and are capable of the first jhana in access concentration only. They are material forms in the body (rupa) but are without thought, morally indeterminate and void; they are not living things but are of the elements of earth or water, heat or air.

Thus, the meditator contemplates as follows.

What is stiff, hard or harsh in him is no more than the sensation of the earth (pathavi) element; that which is fluid and adhesive is the water (apo) element; that which is warm, aging, maturing, ripening is the heat (tejo) element; that which distends or moves is the wind (vayo) element; that there is no soul but only the aggregates of these elements which, together, form his identity.

Awareness of these elements within the human body can also come from awareness of the thirty-two parts of our bodies, especially as they are composed of the same elements. These thirty-two parts are also subjects of meditation and collectively form the Mindfulness of the Body (kayagatasati) subjects.

They are the head, body hair, nails, teeth, skin, flesh, sinews, bone marrow, kidney, heart, liver, midriff, spleen, bowel, entrails, gorge dung, brain, bile, phlegm, pus, blood, sweat, fat, tears, grease, spittle, snort, fluid of the joints, and urine. They are composed of elements only, thus making us aware of their void, non-living characteristics.

In vipassana, a plethora of formations arise from which give feelings such as astral travelling and so on. Whenever there is contact with these elements these should not deceive the meditator into thinking that he has developed supranormal powers, which he has not.

When they manifest themselves he will know that they arise from one of the four stations of mindfulness which is that of the body, feelings, mind and the dhamma. In noting them, he has begun the process of cleansing, which is that of the elimination of the wrongful perception that there is a permanency of living beings. For the rise and fall of the formations are meant to show that we are nothing more than an identity made up of aggregates just as a carriage is an identity consisting of no more than the sum total of its parts.

We can compare this with a butcher selling pieces of beef. We cannot say he is selling a cow, which is already non-existent, though he is selling parts of it. A cow is a conception which was the sum total of all its parts. So too the meditator meditating on the bodily parts further realize that not only are these only bodily parts but not "I" but that they are also themselves only aggregates which will break down into their elements on his death, leaving nothing that he can claim to be himself.

The meditator concentrating on the elements, is aware of the elements within himself. Thus, when the air element manifests itself within him, the result could be the feeling of levitation which some claim they can achieve, the sense of floating or even flying into the sky and astral travel.

When the earth element manifests itself, he may even find bodily parts missing or torn up into its several parts.

When the heat and water elements express themselves, he may suddenly experience heat and profuse perspiration which completely soaks him. Formations which arise when he is in contact with the sense of touch can easily give the feeling of ants biting him all over. These experiences must not be confused with supranormal powers, no matter how strong or real their appearance may seem.

The formations demonstrate their true immaterial and non-permanent nature and help to remove the root of delusion due to ignorance of the truth. As he watches their rise and fall, he will see that he himself is nothing more than a collection of aggregates which will dissolve into their elements on his death.

This brings about detachment from desires and begins the process of "cleansing". Through this, he realizes voidness; rejects false beliefs in the permanence of beings; conquers delight and boredom, develops great understanding, is not exhilarated or depressed and becomes ready for a happy destiny. As it is also part of the process of paticcasammupada, it also affects the kamma.

Since all the four elements are present in the thirty-two bodily parts, mindfulness can easily shift from defining the elements to the bodily parts during meditation. Should this happen, mindfulness must remain with bare attention on the elements and not shift away and attach itself to the objects. For when that happens, he is attached and not abandoning. Since detachment, or abandoning, is part of the cleansing process, he loses the effect of cleansing his mind.

Nor must he not allow his mindfulness to stray to the colour of the bodily part. If he does, he terminates his insight meditation and slips into samatha with red as his subject.

Once, during meditation, I sensed a sudden stiffness and, looking at my arm, I was surprised to find that I could see through my arm as if it was made of transparent plastic. In it, there were two transparent pipes with red bubbling blood gushing through them as being pushed by a huge pump. Blood is red and I suddenly found myself being drawn into noticing its red colour.

Fortunately, there was only a distant aloof awareness and repulsion that we are nothing more than a series of pipes and blood and so I was able to maintain vipassana instead of shifting into samatha.

26

MINDFULNESS OF THE BODY

Mindfulness of the Body and its thirty-two parts is a serenity subject. As a serenity subject, they are treated as objects of repulsiveness. According to the Visuddhi Magga (Ch. VIII), it was introduced by Buddha for monks and samanas and are not suitable subjects for sectarians. It is doubtful if many meditators use this as a particular subject for meditation.

For insight, the attention is directed to the elements, the awareness of the four truths of suffering and where one contemplates on the danger of the bhaya nana. Here the meditator is required to concentrate on the body and its painfulness and suffering, its fragile, impermanent and transitory nature and how unsatisfactory it all is.

Though the body is divided into thirty-two parts, they are all the same idea of uncleanliness and filth which are equally subject to decay. By reflecting on them, the meditator rejects pride and conceit, awareness that he is nothing more than a pile of dirt.

Apart from this effect, it can be an exercise of samatha concentration in the practice of the seven and the ten skills in them. Here, the meditator is required to meditate on each of the thirty-two parts one after the other in forward and reverse order and so on. This itself will take months to complete.

The thirty-two parts are the head hairs, body hairs, nails, teeth, skin, flesh, sinews, bone marrow, kidney, heart, liver, midriff, spleen, lights (two or three pieces of flesh hanging between the breasts above the heart and liver), bowel, entrails, gorge (indigested food in the stomach) dung, brain, bile, phelgm, pus, blood, sweat, fat, tears, grease, spittle, snot (impurity trickling out of the brain) oil, of the joints, and urine.

As meditation subjects they, like the asubha subjects, can give rise only to the first jhana. But practice can be directed towards developing the seven-fold and the ten-fold skills in them as well. However, because of the need for sila, the meditator must constantly note their repulsive nature so as to remove pride and greed and develop detachment.

The seven-fold skill is achieved by verbal recitation, mental recitation, as to colour, as to shape, direction, location, delimitation.

The ten-fold skill requires exercise of the skills in following the order of each of all the thirty-two parts, not too quickly and not too slowly, holding to the subject and warding off all distractions, surmounting the concept of its repulsiveness, successive leaving, absorption, the three suttantas of higher consciousness, calmness and skill in the enlightenment factors.

For meditators who are interested in the skills, the practice itself is set out in the Visuddhi Magga (Chap VIII 49 et seq.) The purpose is to instill in the meditator the repulsiveness and foulness of the subject.

The colour, shape and location are to familiarize the meditator with their identity and location. The delimitation is to establish connection and disassociation, with the rest of the body e.g. head hairs are not body hairs and the organs of the body are delineated as to their locality, such as being around the stomach region, etc.

We recite in proper order, at a deliberate pace, without distraction, surmounting the concept with the awareness of repulsiveness, eventually to concentrate on the parts which appear to be clearer now, in order to arouse absorption (since this subject can induce absorption), till the meditator sees all parts respectively. Thus, as each counterpart sign arises, absorption of the first jhana arises so that he may obtain thirty-two jhanas in the thirty-two parts. This can go on for over a month if he enters one jhana for each day.

Though he may only obtain the first jhana, in this way he can conquer "boredom and delight", "fear and dread", and he can bear "heat and cold".

The purpose of the three suttantas of development of higher consciousness, coolness and skill in the enlightenment factors in the ten-fold skills, are for the purposes of linking energy with concentration.

Higher consciousness means attention to the sign of concentration, of exertion and equanimity to prevent idleness, agitation and to bring about right concentration to destroy the cankers.

Coolness is correct restraint and exertion and encouragement, equanimity means steady calmness in detachment and resoluteness means determination to attain the higher states and to delight in nibbana [A. (iii) 435]. These are the six properties to be used at the right time when they should be present.

Skill is skill in obtaining, developing and holding the sign. He does this by encouraging and feeding the energy factor with profitable thoughts, examples of the Buddha and the disciples. He develops the enlightenment and happiness factors by examples of the Great ones.

He has to maintain correct attitude, ask right questions, keep his basis clean, balance the faculties, avoid unconcentrated persons, cultivate the concentrated, be resolute in practice, avoid the states of loss, follow paths taken by the Buddhas and the great disciples, the greatness of the Master and the Dhamma, perform dana, remove stiffness and torpor, maintain right endeavour and resoluteness, cultivate happiness factors of the Buddha, Dhamma, Deities and maintain virtue, generosity, peace, and holding discourses.

Where, during meditation, the mind strays to their colour, the subject can become a colour kasina [M (ii), MA (iii) 257f, Kayagata sati Sutta (M Sutta 119)].

27
FOULNESS SUBJECTS

There are ten asubha, or foulness, subjects. These all refer to corpses. They are called foulness subjects because the emphasis is on foulness of decay at death. In the time of Buddha, it was easier to come across such subjects which is not so today, due to our laws and custom. Because of this, it can be ignored. However, a description on it would help give us an idea of the extent of detail and care that was applied by Buddha in all his deliberations.

Obviously it is a gruesome subject to look at, much less to concentrate on. Its purpose is to provide a shock and it is precisely for that reason that it is encouraged. It brings home a point forcibly, especially for one interested in the desires of the flesh. For how can anyone not react with repulsion to see a festering or a rotting corpse, especially that of someone we desire? It has a salutary effect and is meant for monks.

Corpses are unpleasant subjects and it is difficult to come across one except at a funeral of a relative or a close friend. Even if such a corpse is displayed, it is difficult to start meditation on them without offending relatives. It is even worse if we should turn up somewhere to make use of an unknown corpse and this can be easily misunderstood.

But it is not impossible to see a corpse and should it be desirable to use it we have first to see if our action can be misunderstood and that there is no suspicion.

It is a subject meant for monks and samanas and it is not suitable for the layman.

Should we insist on using it, we must bear in mind that it is subject to quick change and decay, so that it is important that the patibhaga nimitta be committed to mind as quickly as possible since the corpse can hardly be in a stable state.

Committing its learning image, or the patibhaga nimitta, to the mind requires quick and concentrated action.

The ten subjects are the ten kinds of corpses, being that of the bloated, livid, festering, cut-up, gnawed, scattered, hacked and scattered, bleeding, worm-infested corpse and the skeleton (or heap of scattered bones).

The emphasis is on the foulness, emptiness of life, impermanence of all things and the repulsiveness of it all.

To practise on the subject, the meditator must learn all about it before going there. If he should be going to somewhere strange, he should tell someone about it, for there is a lot of superstition and suspicion about corpses. Should he, as a stranger, be found alone with a corpse, there may be misunderstanding.

The description of the subject is vivid in the Visuddhi Magga and repeating it would be worthwhile. Thus, it is said that not only should he learn all about this subject before going there, but he must know the eleven ways of apprehending the sign, reviewing the path taken and the one he has to take and to come.

He goes to the spot, making certain that he takes precautions to be somewhat leeward to the corpse to avoid the offensive smell, that he is able to identify of the location, the sign of where the body is to be located (for example, a tree to be used as the sign for recognition of the area). This is called the sign of foulness.

Then he looks for the sign in relation to the object itself and its conditions. He does this by noting the condition of the body, that is to see if it is bloated or not, its colour, mark, shape, direction, location, delineation, joints, openings, concavities, convexities, so that it is properly remembered, defined by its characteristics and so forth.

Having noted the sign of foulness and the sign of the object itself, he can then go to the corpse alone after that, with his mind turned inwards, reviewing the path gone by and to come.

Why should he review the path gone by and to come? Because in this way he will have no delusion as to why he has come and so has no delusion as to the object of his coming. By anchoring his mind on the sign (in eleven ways), he anchors his mind on the purpose of his coming.

By reviewing the path, he keeps his mind on the absorption he will obtain, liberation from unprofitable thoughts and achievement of the first jhana, for that is all the subject can provide.

What are the ways of apprehending the sign of the object?

1. By its colour, e.g. is it black, white or yellow.
2. By its mark, e.g. is it young, middle-aged, old.
3. By its shape, e.g. the shape of head, etc.
4. By its direction, i.e. in which direction it is facing.
5. By its location, i.e. in which location related to oneself.
6. By its delineation, i.e. sizing up the size of body parts.

   It is advisable that the meditator should meditate on a body of the same sex Majjhima Commentary; also, the Visuddhi Magga VI 42).

   At this stage, according to the Visuddhi Magga VI43, the counterpart sign, and thus absorption, would appear to the meditator who has cultivated this subject under former Enlightened Ones, kept ascetic practices, threshed out the great primary elements, discussed formations, defined namarupa, eliminated the perception of a being, done ascetic duties, lived the kind life, developed the development, when he contains the seed of Turning Away Formations, and has mature knowledge and little defilement. Only then will the counterpart sign appear to him in the place he is looking for.

   If the counterpart sign does not happen then the meditator continues his attempts by noting the corpse:
7. By its joints, e.g. its 180 joints (or 14 sign joints of 3 in an arm, 3 in a leg, 1 neck, 1 waist joint) are defined.
8. By its openings, i.e. armpit, between legs, stomach, ear, etc.
9. By its concavities, i.e. eye sockets, mouth, base of neck, etc.
10. By its convexities, i.e. its knee, chest, forehead, etc.

11. All round, i.e. body is defined all round. Whether it is bloated; if so, how much, etc.

Once the sign is properly apprehended, and he has only one or two days for it at most, its learning sign should then appear. This sign comes as the remembered image which has been registered in the mind.

It could appear, for example, as a bloated, repulsive object and when this happens he can leave this place for his own lodging with that sign. It is from this sign that the counterpart sign will emerge.

The meditator must make certain that he is well prepared with the characteristics of the surmounting signs and be clear and without delusion. If he is not prepared and non-deluded, there will be resultant visions, such as the corpse moving or rising up to threaten or chase him. That is why he must identify the place and characterize the surmounting sign properly, for there is no object more threatening than a moving or a threatening corpse or skeleton.

Once he has obtained the learning sign, the counterpart sign can arise in him. The counterpart sign is an image devoid of its frightening aspects. For the counterpart sign is a conceptual image and therefore clean of blemishes or actual shape. He can then exercise his mind on this sign for absorption.

Sometimes, due to distraction, the learning sign may be lost. Should this happen and he is not able to return to the area where the corpse was, he will have no alternative but to review the events, the path by which he had gone, visualize the area and in this way to try to recall the sign. This is why he is said to review the path gone by and come by, keeping a track for its purpose of recalling the sign.

As he practises with applied thought and the counterpart sign appears, lust, illwill, stiffness and torpor, agitation and worry, uncertainties are abandoned and he has applied thought and the sign, sustained thought pressing on the sign, happiness, tranquillity, bliss, etc.

At the same time he has access and then absorption as well.

The practice is the same with any of the rest of the ten kinds of corpses and so there is no need to repeat them. But it must be emphasized that this subject is for those who have had practice formerly and have mature knowledge for the subject is such that he might be haunted by the corpse taking on different forms and shapes.

The suitability of which of the ten corpses to use as a meditation subject, however, depend upon the individual temperament of each meditator and it applies as follows.

The bloated corpse suits one who is greedy of beautiful physical shapes as it is a disfigured and bloated shape; the livid corpse suits one desiring beautiful colour, skins and bodies; the festering and smelly corpse is suitable for one greedy of smells and perfumes; the cut-up corpse suits one greedy of compactness; the gnawed for one greedy of the beautiful shapes of the body, breasts, hips and so on; the scattered corpse is suitable for one interested in grace of limbs; the hacked and scattered corpse for one who is greedy of a fine figure as a whole; the bleeding corpse for one greedy of elegance of ornaments and attire; the worm-infested is suitable for one possessive of the body, for he realizes the body is shared by many families of worms; and the skeleton for one greedy of fine teeth and bone structure.

Thus, the meditator, meditating on repulsiveness and foulness of the corpse, choosing the type of corpse to suit his temperament, sees that in the end, everything is subject to death and decay and realises that beauty is but shortlived and so he loses his desires and attachment and is liberated from attachment to desires and realizes that the same ultimate destiny awaits all, whether they be king, prelate or beggar.

Realizing this, he gives up the unprofitable and develops profitable thoughts and gains the benefit of wholesome thinking.

In other words, meditating on a corpse brings about disinterest in beauty of limb, features, perfume and makeup and sex. It is useful for the highly sexed and those taken by physical attractions.

28

REPULSIVENESS OF NUTRIMENT

Everyone likes to enjoy his food and drinks. Sometimes they become greedy and self indulgent and will even tolerate cruelty to enjoy himself. Some may even eat anything if they believe it will benefit their health. Food and drinks are enjoyable and form a pattern of pleasure when they are in fact only good for sustenance.

To perceive them as repulsive is difficult to accept. Yet, it is precisely because they can cause indulgence that they should be considered repulsive. Logically, they are necessities without which we cannot survive. The conclusion is that we must view food as food and not as objects of indulgence. We eat to survive and not as indulgence or craving for flavours. It is gluttony that is wrong.

Again, it has individual essences in its state and is only capable of access without reaching absorption so it is only capable of the first jhana.

Physical nutriment is the subject. This physical aspect concerns perception of what is drunk, chewed, and tasted. It refers to the ten aspects of eating and drinking which is that of chewing, tasting, the going for, seeking, using, secretion, receptacle, what is undigested and digested, the fruit of the above endeavour being that of the flavour, outflow and smearing.

As he goes out seeking for food, he meditates both on the unpleasantness encountered in the going out and in the search for the food, the unpleasant sights and experiences outside his abode and the smells of the filth and so on encountered.

As he eats, he meditates on the food he is chewing and notes how repulsive it all is. When he swallows, he meditates on the secretion of bile and phlegm. When it has gone into his belly, he meditates on where the food has gone to and notes its undigested and repulsive state; and, before digestion, its odorous, fetid and loathsome smells; and, after digestion, how it is turning to excrement and urine, and how the waste products will be discharged out at his several orifices, which is such as to make one ashamed, humiliated and disgusted, whilst the ultimate result of all this will be infestation of worms and diseases.

Here, the meditator rejects indulgence and gluttony for good food as this brings about desire, attachment, contact and rebirth-linking and namarupa.

This makes him aware of repulsiveness. But he can only obtain the access but not absorption because it is a state with individual essence. He soon loses interest in eating for the sake of eating and understands the cause of diseases and the develops mindfulness.

He notes how nutrition originates and is finally discharged from our bodies, results only in awareness of food as a necessity of nourishment. Gluttony and delight in the pleasure of delicacies will fade away.

29

MINDFULNESS OF DEATH

Mindfulness of death is yet another recollection with an individual essence. Absorption is, therefore, not possible but only access (Visuddhi Magga Ch.VIII, 41). Contemplation on this subject is on perception of disenchantment, awareness of impermanence, of non-self, non-delusion and no fear of death. Through it the meditator perceives impermanence, detaches himself from attachments, develops disenchantment and saves himself from delusion.

To meditate, he has to recollect the eight ways of viewing Death:

1. As having the appearance of the murderer. That is to say death will surely come like a killer in the night and there is no way of avoiding it.
2. As the ultimate ruin of success. This means that no matter how mighty or rich a person may be, death will finally overcome all success.
3. By comparison to such as the Great Disciples or Buddha himself, who could not even avoid death, so how can we?
4. By realization that the body is the common property by many others, such as worms and disease.
5. By being aware of the frailty of life. That is to say, that life is impotent and frail and depends upon the elements, bound up by "postures", breathing and nutriment, cold and heat and the primary elements.
6. As to the signlessness of death, its unpredictability and its indefinability. That is so that life has no definiteness as to

span, sickness, time, where it will be put to rest and where is its destiny, because they are indefinite and indeterminate.

7. As to limitedness of the extent. This means the short life span of human beings.
8. As to the shortness of the moment. This is that life consists only of moments of consciousness, each single conscious moment becoming a past immediately it has arisen because it will have ceased before another thought process begins, so that brings about death, which will have occurred at every single passing thought moment.

Thinking in this way, there is disenchantment with all kinds of becoming and attachment to life. Fear of death and permanent dissolution is a constant thought with most people. Hence the normal question also is whether or not there cannot be a way of avoiding death and if there is a life after death.

30

KINDNESS AND LOVE

In contrast to the subjects of repulsiveness and foulness where is rejection of the unwholesome for the wholesome, the subjects of kindness and love, such as the Brahmavihara and Recollections of the Buddha and the deities, are to encourage attachment to the wholesome, thereby rejecting the unwholesome.

The detachment from the pleasures of life as illusions gives the impression that Buddhism is a preparation of death. This is not correct. Though the enlightened person no longer fears death because he has rid himself of unwholesome desires and, though he does not seek hold on to life and no longer fears death, it is not a preparation for death.

Preparation of death implies an acceptance of an inevitability with regret. Buddhism seeks to convince the meditator of the illusion of pleasure which disguises the truth of the impermanency of all aggregates, including the aggregate of life itself.

By establishing practice of the subjects of kindness and love, the desires of the flesh and the unwholesome are rejected and so their formations cease to arise. The formations are due to their preconditioning.

When one is selfish, resultant formations due to selfishness arise. When we rid ourselves of selfishness and develop the Brahmavihara, they cease to arise because the preconditioning is no longer there.

In this way, realizing foulness of the body, the meditator abandons the desires for the flesh, resulting in the loss of desire and non attachment.

With the subjects of kindness and love, of which the Brahmavihara is the most comprehensive group, the opposite approach is made. Whereas the foulness subjects bring about rejection of the unwholesome to give place to the wholesome, the subjects of kindness and love developes the wholesome and thus remove to unwholesome.

The subjects of kindness and love include the Brahmavihara subjects and the Recollections of the Buddha, the Order of the monks, the Dhamma, Liberality, Morality and of the Devas, and of Peace are such subjects.

Through their examples, wholesome behaviour is augmented and thus unwholesomeness is prevented from developing.

The Brahmavihara

The universal kindness Brahmavihara is reflected in the term metta. Like all the Brahmavihara subjects, it does not stop at humans but also refers other living things as well. Thus, his enjoinder "you shall not kill" relates to non-human beings as well.

One cannot be kind, if one is cruel to animals, for instance. Its kindness is kindness is all encompassing nor can it be switched on and off. The all-pervading nature makes employment suitable for the general awareness and development of the meditator.

As his behaviour reflects his inward nature, the improvement of the meditator can be judged by his relationship and behaviour to others around him.

Apart from being called the Illimitables, the Brahmavihara is also known as the Divine Abidings and the Immeasurable States. They are called Brahmavihara because they are the virtues of the brahmas. They are illimitable; for reasons above explained. They are divine abidings because of their divine nature, they are also immeasurable because their effects cannot be measured.

The Brahmaviharas are placed in the order of their own logic being metta, karuna, mudita and upekha, translated as the qualities of lovingkindness, compassion, gladness for the happiness of others and equanimity. Because the steadfastness of metta gives rise to sustained concentration in the first jhana, the presence of joy and bliss in compassion; bliss in the feeling of happiness in the happiness of others and the absence of both joy and bliss gives rise to the fourth. The fourth, equanimity, is the resultant state when the other three jhanas have been established.

They are described as follows in detail.

1. **Lovingkindness (metta)** – Generally, love has many meanings. For example, when one talks of love for a child, it has not the same meaning as love for one's spouse. When one talks of love for a thing, it is not the same as love of a religion.

   Most of these general definitions, however, infer possessiveness or possessive desire of the object of one's love, with a sense of hostility against those threatening the one desired. Even the love of a child infers protection against all others threatening the child and possessiveness. This is not the meaning here. In Buddhism, metta is a universal feeling of lovingkindness without any attachment, applied both universally and to any particular person.

   Metta comes with feeling for the general welfare of beings with detachment; karuna, or compassion, comes with feeling for the suffering and a sense of charity to remove the suffering; mudita, or gladness, comes with gladness when there is an end of the suffering of others or their happiness at the relief of such suffering of others; and upekha is the result of sustained non-distraction of all sense of joy and bliss which result in an equanimity in sustained concentration of the fourth jhana.

   Lovingkindness is not a possessive or demanding love but a universal love with the pure intention of helping others wherever possible with no thought of self gain for oneself. It is kindness for the sake of kindness. Any love with a sense of self-aggrandizement, personal gain or pride, is not permissible.

Explained in another way, lovingkindness removes illwill, hatred and resentment towards others, especially those who have done wrong to the meditator.

It must not arise out of desire, or result in possessiveness. A beginner should not exercise it on a person of opposite sex or one we love dearly, as lust may arise in such a case. Nor should we meditate on a dead person for the sign will be that of a dead body. Nor should we, in the beginning, meditate on someone we hate, for it can arouse anger easily.

The best person to start with is oneself. "May I be happy and free from suffering" or "May I be free from enmity, anxiety and be happy". But this is only the initial step.

Thereafter, he has to recollect gifts, kind words of endearment or encouragement, virtue, and so on, so that he may pervade those persons with lovingkindness, "May all beings be free from enmity, disaffection and anxiety and live happily".

Once he is practised, he can expand his net of lovingkindness to cover a dearly loved friend, a neutral person as a dearly loved friend and a hostile person as a neutral.

Essentially, he has to be mindful of resentment. Even in extreme cases too, the meditator is supposed to control his anger and resentment, for anger at any time under any circumstances is a failure to follow Buddha's teachings.

The importance of lovingkindness is such that the Dhammapada abounds with accounts of the performance of metta by Buddha.

Metta is highest where there is self-sacrifice, the highest form of which is to give up one's life for others. Of course, self-sacrifice is not the only form of metta, it is only the highest.

The lesser forms are those acts done within one's ability to benefit someone else out of lovingkindness.

It must also be done with wisdom. Metta towards a crook is not the same as metta to assist a sangha towards his meditative practice. Helping an arahant towards nibbana has merits not to be found in assistance given to a scoundrel.

2. **Compassion (karuna)** – Compassion removes illwill and lack of feeling and cruelty to others; gladness removes boredom or aversion of others.

   To practise it he should first notice a suffering person, one who is unlucky and unfortunate wrongdoer who is being punished, feeling compassion for his suffering. He should even develop compassion for one who does not know he is suffering and is about to be punished and who is for the time being happy.

   Having thus trained himself, he can go on to feel compassion for those he is neutral towards or towards whom he is hostile.

   Metta has sustained concentration, joy and the bliss of loving. Compassion has the joyous element of sympathy with a feeling of pity for those suffering. There is no more aversion and avoidance of the suffering. Compassion builds a feeling for others and goodwill towards them. One then thinks to relieve their suffering, if possible. With this comes the feeling of charity and so there is joy and bliss accompanying the feelings of goodwill and compassion. Whereas, in the feeling of happiness for the happiness of others, there is only bliss. Hence the first four jhanas are reflected in the order of metta, karuna, mudita, with upekha reflecting the state of calmness thereafter.

3. **Gladness** – When one sees someone else suffering and suffering is relieved, or someone who has achieved happiness of some sort or other and we are glad for them instead of being jealous or grudging in our appreciation or praise of it, we have in us this element of gladness for the happiness of others, this is mudita.

Suffering brings compassion, with compassion comes generosity. With generosity, comes happiness. When one sees this happiness and joins in this happiness, grudge and envy are removed. The feeling of happiness for the happiness of other is present with bliss which is said to accompany mudita. However, the feelings of grudge, envy, hostility or resentment are abolished.

4. **Equanimity** (upekha) – Equanimity is the fourth of the Brahmavihara subjects. It comes only after the three jhanas of metta, karuna and mudita have been achieved. Therefore it comes only when the other three jhanas have arisen. That is to say, when the meditator is able to reach the point of detachment at the fourth state without joy and bliss of karuna and piti.

Thus upekha is the final state after there is metta brings about sustained concentration and the joy of karuna and bliss of mudita have been removed. Upekha is therefore no more then the state of the fourth jhana.

It is stated in the Visuddhi Magga that the first three have surmounting factors and can give rise to the three jhanas although they do not have counterpart signs, whilst equanimity is the fourth jhana that comes after the first three have arisen.

Acts of kindness and compassion are common and should be shown in Buddhists. We observe such acts in those of other religions within animal and social work groups. This is because all humans are dvihetuka persons and such acts of kindness and charity the result of these two roots.

Our regret is that they do not realize that their acts are without wisdom so that they lose the benefit of such acts on their kamma which remain unaffected by their acts. Though they perform humanitarian acts, they lose the opportunity to gain panna.

But, though lack of wisdom prevents the development of panna, they are wholesome acts which can lead to a profitable state upon their realization. For charity, compassion and gladness are the qualities of the Brahma gods from which the name Brahmavihara is obtained.

Because they do not understand the dhamma, they remain in ignorance of the true nature of their acts. Their humanitarian deeds many even be done for wrong reasons. In such cases, the goodness of their acts will actually be cancelled by unwholesome desires.

Brahmavihara acts must be performed. The reasons for performing them must also be understood otherwise it will have no effect upon the consciousness. On the other hand, Buddhists should not grudge to give credit where credit is due, as karuna and mudita would be absent.

Such people are exercising the qualities of the brahmas which, because there is no panna, will have less effect. At least they are better than those who profess knowledge of the dhamma but who do not practice brahmavihara.

There are even cases where those Buddhists who refuse to do any kind act for fear of mixed kamma when, by not taking action commit wrong by omission. Fearing to contaminate their purity, they show no metta and karuna. The sin of omission can be as bad as the sin of commission.

Restraint must mean the correct restraint. Fear of endangering oneself is no excuse. Where the result of an act is mixed, The entire effect is mixed kamma in which the predominant kamma has predominance. Where the Brahmavihara virtues are forsaken due to fear of action, that is not self-sacrifice but self preservation.

The Recollections Subjects or Anussatis

Recollections of Death, of the Body and Mindfulness of Breathing, are subjects of Recollection dealt with separately.

Here we refer to the subjects of Recollection of the dhamma, the Sangha, virtue and Deities are subjects which show and encourage proper positive action through examples. Their meaning is plain and can be discerned from their definitions and there is no need to describe them in detail.

They assist the meditator in his ethics and behaviour and their similarities with the Brahmavihara. But in the classification of the subjects of meditation, they are separated from the Brahmavihara because the Brahmavihara is not a subject of Recollection.

31
MINDFULNESS OF BREATHING

Mindfulness of breathing is the most important and commonly used meditation subject for vipassana. It was used by Buddha himself to gain enlightenment and is thoroughly explained in many of the suttas and the Visuddhi Magga.

So important is it that it is used by the Mahasi Center. There is therefore no reason why such a well documented and much used practice be perverted by attempts to introduce new methods.

In dealing with it we will also refer to the practice of meditation itself because it is difficult to deal with one without describing the other.

Like the kasinas, it has the ability to give rise to all the four jhanas and the counterpart signs as well. They have some common attributes.

However, it is not a totality as it is a recollection, so it is of no benefit for the training of skills as it is not kasina subject.

Because of this, all claims to abhinna through use of Mindfulness of Breathing as a subject is an exaggeration.

As a vipassana subject it is superior and is recommended by the Buddha as the most important subject because practice in it alone, without the use of any other subject, is sufficient to lead to the Path.

Both the Visuddhi Magga and the Patissambhida deal with it at length. Indeed, though there are so many excellent books written on it, that it is advisable to refer to both these writings, especially the Patissambhida, in order not to be confused by the profusion of inaccurate texts.

When Buddha found samatha unsatisfactory in spite of extreme practice, he retired from all company and retraced his meditation to the very beginning and, employing Mindfulness of Breathing as a subject, found attainment after six years.

Concentration, it is said in the Texts, through this subject is both peaceful and sublime, an unadulterated blissful abiding, banishing at once and stilling evil unprofitable thoughts as soon as they arise.

It requires concentration on the internal sign through the recollection of the breathing. Because it is a recollection, though it is suitable for insight, it is not suitable for practice in the skills of samatha.

But, as it can also give rise to the four jhanas, it is therefore uniquely suitable for both practices apart from that limitation.

As a subject, the Texts say, Mindfulness of Breathing is one subject in which the sign becomes less discernible as one progresses higher. It becomes almost imperceptible at the highest stage, like the sound of a gong that is hard and gross at first and then grows subtler and finer until it is hardly perceptible any more except to the finest ear.

So also its counterpart sign which is easy to perceive at first, becomes harder later on.

There are counterpart signs for the in-breath and one for the out-breath which grow fainter and fainter until only the most undistracted, calmest and concentrated of minds can discern the sign of the in- and the out-breath in the higher states. So subtle it is in those states that when this sign is lost there, the meditator can only find it again by concentrating on the spot where it was last lost, for it to be caught when it returns, just as a herdsman would have to wait at the water-hole to recover his lost cattle when they must return for a drink.

Mindfulness of Breathing is the subject most often used today for meditation and it would be convenient to discuss the meditation practice at the same time as this would help understand how this subject is applied.

How does the meditator begin his practice? This is already touched upon earlier but it will do no harm if we now discuss it again in greater detail.

He should have his food one hour earlier to allow for digestion and so that he would not be distracted by hunger. Having washed and cleaned himself and dressed suitably for comfort, he should find a quiet place chosen earlier, sit erectly on a hard and firm platform such as a floor.

If he can he should sit in the lotus or the half lotus position so that his seat will be firm. If he cannot do that, he can just sit cross-legged. A lotus position is where the meditator places both his feet, one on top of the other thigh. A half lotus position is where he places only one foot over the other thigh. These are illustrated in many books on meditation.

The lotus position is the best because it anchors the meditator fully to the ground and he will not fall backwards or forwards or topple in the middle of his meditation. But this requires practice and is neither suitable, possible nor necessary for most beginners.

The half lotus is favoured by many and is a compromise. Again it is also not necessary. It is only important that he is comfortable and is able to concentrate for long periods at a time without the distraction of having to shift his seat from time to time.

Beginners may find it better to use a small cushion in the beginning, provided that it is flat and firm and low enough to be discarded later.

The idea is to have a firm and a steady seat for his meditation.

It is suggested in the Visuddhi Magga that the Brahmavihara should be practised to appease the spirits that abound and to gain a friendly and non-hostile atmosphere around his locality of meditation.

The best place for meditation is a monastery or a meditation center, if there is one, for such places are built for this purpose and the Brahmavihara is practised there and there is no hostility in the neighbourhood.

He begins meditation by holding himself erect, keeping his face forward and his head straight with his eyes closed.

He begins by breathing easily and quietly and normally, for he is not to be distracted by any effort in breathing since his attention must be focused in his breathing in and his breathing out without distraction in any effort.

In this way, his Mindfulness of breathing will be developed and he will become aware that his breathing is not one continuous process but that it has three parts. First, there is the breathing in. Then, there is a pause and then there is a breathing out. On breathing out, he also finds there is a breathing out and then a pause before there is breathing in again.

He will note that it has a beginning and an end of one stage, a pause and then the beginning and the end of the next stage. Thus he notes the cycle of the beginning and end of each breathing without any real respite.

As he breathes in, he notices he is breathing in, and the counterpart sign of this breathing in arises; as he breathes out, he notices he is breathing out and the counterpart sign of this breathing out arises.

In order that he can notice the sign of the breathing in and the breathing out, he keeps his attention on a certain part of his body, such as the nostrils, or his stomach, and he does not follow the cold air in as he breathes in and the hot air going out as he breathes out but keeps his concentration anchored at that particular place.

When he keeps his concentration on his stomach and notes its rise and fall as he breathes in and he breathes out, he keeps his mind there and does not follow the air out. This is what is meant by the expression that the meditator watches the rise and fall as he breathes in and he breathes out.

Later, as he tires of concentration at one spot, he may shift to another spot, provided he maintains the same principle of noting without pursuing.

He may even vary his practice by breathing short and breathing long.

And thus he "breathes long and he breathes short". But he should never pursue his breaths as they move in and out.

He should always keep his mind anchored at the spot where his breath has to pass. For example, he can hold it at the tip of his nostrils, or at his abdomen where he can watch his stomach rise and fall with his in- and out-breaths, maintaining his mindfulness there. But he must never follow the air from his nostrils down to the stomach or vice versa.

Further, the sign of breathing diminishes as the meditator reaches a higher state so that it hardly is discernible as one progress. This makes it extremely difficult for the meditator to maintain contact with the 'sign' of breathing as it becomes subtle so that at times he may lose it altogether. Also, the sign is always coarser at the beginning than at the end of every state, so, although it is recommended and used by Buddha himself, he also suggested that it is most suitable only for the more serious meditator.

As he develops his concentration and his breathing becomes more quiet as his concentration deepens, he reaches the higher states and the counterpart sign of his breathing also grows subtle. Should he lose the counterpart sign, he can wait at that spot where he has lost it to regain contact with it. That is the meaning of the expression waiting at the spot for the cattle to return to drink water to catch them again.

It is useful to remember that the proximate rate of normal breathing is eighteen inbreathe and eighteen outbreathe per minute and that there are three hundred and sixty breaths in twenty minutes. Twenty minutes is therefore a useful unit for the calculation of meditation.

If a minimum session is twenty minutes, three sessions make up one hour.

But he will notice that his breathing slows down as his practice develops and the three hundred and sixty in- and out-breaths will take half an hour or even slightly longer as his experience develops.

It is difficult to sit for even as long as twenty minutes in the beginning.

But once this is achieved there is an internal time clock that will allow us this period of time before waking us from meditation. Time keeping is a distraction but may be necessary to establish our meditation periods in the beginning.

Thereafter, it is not necessary. In any event, not only is it difficult to keep accurate count of time in meditation but it is also a distraction in concentration. It can even prevent us from noting the rise and fall of our formations.

But it is useful to learn to count throughout the period in the beginning to gain the habit of sitting for a certain length of time. It also helps us to know how well we can concentrate, for it is not easy to count up to three hundred without mistakes. But this is a matter of preference and choice. Some meditators do not find this necessary. It is not important if he does not count.

After a short while, he will find it easy to keep the full count without errors but, by that time, it would not only be no longer necessary to count the whole time but it might even be a distraction.

But one can count to ten at a time and repeat the counting to gain concentration.

Once he has sat for a certain length of time before awakening, this period will automatically be the length of his meditation session unless he wills a change in the length of time when that period will then become the period of a session automatically.

He counts at the beginning or at the end of his breath or during the process of his actual breathing. That is to say that he counts "fast" or he counts "slow". But he should not count before the start of the breath because that will give rise to agitation. Nor should he count after because that would give rise to sloth and torpor.

How does the beginner develop this meditation subject? By learning, by questioning, by establishing, by absorption and by characteristics.

We know what is learning, questioning, establishing and absorption, but what is the meaning of the term characteristic? To understand this is to understand the individual essence of Mindfulness of Breathing.

How does he do that? This is done through giving attention to the subject by:

1. Counting,
2. Connection,
3. Touching,
4. Fixing,
5. Observing,
6. Turning away,
7. Purification,
8. Looking back on these.

In detail they mean the following:

1. **Counting** – The beginner counts his breaths to keep his concentration on the breathing. He counts late, or he counts early, whilst keeping his mindfulness on the spot he has chosen to note the rise and the fall of his breaths whether it may be at his nostrils or his stomach. He must note the sign of each in-breath and each out-breath, and he must note that each separately has its own rising and falling, and that they are in fact two separate actions with an interval between them and that there are therefore two distinct movements with a pause in between.

   He counts up to ten, not more, because, if he does that, he will be paying attention to his counting and not to the rise and fall of breathing. So he counts to ten and starts again if need be. Sometimes, the meditator will lose count during the session but that does not matter if he can continue his meditation and the period of his meditating session has already been established.

   In concentrating on his stomach, he notices the falling of his stomach as he breathes out and then he notes the rise as he breathes in. He also notices the pause and the endless repeating of the breathing in and out.

   Should he anchor his attention at the tip of his nostrils, he will observe this breathing out as the sign of hot air touches the tip of his nostrils, the pause and then the sign of cold air as he begins his breathing in.

   However, it is important that he does not follow his breath in and out of himself as that is not "bare" attention. The Patissambhida explicitly says that mindfulness should be anchored only at one point, like the teeth of a saw that remain at the point of the cut on the log at all times during sawing and should not be allowed to go over and beyond the cut.

   This means that we should not allow our concentration to drift away from the initial spot from which we first observed the breath, should it be at the nostrils, throat or at the navel. It should remain there for as long as we can, until boredom makes us shift the anchor of our attention at another more convenient place.

Of course, this shifting is allowed when there is difficulty in concentration. But once shifted, it should remain there for as long as possible.

By the expression that the meditator must not follow his breath is meant that whatever he may do, the meditator must go no further than maintain contact of his breath at the spot where it is observed. He cannot follow the breath as that would be attachment and distraction from his mindfulness.

He should do no more than maintain contact. Further, he must not anticipate his breath before it happens, or try to recollect it after it has passed.

If he does that he will be noting his breathing too soon or too late, leading to agitation or sloth and torpor accordingly.

He must note his breath only at the moment of existence.

2. **Connection** – Connection means sorting the breath, not tranquilization of his mental formations. In this way, he gradually proceeds from concentrating on his consciousness, and delineating it, to mindfulness on impermanence and finally to cessation and to relinquishment of his formations by bringing them to mind and noting but not holding on to them.

   Through Mindfulness of Breathing, the meditator can "achieve the fourth jhana and then, by making that same jhana the basis for comprehension of formations, he can reach arahantship, the highest fruit".

   Here, we can see a reason why samatha meditation is discussed at the same time as vipassana. Having obtained the fourth jhana, the meditator will have trained his concentration to the point where it can be employed usefully for vipassana.

At this stage, he will have developed his concentration enough to try gaining the nanas. He can then be said to turn away from samatha to embark upon observation of the namarupa at the spot he has used and is familiar with, thus to direct his progress towards the noble path of the ariyas, through holding on to the four foundations of mindfulness.

There is no doubt that Mindfulness of Breathing will spread as the subject of meditation because it is not only the best but also the easiest to use.

But we must be careful that practice does not deviate from that set out in the Visuddhi Magga, the Mahasatipathana Sutta and the Patissambhida.

For example, certain teachers hold the view that Breathing must be fast and heavy at all times. But this cannot be so since this would put the meditator out of breath and not only will concentration but mindfulness also be lost.

Breathing can be done slow, fast, and the counting may be at the beginning or the end of the breath, but all these are but variations to prevent boredom for those not yet steady on their course of meditation. These changes are to prevent boredom, not to tire out the meditator.

Breathing must be normal and not distracting from the main subject of the meditation and at the cost of mindfulness.

3. Touching;
4. Fixing;
5. Observing;
6. Turning away;
7. Purification;
8. Looking back on these, only means that the meditator notes the breath touching the spot of his attention as he counts. He merely touches it and fixes it in the sense that he fixes the counterpart sign in absorption observing this in insight meditation, then turning away from the forma-

tions into the Path, gaining purification, which is the fruit of the Path and then he looks back in the sense of reviewing the Path and the antecedents.

All these steps are descriptive of the progress towards the Path through the nanas.

Here, relating to the breath, the meditator is required to note the three signs of breathing without which he knows he has not gained the absorption concentration required.

He lightly feels the breath and the counterpart signs until he is able to distinguish all the three signs. Thus, he looks upon his breath like a saw moving to and fro on a certain part of the trunk it is working on.

He does not allow his mind to move away from the point of sawing. He counts early or late, long or short, but never away from the place of contact.

But he never counts after the event or in anticipation. If he does, he is guilty of torpor and is in anxiety and thus he strays away from his concentration. Thus it is said in the Patisambhida (i 170):

"Sign, in-breath, out-breath, are not objects
Of a single consciousness;
By one who knows not these three things
Development is not obtained.
By one who does know these three things
Development is obtained."

32

KASINAS

The Kasinas, or the Totalities, are the only true samatha meditation subjects. They have no individual essences and can give rise to the four jhanas.

They are the Light, Earth, Water, Fire, the colour kasinas of Blue, Yellow, Red, White and the two of Limited Space and Light kasinas.

Some accounts refer to these colours as those of cyan, yellow and magenta. In that context, they are the subtractive, or secondary, colours. This means that they can produce all the colours of the rainbow.

The earth, water, fire and air kasinas composing the four elements of our body, are propounded by Aristotle as the primary elements that make up universal matter.

Since the colour kasinas make up white light and the elements make up universal matter, except for the last two of space and light kasinas which are mental concepts, we can only marvel at how complete was the system of kasinas, defined some 2,500 years ago.

The term kasina has three interpretations. Firstly, it can mean the mandala, or circle or the bounds of the object. Secondly, it can mean its mental image or mark, known as the nimitta. Thirdly, it can also mean the jhana obtained in that nimitta.

Therefore in discussing the kasinas, it would perfectly be in order if we at the same time discuss the mental images (nimittas) obtained at different levels. At the same time we can discuss the jhanas at the same time for that can be obtained as well, since they intertwine somewhat.

The kasina gives rise to the three nimittas which are important to know for the practice of samatha. When concentrating on the subject, a preliminary image known as the parikamma nimitta is noted. Thereafter, the mind is able to recreate the after-image of the subject which is the replica of the parikamma nimitta with all its blemishes which after-image is known as the patibhaga nimitta.

Finally, from this patibhaga nimitta there will arise the conceptual image translated as the counterpart sign known as the uggaha nimitta.

The uggaha nimitta, because it is symbolic in nature, is an abstract of the patibhaga nimitta without any blemish or particularity.

The uggaha nimitta comes only with absorption concentration. Once he is able to see an image which is divested of its limited objective shape colour and form, the nimitta gains this conceptual form on which the meditator can practise his skills. The Anguttara Nikaya extols the virtues of the practice in the kasinas thereby also suggesting that samatha was accepted as part of the practice of monks.

Buddha adds to this by saying that "in this practice there are many of my disciples who have attained to the summit of the perfection of higher knowledge (abhinna-vosana-parami)".

To indulge in this practice, the meditator has to make for himself one of the kasina subjects on which he is to practise.

Thus, for example, he uses a square dish of earth for the earth kasina; or a bowl of clean clear water for the water kasina; a small fire and a screen with a square hole in it to expose the flame behind it for the fire kasina; or an orifice, such as a crack in the door, through which a light may strike through, for the light kasina.

As in all cases, unless the meditator wants to use colour as a subject, care must be taken to see that the concentration is not diverted to the colour of the subject. Should he inadvertently become conscious of their colour, he would automatically be meditating on the colour kasina instead of on the object. In which case, he must switch his mind back to the original subject.

To use a colour kasina as the subject for his meditation, the meditator would have to find a tray or a dish and fill it with the colour for the kasina which he has decided to use.

In the case of the space or light kasina, the meditator uses the space of a hole in a wall or a window opening, or the light in such a hole in the wall or a window for his subject of space or light kasina.

There have been cases of meditators using the sun as an object of concentration. They do this by staring at the sun in the early mornings. This is dangerous as it might damage the eyes and cause partial blindness. This has happened in the sixties when it was fashionable to use the sun as a subject and it should be discouraged as unnecessary. In the first place, it is not a kasina object. In the second place, it does not stay still but moves. In the third place, the sun changes from red to white as it rises and by that time it could be so strong as to burn the eyes, damaging it. It is easier to use a traditional kasina subject.

Once the meditator is able to bring up the patibhaga nimitta he need not use the physical object anymore. He should do this as quickly as possible especially where the subject is hard to come by or where it could easily change or decompose. An experienced meditator will find this easier. The idea is to have the sign arise in him as quickly as possible. Having obtained that sign, the patibhaga nimitta will arise soon afterwards.

An example of the counterpart sign arises can be seen in the case of the earth kasina. When the image of the earth in a ploughed area arises in his mind instead of the original kasina, this is the counterpart sign that he sees. Again, when the meditator is practising on the light kasina and he suddenly sees the original lighted circle of light on the wall turning into a circle of pure white light, he sees the abstract counterpart sign.

To gain the conceptual or counterpart image, he has first to create the patibhaga nimitta, or the mental after-image of the parikamma nimitta, by looking at and holding the subject in his mind. It often comes after staring at a subject long enough so that when the eyes are shut a sort of after-image appears.

To obtain this after-image, the meditator calls the subject by name, for example, "earth" or "ground" or "light", depending upon which kasina he is using. He does this as he opens and shuts his eyes several times lightly, as if he is blinking.

Once the sign is developed, he sees it, with his eyes open or shut, in replica of the real object.

As soon as this has taken place, he can leave the spot. Should he lose it he must return and start again and recall it. That is to say, when the learning sign has faded away from his mind, he must restart again and again, with sustained and applied thought, till he is able to do it and it does not fade away.

As he practises, the mind becomes detached and concentrated. At first there is upacara, and then there is appana concentration where there is absorption and the counterpart sign arises in its absorptive state.

The uggaha nimitta is therefore the recreated conceptual mental image. Unlike the learning sign, which is the patibhaga nimitta, it is without blemish, purified and has neither the original defined colour nor shape.

At this stage the mind is absolutely still and malleable and, in absorption concentration, there is complete suppression of hindrances and subsidence of defilements.

We have mentioned that even whilst in the state of access concentration, the counterpart sign may arise. This is true, but since access concentration is only the access or gateway into the jhana of absorption, the image is infirm and shaky. For, although the hindrances are suppressed even on the plane of access, the jhana factors are still not strong enough to hold the image firmly. Since it cannot be held for long or firmly enough, practice on it for the skill is impossible in this stage.

But on the plane of absorption there is attainment of the jhana factors. Because of this, the counterpart image can be held firmly. When the jhana factors become strong enough on this plane of absorption, the jhana impulses will be able carry on for a long time, even for a whole day, even if the life-continuum is interrupted. In such a case, the meditator becomes oblivious to his surroundings and may be able to carry on his practice on the counterpart sign.

Therefore, when the counterpart sign arises and absorption concentration does not come immediately, the meditator should try to keep it and hold it so that it will be there in the next session when absorption concentration is achieved, at which event he can immediately practise his skills in it.

Because of this, the lifestyle of the meditator must be carefully monitored and controlled. He should be a concentrated and not a distracted person at all times. He should allow nothing and no one to disturb him as he must not be distracted or become unconcentrated.

He must be careful of his abode, which must be suitable, such as a monastery or a cave. His source of food must also be easy and close by. He must be careful of his speech which must be suitable and he must not involve himself in aimless talk, unprofitable conversation and he must avoid unconcentrated persons.

Not only must conditions suit meditation but he must have food which suits him constitutionally and he has to make sure it is easily obtainable.

He should also stay in a climate suitable for him and maintain suitable postures in sitting, walking, standing and lying down.

All this is necessary because he must cultivate himself and the sign continuously, so that the sign will come immediately on recall without undue delay.

For progress towards abhinna, there are ten kinds of skill he has to develop. A person who is unconcentrated and unskilled will achieve little and claims of supranormal achievements become doubtful if the meditator is not practised in these ten skills. These skills must be practised on each and every kasina.

Samatha concentration also requires balance of the faculties. But whilst the samatha meditator may practise his skills for abhinna in the fourth jhana, the vipassana meditator must hold on to the dhamma and the four foundations of mindfulness where the aggregates will rise and fall, noting their formations without being taken up with them, with sustained concentration.

The conditions for the ten skills which also apply to both meditations, are as follows:

1. **Keeping the bases clean both internally and externally** – For, like a lamp, which requires clean oil and a clean wick to burn well, so also the meditator must be clean, physically and morally, for his formations to become evident. Immoral persons especially will not be able to achieve the correct concentration as he will be distracted by his own desires.
2. **Maintaining balanced faculties** – The faculties are important in all meditation practice.

   These faculties are the faculties of faith, understanding, concentration, energy and mindfulness. The faculties are:
   - Faithfulness – Faith in the Teachings must go with understanding, because a person with faith and little understanding becomes uncritical. Understanding enables the meditator to see the truth and he will not be so uncritical and has groundless confidence. On the other hand, if he has but little faith, he will develop cunning and slyness. With both faith and understanding in balance, he will have confidence with reason and good grounds.
   - Energy – Energy without concentration makes one jump around like a monkey. Yet, concentration without energy creates torpor and laziness. In balance, they bring about concentration with energy.
   - Concentration – Concentration should balance with energy or there will be idleness if there is little energy. On the other hand, there will be agitation where there is energy with little concentration. Absorption will only come with the balance of energy and concentration. In absorption one needs unification, for that is how he reaches absorption.
   - Understanding – Understanding is the fourth faculty required. Understanding here means the understanding of the dhamma which gives rise to panna. Without understanding, the meditator would not be able to penetrate the characteristics of the four formations which is essential to vipassana. It is only with

understanding that faith is balanced with concentration and energy so that the meditator can penetrate the rise and fall of formations.

- Mindfulness – Mindfulness is a faculty that must be ever present in vipassana meditation as it requires awareness of what is happening to us and why. The aggregates manifest themselves through the four foundations and they must be noted. The noting is part on the cleaning process of the consciousness. Without it we would not be aware of the rise and fall from the four stations. It is like the Prime Minister who oversees all other faculties. Mindfulness with its four foundations is the basis of vipassana meditation.

3. Skill in the sign. To produce the sign, to develop it and to protect it as explained above is the meaning here.
4. Exerting the mind when it should be exerted.
5. Restraining the mind when it should be restrained.
6. Encouraging the mind when it should be encouraged.
7. Looking at the mind with equanimity when equanimity is required.
8. Avoidance of unconcentrated persons.
9. Cultivation of concentrated persons.
10. Resoluteness upon that, means resolute upon concentration.

These require no explanation. We may now review the nature of the jhanas to see how they fit into meditation as a whole.

33
THE JHANAS

The jhanas are states of concentration of the meditator. Nanas are insight wisdom achieved by meditation. One deals with concentration, the others show mental awareness of the mind.

In meditation, the meditator, whether he is interested in vipassana or samatha, must first gain concentration of the fourth jhana, which is in the material plane, before he can gain insight or develop abhinna and the supranormal powers.

After obtaining absorption in the fourth jhana, the samatha meditator can practise his skills in the kasinas for abhinna, or leave the rupa plane to enter into the arupa plane for the purposes of obtaining all or any of the other four jhanas.

He has three targets in all. Firstly, he must obtain the four jhanas in the rupa or material plane. Secondly, he may then practise his skills for abhinna or, thirdly, abandon the material plane in an attempt to gain all or any of the four arupa jhana of the immaterial plane.

Thus eight jhanas may be divided into two groups of four mundane and four supramundane jhanas of the material and immaterial planes known as the rupa and the arupa jhanas.

The material jhanas use material subjects for their concentration whilst those of the immaterial plane use the immaterial jhanas.

Whilst the six kasinas are in the physical and the light and perception jhanas are in the mental world, all of them are practised when in the material fourth jhana.

The jhanas rightly belong to the field of samatha though the concentration of the fourth jhana is required for vipassana as well.

Not all subjects can give rise to the four jhanas. Those with inner essences cannot do so, nor can those subjects which do not have the surmounting factors.

Only the kasinas and Mindfulness of Breathing subjects have the surmounting factors to the fourth and only the kasinas are useful for practice in the skills for abhinna.

The four arupa jhanas of space, consciousness, nothingness and non-perception can give rise only to one arupa jhana each. Yet, the space kasina, which is that of the mentality and immaterial sphere is one of the kasinas required for abhinna.

The Four Mundane Jhanas

To obtain the first four jhanas, the mind with its initial and then sustained concentration, with appana and the powers of surmounting, eliminates, one after the other, the states with sukha and piti, to enter the fourth jhana with only upekha and ekaggata, where the meditator can practise his skills for the achievement of the supranormal powers before he abandons them in turn, to enter the immaterial states.

There are, technically, two systems of classification of the rupa jhanas.

One is the fourfold system and the other is the fivefold system.

These two systems come about by the fact that concentration in its first stage is divided into the initial and sustained stages called vicara and vitakka samadhi.

The fivefold system considers that the meditator is in the first jhana where there is the quality of vicara in his concentration without vitakka, so that he is in the second jhana when he has both vicara and vitakka in his samadhi.

The fourfold system ignores the first jhana and considers that the meditator is in the first jhana only when he has both vicara and vitakka in his concentration. In other words, there has to be initial and sustained concentration before he is considered to have reached the first jhana. Other than that, everything else is the same.

Since initial concentration flows into sustained concentration, Buddha himself classifies it into the first jhana so that he uses the fourfold rather than the fivefold system. Thus, in the suttantas, one comes across Buddha referring to the first jhana as the one containing sustained concentration, bliss, joy and calmness.

As this was the system used by Buddha, we will use the fourfold system.

So, with initial and sustained concentration the meditator enters the first jhana with initial and sustained concentration and joy and bliss and calmness.

Through ekaggata and with appana concentration, he surmounts the first jhana and enters the second jhana, with joy and with bliss. Again, through surmounting, he enters the third jhana which is with bliss only and without joy. Finally, again through surmounting, he enters the fourth jhana where there is nothing left in the concentration which becomes unadulterated and filled with detached calmness only.

Thus, it is said, the first jhana contains samadhi, sukha, piti and upekha. With appana he enters the second with ekaggata, sukha and piti. Then, again with ekaggata, he enters the third only with piti. Finally, he abandons piti and enters the fourth which is unadulterated with desires and containing only ekaggata and upekha. The essential element in upekha is detached calmness without distraction of joy and bliss.

The following verse found in the Texts and in the Mahadinna Sutta show the necessity for absorption concentration:

> "Any man who acquires the sign
> In order absorption to gain
> Thus achieves his bolder goal."

Initial and sustained concentration leads to the first jhana. But access and absorption concentration are not matters of the jhana.

They arise when there is already ekaggata. They pertain to the factors of surmounting and the nature of viewing the uggaha nimitta. Access and absorption concentration comes only after ekaggata has been established and there is sustained concentration. Absorption is a sequence to access concentration.

But absorption must be present in every jhana for surmounting the jhana. But it can be achieved only when the subject allows it and it has the surmounting factors. As we already have learnt, the kasinas have such surmounting factors for it up to the fourth jhana.

When the cognitive sign arises, the meditator continues repetitively to avert to the sign, repeating, for example, "earth, earth" when he is concentrating on the earth kasina; or he repeats the word "alokha, alokha" when he is concentrating on the light kasina and so on.

During this period, in one of the series of thought impulsions, on the fourth or the fifth impulsion, absorption arises and the mind moves into the fine material sphere. Those impulsions leading to the fine material sphere are known as access concentration because they are next to absorption consciousness.

Every full thought moment has seven impulsions before it subsides and another thought moment arises to take its place. Based on this, the first impulsion is "the preliminary work", the second is "access", the third is "conformity", the fourth is "change-of-lineage" and the fifth is "absorption".

Since the absorption consciousness comes in the fine material sphere and the meditator is thus in the fine material state, the meditation subject used becomes important because, if he is concentrating on a subject that cannot give rise to the fine material state, he will never get into that state.

He has therefore to find out which subject can or cannot give rise to absorption and what subject can give rise to what jhana.

In the first jhana, the meditator enters into concentration with applied and sustained thought, happiness, bliss born from seclusion, having abandoned the factors of lust, illwill, stiffness and torpor, agitation, worry and uncertainty.

The five factors of the concentration found here in the first jhana are applied thought, sustained thought, joy, bliss and the unification of mind.

And the five abandoned factors of defilements at this stage are lust (which is greed for the various objects, preventing concentration and the abandoning of the sense element), illwill (which prevents uninterrupted thought), stiffness and torpor (which makes the mind unwieldy), agitation and worry (which causes lack of stillness and calm), uncertainty (which prevents concentration) and energy (to mount the attainment).

These five factors of concentration, however, are also found in access concentration as well, but, in that case, their impulsions are weaker and not as strong. This is obvious. They become stronger in absorption concentration.

In the second jhana, applied and sustained thought are absent, since the concentration would have become ekaggata and they will have been absorbed by this single-minded concentration. The second jhana has the factors of joy and bliss. Only when the factors of joy are absent and there are surmounting factors, surmounting can take place and the second jhana is discarded for the third jhana.

In the third jhana, though joy is now absent, there is still the presence of bliss which is born from seclusion. When bliss is overcome the meditator moves into the fourth jhana, where all are absorbed also that the concentration is without any distraction and is therefore detached and calm and thus upekha, which is therefore a detached calmness without the elements of joy and bliss, becomes present.

Pleasure is a condition for joy. Joy is the condition for greed. Greed is the condition for pain (of state of loss). Pain is the condition for grief, whilst grief is the condition for hate. This makes it understandable why the sense of joy and bliss must be absent for the fourth jhana which require their abandonment.

In the fourth jhana, the meditator has ekaggata and equanimity of mind only, all other factors having been abandoned. Ekaggata with equanimity is required for absorption to arise and for the mind to be pliable enough and to be without distraction for practice in the skills required for abhinna.

The fourth jhana is also required by the vipassana meditator. Without this concentration he will not have the pliability of a calm concentration without blemish and distraction, pliable and malleable necessary to note the formations when they arise.

This requirement is referred to in the celebrated Mahanidasana Sutta, which is the discourse between Buddha and Ananda, expounding the theory of paticcasamuppada, the theory of the conditioning and of cause and effect.

In it, Buddha, during his discourse with Ananda, also confirmed the benefits of jhanas when he specifically stated that monks could dwell in cessation (nirodha) with their unified mind for up to seven days, only if they have achieved the eighth jhanas, which he referred to in the Sutta as the eighth deliverance.

Those attaining even the first jhana, can reach the deity level in the Brahma world, should they die at that stage. This is certainly better than rebirth in a state of loss for those who do not believe in meditation at all.

For the others who have not achieved them, it is stated that the practice for the jhanas acts as the proximate cause for Insight whilst practice in the fourth jhana can also give rise to supranormal powers which there are altogether, five kinds.

Firstly, he will develop the ability to transform himself from one to many. This power requires, not only full proficiency in all the eight material kasinas but also skill in all fourteen ways (Visuddhi Magga Chapter 12).

Secondly, he will gain the power of the divine ear, which will enable him to hear sounds up to that which are divine and supranormal.

Thirdly, he will gain the ability to penetrate minds, which means that he will be able to read others' minds and all manner of consciousness both in the sense and the fine material, or immaterial spheres and discern the states of hate, greed (atta), or the extent and type of liberation.

Fourthly, he will have the ability to recollect past lives. This means that he will be able to know the antecedent lives, not only of himself but also, of others. He can even recollect the past aeons of the world's contraction, expansion and its destruction and reformation.

Thus, it was by these special powers, Buddha was able to explain how there have been other worlds and how it has been destroyed eight times before and how it will be destroyed again by the element which is dependent upon which factor of greed, hate or delusion is predominant at the time of such destruction.

In this manner, sixty-three aeons have passed, and the earth has been destroyed, seven times by fire and the eighth by water (was this the great flood that we know of?). The next destruction, as foretold by him, will be destruction by the wind element, which will also in its wake destroy the Subhakinha Brahma world where the life span is sixty-four aeons (Note that a nuclear war could easily fulfil this prophecy).

Fifthly, the meditator can develop the divine eye. This is the power and ability to know the passing away and the reappearance of beings.

With such power he can see the formations of other beings, their states, their nature, their greed, hate and delusion, what sort of state they are now in, their inferior or superior nature and their past and future destinies. He has the divine eye who can see the states of the others which others cannot see, for he sees the material and the immaterial states, their passing and their rebirth. (This perhaps is the inspiration of the Third Eye legends).

Where such powers are claimed, it could be nothing more than mass hypnosis and falsehood. If they are true claims, such powers must be exercised with the dhamma in mind, for, like inherited wealth, it can be quickly dissipated and lost through abuse and unwholesome practice.

Those who attempt to make hay whilst the sun shines, will suffer for their unwholesome practice by entering into states of loss. No one escapes from this law of the dhamma and of cause and effect.

Meditators, who are at the fourth jhana, stand at the end of the material state and he can enter the supramundane states provided he abandons the material fourth jhana.

If he wishes to gain insight, he must abandon samatha practice, although it can be the proximate cause, to enter into vipassana practice.

The Four Supramundane Jhanas

The fifth, sixth, seventh and the eighth jhanas are the jhanas of the supramundane, or immaterial, states. They are called the arupa jhanas because they are jhanas without rupa or materiality.

To attain a higher jhana it is required of the meditator to abandon the lower state. This principle of abandoning is also a principle of vipasanna where an unprofitable state is abandoned to obtain a profitable one. Here, to achieve the immaterial states, the material state has to be abandoned.

He has to abandon so as to surmount. Since he is attempting the immaterial state which is formless, the state of form is abandoned because it is material and has form.

He first rejects the concentration on the physical object he has tried so hard to master and concentrates on the abstract, such as the infinity of space which is the kasina of the fifth jhana.

Having mastered the fifth jhana he also then abandons it as unsatisfactory so as to be able to concentrate on the infinity of Consciousness of the sixth jhana. Then, abandoning that as well, he reaches the seventh jhana of Nothingness and finally to the eighth jhana of Perception and Non-perception. He has to progress step by step, there can be no leapfrogging.

There are those who speak of the seventh jhana of nothingness as the highest form of meditation. This cannot be true.

The reason is that nothingness requires perception. So there is still the element of perception without which there can be no awareness of nothingness. Therefore there is still a further state to be abandoned.

This is Perception which comes with Non-perception. Perception itself has to be abandoned before there is Non-Perception.

Thus the eighth state of Perception and Non-perception is still to be achieved. Only at this state is there nothing else to be done.

In that jhana, the meditator is unable to perceive nothing. He ceases to be aware of existence itself and therefore cannot even perceive nothingness.

At this state, he can obtain cessation or nirodha and is capable of being two-ways liberated if he obtains liberation in vipassana as well, or if he listens to the dhamma.

When the meditator is in the fifth jhana, he uses Space as the subject of meditation. To rid himself of space, he must cultivate Consciousness and so consciousness becomes his subject. Nothingness must be cultivated to rid himself of consciousness. Nothingness then becomes his subject.

Having done that he must rid himself of the Perception with which he has perceived Nothingness. To do that he uses Perception and Non-perception as his subject. Without Perception he would not be able to perceive nothingness. So he gains Non-perception and reaching the state of Non-perception with which he gains nirodha.

Thus, the four immaterial jhanas are obtained through the immaterial objects. Cessation in that state is through suppression of the formations in which he can remain for no more than seven days.

CONCLUSION

Meditation itself was not a discovery by Buddha. Samatha meditation with all its exaggerated claims came before him. He was responsible only for the vipassana technique. Nevertheless, samatha has its uses and was exployed by Buddha and is still practised today. So it is necessary to know that it is. But the problem confronting a student of Buddhism is the fact that interpretation of the texts is not encouraged. Further the lay texts are frowned upon by the religious order and the monks themselves are afraid of heresy and so, dare not give their own interpretation of the texts. This has prevented interpretation and the use of modern vocabulary to translate the texts.

The fear of interpretation is understandable because there will be no end of variations once this is encouraged. Yet, there is a need for it. Some terms such as the term "sectarian" can easily be substituted by the term "layman" though it may be difficult to substitute sense bases and their faculties with other words.

It is precisely this that has made me hesitate to use new and non traditional vocabulary. But all said and done, having set out the text in traditional terms, I would like to do what I feel is justified and substitute modern usage for traditional terms. Thus, for example, can be taken "penetrating the minds of the others" to mean to be the mind reading and mental telepathic communication. One may even consider "the ability to escape from a room through a keyhole" to mean to make one invisible by mass hypnotism and so on.

Such interpretation would make the iddhi-pada powers of samatha more easily acceptable to the modern mind. There is nothing wrong to read this as the power of mind over matter. We know there is such as hypnotism and psychicical powers. We know that the subconscious can be penetrated to deal with hysteria and psychogenic illnesses.

We understand that the subconscious can express its desires through dreams and it is not difficult to assume that meditation allows wish fulfilments to express themselves in the formations and that thought formations are manifestations of our innermost secrets. Why not read the texts that way so as to understand how meditation works?

Such present day knowledge allows us to understand meditation through modern terminology and can put charlatanism in its place. After all, Buddha used the terminology of his day to explain many of his thought processes. We can use what we know today to make it easier to understand what he tried to explain. If it helps us, why not? After all, Buddha was analytical and logical, not mystic and superstitious.

Buddhism originated from the Vedic philosophy. He accepted those beliefs and used it to explain his teaching. That was how the cycle of life came into Buddhism. His contribution was vipassana and how the life cycle could be terminated. He challenged little except the fundamental. He did not even attempt to redefine samatha and its supranormal powers.

He did, however, challenge some of its philosophy such as the concept that Brahma was the Supreme Creator of all living things, maintaining that he happened to be the first Brahma to descend to earth in this era and thus gave the impression that he was the Creator of all things.

His proposition that living beings are born with the three basic roots of greed, illwill and the delusion of the permanency of an ego and their three opposites of anicca, dukha and anatta, as reflected in the acts of the Brahmavihara which are that of lovingkindeness, generosity, charity and detachment is a growth of the theory of opposites. This is not new but the way it is applied seems to be.

The theory of opposites, or yang and yin, was propounded by the Taoists in ancient China. That all men are born either good or bad was an argument also to be found there and occupied a great deal of the time of the metaphysicists of China, especially Mencius.

But his application of this into "wholesome" and "unwholesome" behaviour, thereby redefining "sin" and "purity", is remarkable and new.

Through this idea, he introduced the psychological concept into that of "sin" and separates morality from religious edicts. He was thus the only great "religious" teacher who split the creation of man from the concept of original sin. The Creator is one assumption, but he has nothing to do with our morality. Buddha separated it from this dependency.

To him, lying, killing, taking what is not rightfully yours, committing adultery and drunkenness, are wrong because they are the result of hate, greed or illwill and engender hatred and illwill, therefore it is unwholesome to the mental makeup.

None of the Greek philosophers, Aristotle and Plato, or even Marx, with his lialectic materialism, dealt with the problem of the individual in their concept of universal or common good. Somehow, they did not attempt to explain how this concept of universal good applies to individuals and the need to change the sense of values and its scale in the individual before concept of universal good can be achieved. This appears to be an important factor of the failure of Communism. It never created a new man.

I believe that there can be no new and bold society without changing the sense and values of the individual that comprise the state. I think most will agree with that. For no philosophy could explain why and how the individual should strive to do good or bad, apart from the explanation that wrongs are sinful. The Chinese stated the problem that men are born either good or bad without attempting to explain why this is so.

To me this was a missing link in our thinking. I found this missing link when I came across the English translations of the Tipitaka by the Buddhist Society of England and the 1958 English translation of the Visuddhi Magga by the great German monk Bhikkhu Nanamoli.

It filled the missing link. Since it is the indivduals that make up a society, the quality of the individual can influence the quality of the society. The health of the society depends upon the health of its individuals. What is healthy is what is wholesome, and that is behaviour that is the opposite of greed, illwill and the delusion of a permanent ego. So far that is nothing new. What was new is the argument that all voluntary acts have a volition which arise according to the inner nature of the doer which is self perpetuating.

This cycle can be terminated through meditation which allows us to look into our subconscious and cultivate what is selfless, kind and sympathetic to all living creatures and without ego.

The Abhidhamma is therefore a unique tome on ethics and the meaning of "good" and "bad" and should not be ignored in any study on ethics and philosophy. Further, it sets out a practice which have developed a personality that is wholesome and constructive.

Nothing results without a cause, we are what we are because it is what we have made ourselves to be. Everything we do is the result of a cause which, in its turn, becomes the cause of the next resultant act. It is attachment, due to desire, which is the cause of the action and it results repeatedly becomes a habitual.

This creates a cycle of demands and satisfaction which ultimately becomes our nature. So we can blame no one but ourselves for what we are.

A person fond of food could easily become a glutton. A person who enjoys killing for sport will go out his way to find blood sports. Similarly, a cheat will continue to be a cheat and a person who takes drugs habitually becomes a drug addict.

Metaphorically, if we behave like greedy pigs, we will become greedy pigs. Carried further, we might even be born pigs, such is the similarity between the two.

Once we are able to dissociate ourselves from these desires, the habit will stop and our nature changed. That is to say, if the inherent characteristics are not too strong and they are such as can be changed. Basically, however, a person's nature cannot be changed unless there are also in him the seeds for the change.

This is explained by the terms kamma and paramis, which are past meritorious acts. Thus, inherent characteristics like kamma which, unlike physical characteristics, do not come from genes. Kamma is in the consciousness brought over from a past life just as a flame is passed from one base to another, taking on new characteristics as it switches from oil to wood. In itself, it has resultant effects which have to be executed in spite of all efforts to the contrary. In this sense it is "fated". But kamma can be slight or mixed and can be avoided.

In this sense it is not "fated" and can be removed by "virtuous" behaviour. Paramis are past meritorious acts which provide the base for improvement. This has to be present as the basis for the correct desires and the ability to obtain progress.

The idea of the continuing cycle of life is the logical extension of the argument that there is nothing which is not the result of a cause. As long as there is desire and attachment, there is birth. This repeats itself even to life itself.

Whether we accept the concept of different planes of existence to the real or metaphorical, is really not relevant to the argument. We do find company that reflect ourselves. Gangsters, for example, tend to be with other gangsters.

But unwhole behaviour brings about anger, pain, anguish, stress, anxiety, agitation and restlessness. We are at odds with ourselves all because of our greed, illwill and ego. Wholesome behaviour, however, develops the opposite and, therefore, inner peace. This explains the title of this book.

We can realise this through meditation with mindfulness which allows us to contact our innermost selves and see for ourselves the thought formations coming out of the subconscious. By noting them and not reacting, we learn to detach ourselves from them. Whether we believe in the other aspects of Buddhist beliefs, it is necessary for us to understand the dhamma since it explains the theory of meditation and explains its contacts and manifestations.

Apart from this we have to always bear in mind that miracles are not to be expected but realisation of the truth. It should also be remembered that progress depends upon kamma and not all behavioral patterns can be changed.

Firstly, certain behavioral patterns, which vary from person to person and which are known as postures because they have no kammic meaning, e.g. the way one stands, walks, seat or the manner of behaviour (such as Sariputtra who was accused of arrogant behaviour which was explained by Buddha to his disciples as a non kammic posture resulting from previous life as a nobleman) are irrelevant and inconsequential to kamma.

Secondly, the resultants of heavy kamma cannot be avoided, no matter what we do. In other words, the punishment is already fixed and it will inevitably come no matter what we do. This is the usual meaning of the term kamma.

Thirdly, progress depends upon if there is sufficient paramis in us. The idea of paramis is that our propensity in us to develop depends largely upon how practised we are on acts of virtue. The supporting base of development in virtue depends upon how much we have practised it and how strong is its base. This is understandable since every result is due to a cause and the stronger the cause the better the result.

All this that makes study of Buddhism and its meditative exercise fascinating. Apart from vipassana, which develops virtue, samatha can result in powers of perception and feats, some of which are still beyond the ordinary comprehension. Imagine the ability to remain alive confined in a glass case for days and imagine the still perfectly composed body of the monk in Chiengmai, Thailand, who was supposed to have died during meditation. The understanding of power of mind over matter of samatha is unfolding.

The quaint language of the Pali texts, does not reduce the astounding perception set out so long ago. It was at a time when science was at its infancy. When we examine its planes such as materiality and immateriality, its different forms of existence, its Aristotlelian definition of the four elements, its elements and aggregates, the kasinas, to name but a few, we wonder if our discovery that everything we know of are different expressions of energy wave forms and patterns, were not known to them.

Consciousness itself, which can transmit itself from life to life would also appear to be an energy force, a life force which the Chinese refer to as the chi. When we read of such as the ability to reach into the past and future, we wonder if this comes from the concept of time which has no beginning or end; a concept that "time past, present and future is time is".

But, as Shakespeare puts it through Hamlet, there are more things in heaven and earth than we know of. Much can still be learnt but it requires a lifetime's practice and there is no short cut.

Meditation can still unravel many secrets and the limits of the power of the mind. It is a subject that must be experienced to be understood. Many things still remain a mystery waiting to be solved. But one thing is certain, the mind has power over many or our illnesses such as even the power to remain healthy or grow sick and die, as is now discovered to be prevalent in retired persons and those who feel unwanted. There is in us, the ability to reach inner peace. But, to each his own.

Schedule I

SAMATHA MEDITATION

Rupa states	1st jhana	concentration with vicara, joy and bliss
	2nd jhana	concentration with joy and bliss
	3rd jhana	concentration with bliss
	4th jhana	concentration with upekkha
		practice abhinna or go to arupa
Arupa states	5th jhana	space kasina
	6th jhana	consciousness kasina
	7th jhana	nothingness kasina
	8th jhana	perception @ non-perception kasina

Schedule II

VIPASSANA MEDITATION

Purity of views		Purity of citta
Sila and Bhavanga are the first 2 Purities without which the other Purities cannot be obtained.	sila samadhi	Note that sila and bhanga are also developed right through to Arahant.
These 3 are nanas of the 3rd Purity of Views (dithi visuddhi), where he can rightly discern namarupa and enters the Purity of Over-coming Doubts (kankhavitarana visuddhi).	1. namarupariccheda nana 2. pacchaya-pariggaha nana 3. samasananna nana	Basic understanding and concentration up to the equivalent 4th jhana has to be obtained at 4th nana.
He gains 4th Purity (kankhavitarana and becomes chulia sotappan and moves into the 5th Purity of Knowledge and Vision of what is the correct Path.	4. udayabhaya nana	Cleansing power begins. He sees the 10 defilements of meditation he must abandon if he wishes to progress.
The 5th Purity of Knowledge (magga magga nanadasanna visuddhi) is the result of contemplation of impermanence, pain and suffering, voidness after which he moves to the 6th Purity of Pattipada nanadassana visuddhi.	5. bhanga nana 6. bhaya nana 7. adinava nana 8. nibbida nana	These 3 nanas of part of the 5th Purity are often grouped together because they are different aspects of the same thing.

Schedule II (cont'd)

Purity of views		**Purity of citta**
All these nanas lead into one another and can be quite hard to distinguish. After the sankharupekkha nana in fact the meditator is carried into the anuloma or conformity state and then into gotrabhu nana which is the change-of-lineage almost by the tide, as it were. The anuloma and the gotrabhu is the 6th Purity which leads to the Path which is the 7th Purity of Knowledge and vision of the Path.	9. munchitukamyata nana 10. patissandha nana 11. santhana nana 12. sankharupekkha 13. anuloma nana 14. gotrabbhu nana	Terror, danger, misery of (5), (6) and (7) lead into the 6th Purity, starting with disgust (7) and search for deliverance (9). Then comes reflection (10) leading to equamity (12) which is sometimes divided into 3 aspects of (12)
The cleansing process continues even in ariya states. Only the arahant has achieved full purity (See Schedule III for full diagram). Path means the 1st, 2nd and 3rd or 4th path as the case may be (for impulsions of attainment see Book 1Ch. 15).	15. the path 16. phala 17. reflection	Each ariya state has its own Path, Phala and Reflection. Purification continues in each ariya state till the arahant who reaches perfection where his acts no longer have resultant kammic effect (kriya).

Schedule III

ELIMINATION DEFILEMENTS

(Explanatory Notes)

FETTERS	There are ten states in fetters divided into five lower fetters and five higher fetters. The lower fetters are the courser ones and the higher fetters are the subtle ones. The lower ones are those fetters of coarse material form. The higher ones are the fetters to the kamma and fine material form. They are set out in the schedule.
DEFILEMENTS	Again there are ten states in all. They are so called because they are themselves defiled and because they defile the states associated with them. The ten states are already in the schedule.
WRONGFULNESS	There are eight states again set out in the schedule. They are so called because they occur wrongly.
WORLDLY STATES	There are eight dealing with the states in society set out in the schedule.
AVARICES	There are five, again dealing with society and social belongings.
PERVERSIONS	There are three dealing with the mind and perversions.
TIES	There are four dealing with greed and trying us to our greed and the mental and material body.
BAD WAYS	It means doing what ought not to be done and not doing what ought to be done out of desire, hate, delusion and fear. They are bad ways because they are not noble.

Schedule III (cont'd)

CANKERS (ASAVAS)	They are the sort of greed and desire which bring out into the unguarded mind the wrongful desires and so on. Floods, Bonds and Cankers have in fact the same meaning.
HINDRANCES	There are five in all again delaing with illwill, agitation, doubt, etc. in the sense of obstructing, hindering and concealing from the consciousness.
ADHERENCE	It is a term for wrong view and attaching to because it misses the understanding of Dhamma and attaching to the wrong view.
CLINGINGS	There are four attached to the sense-desires.
INHERENT TENDENCIES	There are seven which are anusayas. They are causes of greed for sense-desire and so on.
STAINS	There are three. They are dirtiness, attached to greed, hate and delusion. They are so called because they are dirt.
UNPROFITABLE COURSE OF ACTION	There are ten dealing with the eight full noble path.
UNPROFITABLE THOUGHT-ARISINGS	There are twelve consisting of eight rooted in greed, two rooted in hate and two rooted in delusion.

GLOSSARY

Abhinna	Direct Knowledge, related to samatha.
Absorption Concentration	Appana.
Access Concentration	Concentration leading to absorption.
Adinava nana	The insight knowledge of deliverance from the suffering of the world.
Adhipanna	Higher insight, higher understanding.
Adinava	Danger, Insight knowledge of danger (adinanana).
Adosa	Without illwill or hatred.
After-image	The conceptual image, patibhaga nimitta.
Aggregates	That leading to the formations, khandhas.
Ahirika	Shamelessness.
Alobha	Without greed.
Alokha	Light.
Amoha	Without delusion wisdom.
Anagami	The second highest of the ariyas.
Anatta	Without concept of self, the permanent soul, or ego.
Anicca, Dukha, Anatta	Impermanence, Suffering, impermanence.
Anapana	Breathing.
Anatta	Non-self.
Anna	Final Knowledge (referring to the Arahant).
Anuloma	Comformity stage in the development of Insight (anuloma nana), Conformity with the arising of Dependant Origination.

Anusayas	Arisings, inherent, the seven underlying tendencies.
Appamana	Measureless.
Apo	Liquid or Water element.
Appana	Absorption, absorption concentration.
Arahant	Highest ariya, person who had done everything that should be done.
Aramanas	Object of consciousness or its concomitants, subject of awareness.
Ariya	The attainers of the Path, the four Noble ones.
Arupa	The Immaterial, the immaterial states.
Asavas	The cankers, taints of unwholesomeness.
Asevana	Cultivation, repetition.
Asubha	Foul, foulness, ugly.
Atta	Self, ego.
Avijja	Ignorance.
Ayatanas	Field of the senses expressing psychological relationship between mind and matter, e.g. cakkhu-ayatana and rupa-ayatana, meaning the sense of sight and feeling.
Bala	Power.
Bhanga	Dissolution.
Bhanga nana	Insight of ultimate dissolution of all things.
Bhava	Becoming, existence, birth.
Bhavana	Mental culture, meditation.
Bhavanga (-sota)	Life-continuum.
Bhaya	Terror, danger.
Bhaya nana	Insight knowledge of Danger.
Bhikku	Bhuddist Monk.
Bojjhangas	Mental constituents for full enlightenment – (seven pertaining to: Mindfulness constituent, satisambojjhanga; Dhamma investigation constituent, Dhammavicayasambojjhanga; Energy constituent, viriyasambojjhanga; Zest constituent, Pitisambojjhanga; serenity constituent (Passadhisambojjhanga; concentration constituent, Samadhisambojjhanga; equanimity constituent, upekhasambojjhanga).

GLOSSARY

Brahmavihara	The virtues of the Brahmas, Divine Abidings, Illimitables.
Caga	Generosity.
Cakkhu	Eye (*see* Dibba-chaku).
Canons	The Tipitaka (the three baskets of Bhuddist texts).
Carana	Conduct.
Cetana	Volition, intention of acts.
Cetasikas	Consciousness concomitants (those accompanying consciousness of feelings, perception and formations), kusala and akusala concomitants).
Chulia sottapan	Meditator achieving udayabhaya nana (thus assured of rebirth in a happy realm).
Citta	Mind, consciousness.
Cittavithi	Cognitive series of consciousness.
Dana	Gift, offering.
Dhamma	The Dhamma, Law preached by Bhudda.
Dhammapada	Stories of the Dhamma, a basket of the Tipitaka.
Dhatu	Elements; also, ore.
Dibba-chaku	Divine eye.
Dithi	View.
Dosa	Hate, illwill.
Dukha	Suffering in the sense of loss and misery because all things are transitory and impermanent.
Dvihetuka	Person with two roots of past metta and karuna but without sasana.
Ekaggata	One-pointed concentration.
Gandatanha Gati	Destiny, destination on rebirth.
Gotrabhu	Change-of-lineage (-nana) the entrance to the Path of the ariyas.

Hetu	Root, root cause.
Hinayana	Smaller of the two sects of Buddhism, purist school believing in meditation for personal salvation. Opposed to the Mahayana (or bigger) school, practised in China and elsewhere.
Iddhi	Power, supranormal powers.
Indriya	Faculty.
Jara	Ageing.
Jara-marana	Ageing and death.
Jati	Birth.
Javana	Impulsion of consciousness, speed.
Jhanas	States of samatha meditation.
Kamma	Result of all effects from causes; result of paticcasammupada; fate, fated.
Kamma-bhava	Kamma-process becoming.
Kamma vipaka kamupadana	Resultant of kamma.
Karuna	Compassion for suffering of others, reference to lack of greed.
Kasinas	The ten Totalities of samatha meditation.
Kaya	The body, group, order.
Khandas	Aggregates from the five sense bases which give rise to formations.
Kilesas	Defilement, defilement hindrances to progress of meditation.
Kriya	Causeless acts of the arahant.
Kukucca	Worry.
Kusala	Profitable, wholesome (consciousness).
Labha	Gain.
Lobha	Greed.
Loka	World.
Lokiya	Mundane, as opposed to the lokuttara.
Lokuttara	Supramundane state of the ariyas (or supramundane states of the ariyas, or related to the Path, fruition, nibbana).

Maccariya Avarice.
Mala Stain.
Mandala The circle used as a device in a kasina.
Manodvara Threshold, state of consciousness between bhavanga and muthivithi.
Miccha Wrong.
Middha Torpor.
Metta Benevolence, Lovingkindness, one of the four Illimitables.
Moha Delusion, false belief giving rise to the concept of Atta.
Mudita Gladness (at others'success), one of the four Illimitables.

Nama Mentality.
Namarupa Mentality-materiality of the five aggregates.

Namaruparicheda nana Insight to the definition of namarupa.
Nanas Insight knowledge from vipassana.
Nibbana Cessation of the formations, Nibbana, extinction of the three roots of greed, hate and delusion.
Nimitta Sign.
Nirodha Cessation.

Panna Insight knowledge.
Paramis Perfection.
Parikamma nimitta Sign of actual object of concentration.
Parinibbana Attainment of Nibbana.
Pariggaha Discerning, Inclusion, embracing (as definition of right speech).
Pariccheda-rupa Delimiting materiality.
Parikamma nimitta The thought impression of the object of concentration, the preliminary mark, the subject itself, from which the exact mental image of the object, the Uggaha nimitta, or the learning sign, arises.
Paritta Small, limited (in the sense sphere).
Passadana Clarification, confidence.
Passadhi Pathav Tranquillity.

Paticcasammupada	Dependant origination.
Pattibhaga nimitta	After-image, conceptual image, in abstract form without the blemishes.
Phassa	Contact.
Piti	Zest, joy.
Phala	Fruit of the Path, fruit of cause.
Puthujjana	Ordinary mortal.
Raga	Lust, greed.
Rasa	Taste, flavour, essential juice.
Rupa	Materiality (aggregate, visible datum, object or matter).
Rupa-kaya	Material body.
Rupakhandha	Material aggregate.
Rupavacara	Fine material sphere.
Saddha	Faith.
Sakadagami	Ariya, of the third order.
Salayatanas	The sixfold base of contact.
Samadhi	Concentration.
Samatha	Serenity.
Samsara	Cycle of rebirths.
Sanna	Perception, sign, signal, label, restrained.
Sangha	The community of the Order, monks of the Order.
Sankhara	Formations.
Sankharupekha	Equanimity about formations.
Sasana	Dispensation.
Sila	Virtue.
Sottapan	Ariya, of the fourth order, Stream-Enterer.
Sukha	Pleasure, joy.
Sukha-vipassaka	Dry-visioned attainer, a bare attainer, one who attains withouth previously attaining jhana.
Sunna, sunnata	Void, voidness.
Tanha	Craving.
Tejo	Water.
Tihetuka	Person of three roots, one with understanding of the sasana.

Udayabhaya	Rise-and-fall.
Udayabhaya nana	Insight of the rise-and-fall of formations.
Uggaha	Anything to be learned or studied.
Uggaha nimitta	The learning sign appearing after the parikamma nimitta.
Upacara	Access, preliminary (concentration), apprach, neighbourhood.
Upadana	Clinging (to formations).
Upekha	Detached calmnesser.
Vayo	Air.
Vedana	Feeling of pleasure, or pain, or neither.
Vicara	Sustained thought.
Vihara	Dwelling place, abode, monastery.
Vimokha	Liberation.
Vimuthi Magga	Path to Deliverance or Freedom, book on meditation surviving in a Chinese verion only.
Vinnana	Consciousness, cognition.
Vinaya	Discipline, vinaya Prtaka Book of Discipline for monks.
Vipaka	Resultant effect of kamma.
Vipassana	Insight of impermanence, pain and suffering, non-self.
Viraga	Fading away of greed.
Viriya	Energy.
Visudhi magga	Path to Purity.
Visudhi	Purity.
Vithi	A state of consciousness.
Vithi-citta	Consciousness in the cognitive series of states.
Yogi	Meditator.

BIBLIOGRAPHY

The text, wherever possible, is taken from the original authenticated Pali Text published by the Pali Text Society of London.

The spelling is based upon that used by the Theravadians so Nibbana is not Nirvana which is Hindu and Sanskrit.

A Translation of the Katha-Vatthu from the Abhidhamma-Pitaka, *Points of Controversy or Subjects of Discourse,* The Pali Text Society, London, 1973.

A Translation of the Katha-Vatthu from the Abhidhamma-Pitaka, *Psalms of the Early Buddhists I – Psalms of the Sisters,* The Pali Text Society, London, 1961

Anguttara-Nikaya, *The Book of The Gradual Sayings or More-Numbered Suttas Vol I (Ones, Twos, Threes),* The Pali Text Society, London, 1970.

Anguttara-Nikaya, *The Book of The Gradual Sayings or More-Numbered Suttas Vol II (The Book of the Fours),* The Pali Text Society, London, 1962.

Anguttara-Nikaya, *The Book of The Gradual Sayings or More-Numbered Suttas Vol III (The Books of the Fives and Sixes),* The Pali Text Society, London, 1961.

Anguttara-Nikaya, *The Book of The Gradual Sayings or More-Numbered Suttas Vol IV (The Books of the Sevens, Eights and Nines),* The Pali Text Society, London, 1965.

Anguttara-Nikaya, *The Book of The Gradual Sayings or More-Numbered Suttas Vol V (The Book of the Tens and Elevens)*, The Pali Text Society, London, 1961.

Anguttara-Nikaya, *Sacred Books of The Buddhists Vol II*, The Pali Text Society, London, 1977.

Anguttara-Nikaya, *Sacred Books of The Buddhists Vol III*, The Pali Text Society, London, 1977.

Anguttara-Nikaya, *Sacred Books of The Buddhists, Vol XXIX, (Birth-Stories of the Ten Bodhisattas and the Dasabodhisattuppattikatha)*, The Pali Text Society, London, 1975.

Ashin Silanandabhivumsa, *The Venerable Mahasi Sayadaw Biography*, translated by U Min Swe (Min Kyaw Thu).

Bhadantacariya Buddhaghosa, *The Path of Purification (Visuddhimagga)*, translated from the Pali by Bikkhu Nanamoli, Buddhist Publication Society, Kandy, Sri Lanka, 1979.

Dhammadana, *A Discourse on Sallekha Sutta*, Buddhasasana Nuggaha Organisation, Rangoon, Burma, 1981.

Dhammadana, *Biography of the Venerable Mahasi Sayadaw*, Buddhasasana Nuggaha Organisation, Rangoon, Burma, 1981.

Dhamma-Sangani, *A Buddhist Manual of Psychological Ethics*, The Pali Text Society, London, 1974.

Dhatu-Katha, *Discourse on Elements*, The Pali Text Society, London, 1962.

Dhatu-Katha, *Compedium of Philosophy*, The Pali Text Society, London, 1967.

J. Auboyer, J.L. Nou, H. Dumoulin, Introduced by Huston Smith, *Buddha: A Pictorial History of his Life and Legacy*.

Kathavatthuppa-karana-Atthakatha, *The Debates Commentary*, The Pali Text Society, London, 1969.

Kathavatthuppa-karana-Atthakatha, *Buddhist Legends*, The Pali Text Society, London, 1969.

Khuddakapatha, *The Minor Readings (The First Book of the Minor Collection)*, The Pali Text Society, London, 1978.

Majjhima-Nikaya (Mulapannasa), *The Collection of The Middle Length Sayings Vol I – The First Fifty Discourses,* The Pali Text Society, London, 1976.

Majjhima-Nikaya (Mahijmapannasa), *The Collection of Middle Length Sayings Vol II – The Middle Fifty Discourses,* The Pali Text Society, London, 1957.

Majjhima-Nikaya (Uparipannasa), *The Collection of The Middle Length Sayings Vol III – The Final Fifty Discourses,* The Pali Text Society, London, 1967.

Nyanaponika Thera, *Malaysia Heart of Buddhist Meditation,* Rider Pocket Edition, 1983, Guernsey Press Co. Ltd, Guernsey, Channel Islands.

Paticcasamuppada, *A Discourse by the Venerable Mahasi Sayadaw of Burma,* translated by U Aye Maung, March 1982.

Patisambhidda-Magga, *The Path of Discrimination,* The Pali Text Society, London, 1982.

Patthana, *Conditional Relations,* The Pali Text Society, London, 1969.

Petakopadesa, *The Pitaka-Disclosure,* The Pali Text Society, London, 1964.

Petakopadesa, *Milinda's Questions Vol II,* Luzac & Company Ltd, London, 1969.

Petakopadesa, *The Inception of Discipline and The Vinaya Nidana,* Luzac & Company Ltd, London, 1962.

Puggala-Pannatti, *Designation of Human Types,* The Pali Text Society, London, 1969.

Sanyutta-Nikaya, *The Book of The Kindred Sayings or Grouped Suttas, Part I (Kindred Sayings with Verses – Sagatha-Vagga),* The Pali Text Society, London, 1971.

Sanyutta-Nikaya, *The Book of The Kindred Sayings or Grouped Suttas, Part II (The Nidana Book – Nidana-Vagga),* The Pali Text Society, London, 1952.

Sanyutta-Nikaya, *The Book of The Kindred Sayings or Grouped Suttas, Part III,* The Pali Text Society, London, 1954.

Sanyutta-Nikaya, *The Book of The Kindred Sayings or Grouped Suttas, Part IV,* The Pali Text Society, London, 1956.

Sanyutta-Nikaya, *The Book of the Kindred Sayings or Grouped Suttas, Part V (Maha-Vagga),* The Pali Text Society, London, 1965.

Sanyutta-Nikaya, *The Minor Anthologies of The Pali Canon, Part II,* Printed by London Geoffrey Cumberlege Oxford University Press, 1948.

Sanyutta-Nikaya, *The Minor Anthologies of the Pali Canon, Part III,* The Pali Text Society, London, 1975.

Sanyutta-Nikaya, *The Minor Anthologies of The Pali Canon, Part IV,* The Pali Text Society, London, 1974.

Sutta-Nipata, *Woven Cadences of Early Buddhists.*

Sutta-Nipata, *English-Pali Dictionary,* The Pali Text Society, London, 1970.

Sutta-Nipata, *Concise Pali-English Dictionary,* U. Chandradasa De Silva Ahangama, Colombo, 1968.

The Jataka, *Stories of the Buddha's Former Births,* The Pali Text Society, London, 1969.

Vimuttimagga, *The Path of Freedom,* Buddhist Publication Society, Kandy, Sri Lanka, 1977.

Vinaya-Pitaka (Suttavibhanga), *The Book of The Discipline Vol I,* The Pali Text Society, London, 1969.

Vinaya-Pitaka, *The Book of The Discipline Vol II,* The Pali Text Society, London, 1969.

Vinaya-Pitaka (Suttavibhanga), *The Book of The Discipline Vol III,* The Pali Text Society, London, 1969.

Vinaya-Pitaka (Mahavagga), *The Book of The Discipline Vol IV,* The Pali Text Society, London, 1962.

Vinaya-Pitaka (Cullavagga), *The Book of The Discipline Vol V,* The Pali Text Society, London, 1963.

Vinaya-Pitaka (Parivara), *The Book of The Discipline Vol VI,* The Pali Text Society, London, 1966.

Visuddhimagga, *The Path Of Purification,* Buddhist Publication Society, Kandy, Sri Lanka, 1979.

Visuddhimagga, *Discourse on Paticcasamuppada,* Buddhasasana Nuggaha Organisation, Rangoon, Burma, 1982.

W.F. Jayasuriya (Dr.), *The Psychology and Philosophy of Buddhism, An Introduction to the Abhidhamma*, Ceylon, 1976.

W.F. Jayasuriya (Dr.), *Psychology and Philosophy of Buddhism,* Buddhist Missionary Society Publication, Kuala Lumpur.

INDEX